Detained without Cause

Muslims' Stories of Detention and Deportation in America after 9/11

Irum Shiekh

palgrave
macmillan

First published in 2011 by
PALGRAVE MACMILLAN®
in the United States—a division of St. Martin's Press LLC,
175 Fifth Avenue, New York, NY 10010.

Where this book is distributed in the UK, Europe and the rest of the world,
this is by Palgrave Macmillan, a division of Macmillan Publishers Limited,
registered in England, company number 785998, of Houndmills, Basingstoke,
Hampshire RG21 6XS.

Palgrave Macmillan is the global academic imprint of the above companies
and has companies and representatives throughout the world.

Palgrave® and Macmillan® are registered trademarks in the United States,
the United Kingdom, Europe and other countries.

ISBN: 978–0–230–10381–8 (hardcover)
ISBN: 978–0–230–10382–5 (paperback)

Library of Congress Cataloging-in-Publication Data is available from the
Library of Congress.

A catalogue record of the book is available from the British Library.

Design by Newgen Imaging Systems (P) Ltd., Chennai, India.

First edition: March 2011

10 9 8 7 6 5 4 3 2 1

Printed in the United States of America.

This book is dedicated to my mother,
Sitara Jabeen Butt, and my family elders.
Their sense of social justice has been a guiding force
for me throughout my life.

Contents

Illustrations

Graphs

Figures

Acknowledgments

This book could not have been possible without the help of my close friend and editor Aisha Mohammed. She read the manuscript closely several times throughout the lengthy writing process. Often, I would give her a chapter when I could not work on it anymore. Weeks later, she would return it with her highlighted edits and supportive suggestions. Her constructive comments were revitalizing, and I would revisit the material with a new vigor. Every writer needs an editor like her: someone who is politically savvy, possesses the ability to think clearly, and has a strong command of diction. I am glad that she had my back in writing this book.

If Aisha was my writing companion, Adem Carroll was my research guide. He connected me to detainees while some of them were still in various detention centers. Without his connections, it would have been very difficult to complete my research. Former detainees recognized Adem's hard work, and referencing his name allowed me to create trusting relationships with them.

At the ethnic studies department of the University of California at Berkeley, my dissertation advisor and academic mentor, Elaine Kim, understood the political significance of this research and established a fortress of support around me. This guarded me and created a supportive space in which I felt comfortable taking risks and advancing my scholarship. She also wrote hundreds of reference letters and opened new doors for me. Michael Omi met with me personally several times, gave specific written comments, and discussed theoretical concepts. Ronald Takaki believed I had the ability to tell stories very early on in my academic career. He closely reviewed several of the book chapters and also insisted that I approach this project as a series of oral histories. Sadly, he did not live to see the published book, but I perfected my art of telling stories with him. Jane Singh, a friend and mentor, stayed by me through thick and thin. She nudged me to finish the book and invited me to her class for lecture and discussion. Jerry Takahashi and Stephen Small gave invaluable insights based on their publication experiences.

The University of California at Berkeley (UCB), in general, and the Department of Ethnic Studies, in particular, were politically charged places in which I was able to undertake such a research project right after 9/11—several faculty members and graduate students invited me to speak to their classes and at conferences and symposiums. They helped me hone my conceptual framework. At UCB, these individuals include but are not limited to Wali Ahmadi, Amatullah Alaji-Sabrie, Palo Baccahhatt, Nerissa Balce, Sylvia Chan, Catherine Choy, Loan Dao, Huma Dar, Harvey Dong, Rondi Gilbert, Evelyn Nakano Glenn, Jane Mauldon, Minoo Moallem, Priya Kandaswamy, Jaideep Singh, Victoria Robinson, Timothy Randazzo, Rashmi Sadana, Nitasha Sharma, Shaden Tageldin, Fouzieyha Towghi, Wesley Ueunten, Khatharya Um, and Ling-Chi Wang.

At the University of California at Los Angeles, the Institute of American Cultures, Asian American Studies, and the Center for Oral History offered me a post-doctoral fellowship to write this book. I owe thanks to Don Nakanishi for spreading the word about my research, sharing his research experience, and writing countless letters of support; Melany De La Cruz for her creative thinking, initiative, and trust; Shirley Hune for making time to discuss my research; Russell Leong for inviting me to write an article for Amerasia Journal; and Lane Hirabayashi and Dawn Setzer for organizing a photo exhibit that allowed me to juxtapose the experiences of 9/11 detainees with the Japanese American internment experience. Teresa Barnett, director of the Center for Oral History, was instrumental in connecting me with my publisher at Palgrave. She also organized workshops around oral histories and included my manuscript for discussion, read my book chapters, and gave specific feedback. In addition, Horacio Roqueramirez and other post-doctorates working on oral history projects in the year 2006–2007 offered their feedback as oral history scholars. Susan Plann offered her ear and support as a friend and as an oral historian. Many others—including Keith Camacho, David Manuel Hernandez, Sondra Hale, Stacey Hirose, Grace Hong, Marjorie Lee, Valerie Matsumoto, and David Yoo—took keen interest in my work and provided support in numerous ways.

Rachel Meeropol from the Center for Constitutional Rights read my manuscript chapters and offered her legal expertise. She and Matthew Strugar met with me several times to discuss the *Turkmen* lawsuit and kept me updated. Many other private and civil rights attorneys, legal experts, and staff members took their time to discuss specific cases, including Rowley Clan, David Cole, Riva Enteen, Nany Hormachea, Aziz Huq, Lucas Guttentag, Subhash Kateel, Sin Yen Ling, Sandra Nichols, Heba Nimr, Aarti Shahani, Michael Schneider, Wendy Sherman, Martin Stolar, Rebecca Thornton, Rachel Ward, Khurrum Wahid, and Steven Watt.

Several organizations and individuals that work with detainees provided me resources, contacts, and/or access to their records for my research. They include but are not limited to American Civil Liberties Union, American Friends Service Committee, Desis Rising Up and Moving, Families for Freedom, Islamic Circle of North America, Human Rights Watch, and Muslim Community Services.

My family in the United States, Pakistan, and Egypt provided me resources and emotional and financial support to complete my research and write the book—more specifically, they trusted me and knew that what I was doing was something that needed to be done. My older sister-in-law, Amla, connected me to people who wanted to tell their stories, while my younger sister-in-law, Brenda, offered legal expertise for correcting the legal language in my book. My nephews Abdu and Amir shared their stories of racial profiling and allowed me to understand the experiences of young American Muslim males after 9/11. My husband, Ahmed, who migrated to the United States after 9/11 on a visiting visa and later became a legal resident, allowed me to personally experience the complicated and torturous mazes of immigration laws—he called himself a "lab animal" for my research, and I appreciated his sense of humor. My sister, Arfa, opened her house for me to stay whenever I needed it, asked pertinent questions about my research, and organized housing for me in Hyderabad, India. My brother Anjum persistently supported me throughout the writing of this book and provided me free international air travel privileges. My younger brother Shoaib's support provided me the confidence to undertake risks and follow my dreams and passions. My nieces Aisha, Amna, and Shaheena read my chapters, listened to my grumbles, and were my confidants and comrades. My young nephews and nieces Usman, Ikhlas, Aber, Rabail, Fatima, Carrie, Martin, Oliver, and many more inspired me to work toward a future in which they won't have to experience racial and religious discrimination. Overall, I felt I had strong wings supporting me as I traveled across the globe to meet with former detainees scattered all over the world and came back home to California to share my experiences with a strong network of support.

My friends both academic and nonacademic created a space for me to brainstorm and develop myself both personally and academically—Casey Peek, a comrade filmmaker and close friend, cooked for me after I went to his apartment to chill after a strenuous writing spell; Roshi Sirjan, my personal legal advisor, visited jails with me; Grace Shimizu invited me to discuss my research on a speaking tour in Japan; Susan Davies traveled with me to Pakistan and shared hours of her personal interviews with Ansar Mahmood; Rondi Gilbert, a friend for over 20 years, organized housing in Brooklyn, NewYork, at the home of his brother Gil, who volunteered to film the Metropolitan Detention Center (MDC) jail for me; Arnold Garcia published my photos in his journal; Nawal Ammar, Vivian Chin, and Fariha Khan invited me to speak about my research; my childhood friend Zihada Malik from Pakistan helped me to locate former detainees; and Farzana Zhaid from Pakistan took care of me when I was sick and felt as if I was going to die. Other friends and mentors to whom I am grateful for their continuous support include but are not limited to Michael Ames, Fe Liza Bencosme, Nigel Barboza, Faul Bakrania, Puja Bhatia, Eunice Cho, Anita Comelo, Elspeth Duncan, Riva Enteen, Rajesh Gautam, Nadine Ghammache, Carol Hamilton,

Julie Luna, Belinda Lum, Sunaina Maira, Kathryn Nasstrom, Susan Shulman, and Keagan Wethington.

Many individuals opened their homes and allowed me to stay with them in different parts of the world. Thanks to my elder brother Basharat; because of his connections, I stayed for months with Neela and Tanveer in Virginia. During this stay, Neela became my close friend, cooked delicious Pakistani food, took care of me, and provided me additional personal connections to her sisters, brothers, and nieces in Queens, Long Island, and Staten Island, where I stayed for free and completed my research. James Ridgeway connected me to Tami Gold in Brooklyn, where I stayed for weeks and enjoyed her hospitality. Susan Davis and Rajesh Barnabas provided additional housing in upstate New York. In Pakistan, my aunts, uncles, and cousins and especially Kishwar provided me the home base to travel back and forth throughout the country. My friend Zihada Malik connected me to her sister-in-law, and my niece Aisha's mother-in-law, Parveen Ahmed, connected me to her childhood friend Nuzhat Jamali to arrange housing in Karachi. Rana in Hyderabad, India, offered her house, and in Egypt, Sal-Din helped me with housing.

Thanks to Linda Shopes, Bruce Stave, Chris Chappell, Norman Silber, Samantha Hasey, and Sarah Whalen for trusting my scholarship and working diligently at Palgrave Macmillan to publish the book.

Last but not least, I owe thanks to the former detainees who shared their stories with me. Without their trust, I would not have been able to write this book. There are many whom I interviewed whose stories are not included in the book. However, their voices stayed with me as I wrote this book. Several of these individuals helped me to connect with additional 9/11 detainees and, therefore, they were my research guides. I thank them for their courage in speaking up, telling their side of the story, and guiding me. I am grateful for their trust as I tried to be a vehicle for conveying their stories. I appreciate their patience in waiting to see the final publication of the book.

The funding for this project was provided by the University of California at Berkeley, the University of California at Los Angeles, the Soroptimist International Founder Region Women's Fellowships, and my family. Thanks!

Series Editors' Foreword

The tension between national security and civil liberties has a long history in the United States, as Irum Shiekh briefly describes in the introduction to this volume. Immigrants often feel the brunt of the national anxieties that fire such tension with the resulting constriction of their constitutional rights. Profiling facilitates the characterturing and scapegoating of foreigners, as well as ethnic and racial groups. African Americans are quite familiar with the phrase, "driving while black," which describes the situation of being stopped or ticketed in disproportional numbers because of race. After the 9/11 terrorist attacks in 2001, the interviews in this book suggest that "detained without cause" may have had a similar but even more devastating effect.

Understandably, Americans showed great concern after the attack on the World Trade Center (WTC). Many grieved for the lives lost. Fear flourished as a foreign entity, Osama bin Laden's and Ayman al-Zawahiri's al-Qaeda, penetrated American security on a massive scale for the first time since the bombing of Pearl Harbor, which began the nation's entrance into World War II in 1941. In the wake of the destruction of the Twin Towers, the government rounded up almost 1,200 "special interest cases"—a euphemism, in many instances, for innocent individuals who resembled in physical appearance and religion the 19 hijackers who crashed planes into the WTC and Pentagon. Many were detained for questioning, some for long periods of time under difficult circumstances in places like Manhattan's Metropolitan Detention Center. A number were deported, not because of any connection to al-Qaeda but because of immigration violations.

Irum Shiekh traveled to far-off lands to speak with some of her subjects who were exiled from America. She did so to humanize their stories. In all, she recorded 40 narratives, and from these she selected the six interviews that follow in these pages. Shiekh also undertook extensive research into the written documents related to each of her subjects. Hers is an oral history with purpose. She desires that readers, especially progressive lawyers, use her material to reopen cases and, at a minimum, clear the names of the people involved. Moreover, she desires the government pay reparations to the former detainees and issue an apology for violating their civil, legal, and human rights. Whether the reader agrees with the author's goals is for the individual to decide. However, one cannot deny the power of her interviews.

With this volume, we offer not only a good example of advocacy oral history but also enhance our series' scope to consider U.S.–Middle East relations, although through the prism of domestic events. The Palgrave Studies in Oral History series includes several other works that concern abridgement of human rights, including Susana Kaiser's *Postmemories of Terror*, Diana Meyers Bahr's *The Unquiet Nisei*, Tamar Morad et al.'s *Iraq's Last Jews*, and Suroopa Mukherjee's *Surviving Bhopal*. The geographic range of these books, as well as the variety of subjects they cover, reveals the scope of the series, which aspires to bring the best of oral history method and substance to its readers, as well as advance theoretical discussion in the field.

Bruce M. Stave
University of Connecticut

Linda Shopes
Carlisle, Pennsylvania

Introduction

I was inspired to research the topic of post-9/11 detentions because the FBI investigated two of my own brothers. Anjum Shiekh, a pilot for United Airlines, was in Buenos Aires, Argentina, on a scheduled business stay on the night of September 11, 2001. The next day, five or six FBI officials investigated him. Even after confirming that Anjum had served in the U.S. military for over 20 years and was a retired U.S. Air Force officer and pilot, the officials were not satisfied. They wanted to search his Florida residence. Because all flights had been cancelled, Anjum could not fly home from Argentina immediately. Officials insisted on searching his apartment in his absence, threatening to break down the doors if necessary.

On September 13, after obtaining his reluctant consent, dozens of FBI agents in blue jackets sealed off his one-bedroom apartment and the adjoining streets with yellow "do not enter" tape. Floodlights lit up the night, turning the scene into a circuslike performance that attracted a curious audience. On September 17, WPLG-TV in Miami aired a story about Anjum and published it on their website. The headline read, "FBI Investigates Mysterious United Airlines Pilot: Anjum Pervaiz Shiekh Vanished Two Days Before Attack." Listing Anjum's name and address, the article referred to the Urdu novels the FBI agents had found as "potential terrorist paraphernalia" that "included pictures of what appeared to be Arab women waving guns."[1]

Anjum was not arrested, but his ordeal did not end with the search. As a pilot, he had flown his private plane frequently before 9/11. But after 9/11, law enforcement officers[2] stopped him each time, when someone at the airport noticed his "Muslim looks" or "Muslim accent" and called to "feel safe." Disgusted by the racial profiling,[3] he ended up selling his plane.[4]

My second brother, Shoib Ellahi, a successful businessman in California, was investigated by an FBI agent in April 2002. During the interview, the agent asked him about a business-related fund transfer that he had made in Pakistan. She also solicited his opinion on the September 11 attacks and then scrutinized him as he responded. His telephone lines were tapped for months; he could still be under surveillance.

Neither of my brothers was arrested. I believe that their U.S. citizenship and socioeconomic status prevented their detention. However, the fact that they could be discriminated against and perceived as a threat because of their ethnicity and religion, despite having spent approximately 30 years in a country that they helped to build, cannot but remind me of the Japanese Americans who, during World War II, were harassed and ultimately sent to internment camps because of their race and national origin.[5] I have heard similar stories from family friends who were subjected to investigation and detention by the government simply because of their ethnicity and religion. My fieldwork has confirmed this pattern of racial profiling. One interview after another established that after September 11, law enforcement officers targeted Muslim-looking men[6] under the guise of national security and curtailed the freedom of innocent individuals. At the same time, the government continued to affirm that these detentions and deportations were important legal steps toward ensuring national security.[7] This duplicity, which resulted in the uprooting of thousands of individuals rendered guilty by their religious and ethnic affiliations, inspired me to document the voices of 9/11 detainees and to examine the detention and deportation process.

Unfortunately, the wartime emergency of 9/11 was not the first time that the U.S. government created scapegoats and detained innocent individuals in the name of national security. Many historians and scholars have documented that politicians have repeatedly used the concept of national security as an excuse to target vulnerable populations and to portray them as enemies for political gains.[8] In the following section, I provide a quick historical overview of wartime emergencies in the twentieth century in which the civil liberties of immigrants were curtailed in the government's so-called pursuit of national security. The purpose of this discussion is not to be exhaustive but to contextualize 9/11 detentions within U.S. history.

This historical context adds credibility to the voices of the detainees in this book. U.S. historical archives have demonstrated that politicians have often tried to take advantage of wartime emergencies, and it is hard not to conclude that instead of a real threat of terrorism, similar motivations led to the unlawful detentions of thousands of Muslim-looking individuals after 9/11. This historical overview also allows readers to see that although wartime emergencies share many similarities, the way the government carried out its operations against various groups differed from one historical period to another. For example, after the Pearl Harbor attacks, the government rounded up and interned over 100,000 Japanese Americans. In contrast, after 9/11, the government implemented a much narrower sweep and rounded up over 1,000 individuals based on their immigration status and Muslim appearance. The differences in strategy allow the government to suggest that it is not repeating its mistakes and that it really is pursuing criminals and terrorists. Despite these differences, one element clearly stands out: immigrants are vulnerable subjects who are much easier to harass and detain legally. In essence, the tradition of creating domestic enemy aliens is a cornerstone of U.S. domestic policy in wartime.

Wartime Emergencies in the Twentieth Century

The tradition of labeling immigrants as "enemy aliens" and detaining political dissenters in the United States dates back to the 1790s. The French Revolution and the subsequent turmoil in Europe raised fears about foreign political intrigue and influence. The Federalist president John Adams enacted the Alien and Sedition Acts of 1798, which allowed the government to deport aliens considered dangerous to the peace and safety of the United States.[9] Over a century later, fear of the Russian Revolution infiltrating the United States led Attorney General Mitchell Palmer and his assistant John Edgar Hoover to target radicals and Communists under the Espionage Act (1917) and the Sedition Act (1918).[10] During an episode generally known as the Palmer Raids, approximately 3,000 immigrants from Russia and Eastern Europe were rounded up under the threat of Communism and labeled as "Reds."[11]

These raids took place in several cities during 1920–1921 and targeted Union workers and foreigners. The vast majority of detainees were eventually released, but the anarchist Emma Goldman and 247 other people were deported to Russia. According to the historian Howard Zinn, "Pains were taken to give spectacular publicity to the raids, and to make it appear that there was great and imminent public danger....The arrested aliens were in most instances perfectly quiet and harmless working people."[12] Palmer legitimated these raids by creating a climate of fear; he implied that Communists were planning to overthrow the American government after the Russian Revolution.[13]

The practice of creating enemy aliens came to the forefront during World War II. After the Japanese attack on Pearl Harbor on December 7, 1941, President Franklin Delano Roosevelt (FDR) signed Executive Order 9066, which authorized the secretary of war to designate military areas "from which any or all persons may be excluded as deemed necessary or desirable."[14] By August 1942, over 110,000 Japanese Americans, two-thirds of whom were U.S. citizens, were removed from California, Washington, Oregon, and Arizona and interned in camps located mostly in remote areas of the Midwest and the Southwest. Lieutenant General John L. DeWitt, the commander of one of these areas, declared, "In the war in which we are engaged, racial affiliations are not severed by migration. The Japanese race is an enemy race....A Jap is a Jap."[15]

Internally, the government had not reached a consensus on the threat that Japanese Americans posed. Only two days before FDR signed Executive Order 9066, Attorney General Francis Biddle informed the president that there was "no evidence of any planned sabotage."[16] Both the attorney general and the secretary of war argued against internment on the grounds that the demand for the program was based on public hysteria and racial prejudice. Nonetheless, to appease public fears, FDR signed the order.[17]

Along with the Japanese, German and Italian nationals were also considered "dangerous enemy aliens." A limited number of persons of German and Italian heritage were imprisoned; however, the mass internment of Japanese Americans was unparalleled in American history.[18] Many scholars argue that race was the key factor in the large-scale detentions of Japanese Americans,[19] which were not limited to Japanese living within U.S. borders. Government officials also captured ethnic Japanese from Latin American countries to be used in exchange for American prisoners of war captured by Japan. Over 2,000 Japanese individuals from 18 Latin American countries were brought to the United States and imprisoned in internment camps along with Japanese Americans.[20]

A decade after World War II, U.S.-Soviet relations had started to deteriorate, and Communists and socialists were again scapegoated during the witch hunt led by Senator Joseph McCarthy.[21] Unlike the events of the early 1920s, citizens were also under suspicion in the 1950s, along with immigrants. The fear of a nuclear war turned the "hot" war into a long cold war, in which affiliation with Communism or socialism became a national security issue and a source of suspicion. The Internal Security Act of 1950 made membership in Communist or totalitarianist organizations grounds for exclusion, deportation, or denial of naturalization. Senator McCarthy, as chairman of the Senate Committee of Government Operations, which included the Senate Permanent Subcommittee on Investigations, used the anti-Communist platform to accuse thousands of people of espionage, leading to the arrests and deportations of thousands.[22]

During this time frame, the loyalties of over 10,000 American citizens of Chinese descent were also questioned because their ethnicity was considered an alleged risk to national security. Many were "hunted down, arrested and deported."[23] Three laundrymen, for example, were imprisoned for six months for sending money to their families in China on the allegation that they were trading with the "enemy," as defined by the Enemy Alien Act of 1917.[24]

More recently, Muslim Americans have become the new enemy aliens after the 9/11 attacks, in spite of the fact that they have been inhabiting U.S. soil almost since the founding of the nation. A quick overview of the history of Muslims in the United States allows us to discern those historical moments when U.S. political interests converted immigrants into enemies.

History of Muslims in the United States

The history of Muslims in the United States is rich and diverse and includes legacies of slavery, migration, and conversion. Many scholars have identified Muslim names, Arabic scripts, and slave narratives written by Muslims in slave trade records that date back to 1530.[25] Although the exact number of Muslims brought from Africa as slaves is not known, scholars' estimates have ranged from 7 to 10 percent because slaves were brought from predominately Muslim countries such as Morocco, Senegal, Gambia, Guinea, Mali, and Niger. Scholars[26] have discovered lists of slave names, birth and death notices, family and church documents, advertisements for runaways, and other literary texts and notes describing exceptional slaves who read and wrote in Arabic, prayed five times a day, and observed strict diet codes. This initial wave of Muslims, however, did not flourish under the harsh living conditions slavery imposed.

The Muslim immigrant experience from the Middle East can be traced back to the 1890s. The first wave came from a region called the greater Syrian area and consisted of primarily farm workers. They were pushed to migrate to America by the economic hardships caused by the opening of the Suez Canal in the mid-nineteenth century, which rerouted world traffic from Syria to Egypt. Generally identified as Syrian, Syrian-Lebanese, and Ottoman subjects, most of these young immigrants were not highly educated and were male laborers intent on making a quick dollar and returning home. Lacking in training, capital, and English-language skills, many became peddlers. In the words of the scholar Michael Suleiman,

> With a few words of English learned on the run, a suitcase (Kashshi) full of notions (e.g., needles, thread, lace) provided by a better-established fellow Lebanese or other Arab supplier, probably a relative who helped bring them to the New World, many new arrivals often were on the road hawking their wares only a day or so after they landed in America.[27]

As the peddling industry dwindled because of industrialization in the 1920s and 1930s, many of these peddlers opened small grocery stores, restaurants, and coffee shops. Ford Motor Company in Dearborn, Michigan, and the shipbuilding industry in Quincy, Massachusetts, were the two major industrial forces that took advantage of the cheap labor provided by these young male immigrants.[28] These early immigrants appear to have fitted comfortably into America, for the most part, with their children and grandchildren.[29]

Many scholars have noted that there is no continuity between the Islam practiced by African Muslims and the Black Muslim movement founded by W. D. Fard as the Nation of Islam in Detroit in the 1930s. After Fard's mysterious disappearance in 1934, the Nation of Islam flourished under the leadership of Elijah Muhammad until the leadership of Malcolm X transformed it into a powerful movement during the 1950s and 1960s. During this time, the FBI placed Malcolm X under heavy surveillance and blamed the Nation of Islam and other African American groups for fostering radicalism. After Malcolm X's assassination in 1965 and Elijah Muhammad's death in 1975, Wallace D. Muhammad[30] and Louis Farrakhan assumed leadership of the Nation of Islam.

The end of colonization in the 1940s in the Middle East and the subsequent emergence of nationalism shaped Muslim identities in relation to specific nation-states, and immigrants started to see themselves as Syrian, Lebanese, and

Jordanians instead of the larger Syrian or Ottoman identity. These immigrants tended to be secular in orientation and were committed to Arab nationalism and socialism, which started to emerge in the Arab nations in the 1950s and 1960s. The dismemberment of Palestine and the creation of the state of Israel created hundreds of thousands of Palestinian Arab/Muslim refugees, some of whom eventually found their way to the United States.

The U.S. government relaxed its immigration policies in 1965, in part because the cold war and the Korean and Vietnamese conflicts had created a severe shortage of qualified engineers, doctors, and professionals in the United States. Some of the highly educated populace of the Indian subcontinent and the Middle East, who were looking for opportunities to use their education and skills in a technologically advanced environment, took advantage of this urgency. This transnational pattern of supply and demand brought a new wave of Muslims from South Asia and the Middle East. "They were neither poor nor uneducated; on the contrary, they represent the best, educated elite of the Muslim world who see themselves as helping develop America's leadership in medicine, technology, and education."[31] Many of these immigrants settled in large urban centers such as New York, Detroit, Los Angeles, San Francisco, Philadelphia, and Chicago and worked as doctors, engineers, computer programmers, and business entrepreneurs. After the Russian invasion of Afghanistan in 1979 and the Shah's overthrow in Iran, additional waves of Muslims came to the United States. Most of the Afghanis and Iranians settled in California and further diversified America's Muslim population in terms of social status, language, and culture.

After the initial wave of migration of highly qualified male professionals, family reunification, visa lottery programs, and familiarity with U.S. immigration laws sparked a second wave of migration—consisting of women and less educated people from working-class backgrounds—and further diversified the Muslim American population. Although U.S. immigration policies became more stringent with the passage of time, by the 1990s the establishment of a large Muslim community in the United States provided a network for individuals to obtain student, visitor, or asylum visas. Many of these individuals with temporary visas came to the United States and disappeared among immigrant communities after their visas expired, leading them to remain undocumented and missing from official census counts. A growing number of these immigrants are working for convenience stores, gas stations, and taxi companies,[32] even though they come from educated and middle-class families in the Middle East and South Asia. Generally, the relatively high cost of airfare to the United States and unfamiliarity with English prohibit very low-income and uneducated South Asian and Middle Eastern individuals from migrating to the United States. Today, there are 2–7 million Muslims[33] in the United States consisting of Arabs, South Asians, African Americans, Africans, Central Asians, East Asians, individuals from other nations, and converts.

9/11 Detentions: Historical Context

As this historical overview illustrates, the immigration of Muslims to the United States is not a new phenomenon; Muslims have been part of American history as slaves and immigrants since the country's inception. As people of color, they experienced discrimination just as many other immigrant groups faced; however, a strong anti-Muslim sentiment is relatively new; it started to emerge in the American public consciousness at the end of World War II. Many scholars have observed that the image of Muslims as dangerous terrorists—and therefore subject to detainment and deportation—has been rooting itself in the popular imagination since the advent of the cold war in general and since shifts in U.S. foreign policy in the Middle East after 1967 more specifically.[34] The United States' economic (primarily oil-related), military, and political interests in the Middle East have been instrumental in fanning these anti-Muslim sentiments.[35]

Along with these strategic interests, orientalism[36]—a subjective and stereotypical image of the East from the Western perspective[37]—has left very little room for perceiving Muslims as anything but fanatical males and oppressed females. The media scholar Jack Shaheen notes that

> ever since the camera began to crank, the unkempt Arab has appeared as an uncivilized character, the cultural Other, someone who appears and acts differently than the white Western protagonist, someone of a different race, class, gender or national origin.[38]

With the passage of time, the stereotype of the "unkempt Arab" has evolved from an unruly and uncivilized barbarian to an oily, opulent sheikh to a fundamentalist, fanatic terrorist—but the status of the Arab as Other has stayed constant.[39]

Anti-Muslim sentiment has motivated the government to adopt policies and programs that have curtailed the civil liberties of Muslims before and after 9/11. Many scholars have documented FBI sting operations, tactics, and surveillance programs that targeted Muslims and Arabs before 9/11, including Operation Boulder, Operation Abscam, and the Registration Program of 1979 for Iranian nationals.[40] More recently, the 1996 Anti-Terrorism and Effective Death Penalty Act (passed on the anniversary of the Oklahoma City bombing) includes sections that have severely impacted the civil liberties of Muslims in the United States. This act allows the government to present secret evidence against suspected alien terrorists without providing the defendant a chance to respond to the evidence. Immediately after passing the act, the State Department also designated 30 groups as "terrorist organizations," of which more than half were Arab and Muslim groups.[41] Providing material support to any of these groups is grounds for arrest under the 1996 act.

Secret evidence including rumors, innuendoes, and faulty translations has been disproportionately used to prosecute Arab and Muslim immigrants. The religion scholar Kathleen Moore asserts that through the 1996 law, "Congress effectively has created a new class of persons who are defined as deportable merely because of their association with a disfavored group, not because they personally committed a terrorist act."[42]

The combined impact of foreign policy, global politics, domestic enforcement policies, orientalism, and the shift from the cold war to a holy war has increasingly contributed to creating the image of Muslims as terrorists who are barbaric, savage, fundamentalist, and inhumane. Some political analysts have argued that Islam is the West's new evil empire. According to Suad Joseph, "Islam is frequently represented as a militaristic religion bent on jihad (holy war), inherently and historically hostile to the democratic, capitalist, Christian West."[43] John Esposito writes, "Fear of the Green Menace [the green color is associated with Islam] may well replace that of the Red Menace of world communism.... Islam is often equated with holy war and hatred, fanaticism and violence, intolerance and the oppression of women."[44]

Although an anti-Muslim climate was already present before 9/11, the attacks on the World Trade Center and the Pentagon provided the catalyst for rounding up and deporting over 1,000 Muslims in the three months after 9/11. These 1,000-plus individuals were primarily arrested on minor immigration charges and framed as terrorists, and an overwhelming majority of them were deported on minor immigration/criminal charges.

Patterns of Post-9/11 Detentions

The term "9/11 detentions" refers to the cases of individuals from predominately Muslim countries who were arrested after 9/11 on the suspicion of terrorism but were held under unrelated immigration or criminal charges. Immigration officials categorized these individuals as "Special Interest Cases" because of their suspected involvement with the 9/11 attacks.[45] The total number of 9/11 detentions is unknown because of the secrecy surrounding these cases, but two months after the attacks occurred, government officials acknowledged that 1,182 individuals had been detained for questioning.[46] Later, the government stopped releasing the total number of detentions because of complications in counting.[47] Even though detentions of individuals in connection with the 9/11 attacks continued after the release of the initial figure, my analysis is based on the 1,200 detentions that occurred in the immediate aftermath of 9/11.[48]

The Office of the Inspector General's (OIG) report[49] defines 9/11 detainees as "aliens held on immigration violations in connections with the investigation of the September 11 attacks."[50] Of the 1,200 aforementioned cases, the report focuses on 762 individuals arrested for immigration violations between September 11, 2001, and August 6, 2002.[51] In my analysis, I also include individuals convicted of minor criminal[52] charges along with those convicted of immigration violations.[53]

9/11 Detainees: Demographics

The OIG report provides a demographic breakdown of the 762 "Special Interest Cases" included in its analysis. Most of the individuals are from predominately Muslim countries such as Pakistan, Egypt, Turkey, Jordan, Yemen, Saudi Arabia, Tunisia, Syria, Lebanon, Iran, Algeria, Guyana, Bangladesh, and Afghanistan.[54] The demographic breakdown also identified British and French citizens, most of whom were naturalized citizens originally from countries such as Pakistan, Egypt, and Algeria.[55] The Human Rights Watch report presents a similar demographic breakdown, which showed that most of the "Special Interest Cases" came from Pakistan, Egypt, and Turkey.[56]

It is difficult to understand why law enforcement officers specifically targeted individuals from Pakistan (33 percent of the 762 individuals included in the OIG analysis) when none of the 9/11 hijackers were from Pakistan.[57] The only explanation that I can offer is that most of these Pakistanis were employed in low-paying jobs in public spaces and stood out because of their brown skin color. Their socioeconomic status often meant that they were not fluent in English and probably could not afford lawyers. This made them vulnerable to questioning by law enforcement officers. Later, their Muslim names and heritage along with expired visas or fake identification cards resulted in their detention. Even though most of the 9/11 hijackers were from Saudi Arabia,[58] the number of Saudi individuals arrested[59] is relatively low owing to their higher socioeconomic status and the fact that most of them work in offices or respectable institutions where they could not be easily questioned.

The majority of the 762 arrests included in the OIG report occurred in New York (491, approximately 62 percent). Even though the metropolitan area in Detroit, Michigan, has a large population of Arabs and Muslims,[60] the number of arrests there remained relatively low.[61] During my trip to Dearborn, Michigan, in 2003, I interviewed some local community organizers,[62] and they informed me that the FBI worked closely with them to identify any suspicious activity. Law enforcement officers arrested a few individuals, but they did not round up people like they did in New York and New Jersey.[63] The OIG report found that the guards at the Metropolitan Detention Center (MDC) in Brooklyn, New York—who had lost relatives, friends, and colleagues on September 11—harbored anger and vengeance toward the detainees and were "high on adrenaline," which created an "emotionally charged environment."[64] This would help to explain why 60 percent of the arrests occurred in New York.[65] San Diego, California, and Southern Florida should have been hotspots for arrests since most of the hijackers had settled in both of these areas.[66] However, the actual number of arrests from both California and Florida remained relatively low.[67] Law enforcement officers focused on the area impacted (New York) even though it was not the area most likely to yield relevant information. These were ineffective intelligence tactics.

A report produced by the Migration Policy Institute in 2003 includes statistical analysis of 406 individuals arrested after 9/11.[68] This report sheds additional light on the demographics of 9/11 detainees and points out,

> Of the detainees for which information about the total amount of time spent in the United States was available, 34.6 percent had been in the United States between one and five years, and 46.5 percent had been in the United States at least six years, suggesting that the majority of the detainees in the sample had significant ties to the United States and roots in their communities. Additionally, of all the detainees, approximately 23 percent had a spouse and/or children in the United States and approximately 21 percent had extended family in the United States.[69]

Methods of 9/11 Arrests

The overwhelming majority of September 11 arrests occurred through tips and racial profiling; the general public called and reported suspicious people, and law enforcement officers stopped and questioned individuals based on their race and religious profile. This means that individuals who slightly resembled the 19 hijackers—those whom officers perceived as being from the Middle East—were subject to surveillance, questioning, scrutiny, and detentions. According to the OIG report, the attorney general directed the FBI and other federal law enforcement personnel to use "every available law enforcement tool" to arrest persons who "participate in, or lend support to, terrorist activities."[70] One of the principal responses by law enforcement authorities after the September 11 attacks was to use federal immigration laws to detain aliens suspected of having possible ties to terrorism. The journalist Steven Brill states,

> [Attorney General John] Ashcroft told [FBI director Robert] Mueller that any male from eighteen to forty years old from Middle Eastern or North African countries whom the FBI simply learned about was to be questioned and questioned hard. And anyone from those countries whose immigration papers were out of order—anyone—was to be turned over to the INS [Immigration and Naturalization Service].[71]

As a result of these policies, within two months of the attacks, law enforcement officers had detained, at least for questioning, more than 1,200 citizens and aliens nationwide.[72]

For field officers untrained in terrorist intelligence[73] and unfamiliar with Muslim cultures,[74] the term "suspicious people" translated as Muslim-looking individuals—individuals who looked like the 19 hijackers regardless of whether they were Muslims, Christians, Sikhs, Hindus, or Jews. Instead of using pertinent intelligence, evidence, or knowledge about Muslim communities living in the United States, law enforcement officers used racial profiling and depended on tips[75] made by fearful and paranoid citizens. The Human Rights Watch report titled *Presumption of Guilt* provides several examples of such arrests. One of them was Osama Sewilam, who

> upon arriving at the Newark, New Jersey train station, on October 11, 2001 asked a policeman for directions to his immigration attorney's office. The policeman asked him where he was from, and he replied, "Egypt." The police-man asked him if he had a visa. He said it had expired and that was why he was going to see his lawyer. The policeman took him to the police station and called the FBI. Sewilam was deported on March 15, 2002.[76]

Because of this racial profiling, many non-Muslims—including Arabs, Latinos, and Indians, especially Sikhs and Hindus—were stopped and questioned. Depending on the vulnerability of the suspected individuals and the attitudes of the individual law enforcement officers, some of these non-Muslims were also arrested. For example, Purna Raj Bajracharya, a Nepalese Buddhist man, was arrested on October 25, 2001, in downtown New York for videotaping build-ings. Officers suspected that he might be a terrorist and imprisoned him on the ninth floor of the MDC in Brooklyn. Purna was deported to Nepal in January 2002 for an immigration violation after an FBI officer intervened.[77] Another example is Sher J. B. Singh, a 28-year-old Sikh man with a turban and a beard. He was arrested on a train on September 12, 2001, for carrying a Kirpan, a short blunt ceremonial sword that all Sikh men are mandated to carry by religious doc-trine. Later he was charged with carrying a concealed weapon.[78]

Often, as revealed by the narratives included in this book and several other reports published about the 9/11 detentions, law enforcement officers used racial profiling to stop individuals and then followed up with specific questions to con-firm their religious identities. For example, Nabil Ayesh's narrative in this book shows that after he tried to highlight his Israeli nationality, officers asked him whether he was an Arab or a Jew. Nabil's case also illustrates that for uninformed law enforcement officers, *Arab* was synonymous with *Muslim*.

Along with racial profiling, tips from the general public were another pri-mary cause for investigation and detention. Tips were collected from FBI hotlines and Internet sites established right after 9/11. Through announcements and the media, the FBI encouraged the general public to report "suspicious persons." The OIG report notes

> By September 18, 2001, 1 week after the attacks, the FBI had received more than 96,000 tips or potential leads from the public, including more than 54,000 through an Internet site it established for the PENTTBOM case, 33,000 that were forwarded directly to FBI field offices across the country, and another 9,000 tips called into the FBI's toll-free "hotline."[79]

Like the arrests based on racial profiling, most of the tips were based on fear, ignorance, and hearsay. Most of the callers attributed suspicious activities to "Arab men." The OIG report provides examples of such tips. One of the callers

> told the FBI that "two Arabs" rented a truck from his —— —— vehicle rental business on September — for a one way trip to a ———— city, and then returned it — minutes later having gone only – miles. They were, according to the caller, "extremely nervous," and did not argue when told they would not be refunded the hundreds of dollars they had paid for the rental.[80]

A few days later, the "suspicious" Arabs were arrested from their apartment and classified as having connections with the September 11 attacks. The FBI whistle-blower Coleen Rowley describes the typical FBI hotline tip received immediately after 9/11:

> The most common "citizen tip" we receive is something to the effect of, "I don't want you to think I'm prejudiced because I'm not, but I just have to report this because one never knows and I'm worried and I thought the FBI should check it out." This precedes a piece of general information about an "Arab" or "Middle-Eastern" man who the tipster lives by or works with that contains little or nothing specific to potential terrorism activities.[81]

One of the FBI agents I interviewed also mentioned that the FBI started to develop investigation strategies only after the number of hotline tips started to decline and they had time to think and strategize. Before that, tips from "concerned citizens" were the primary source for triggering the investigation process. Prior to 9/11, these kinds of tips were generally ignored, but after 9/11, policies changed. Rowley quotes the FBI spokesman Bill Carter to note changes in the FBI's attitude:

> At one time, when information came to us, a lot of times based on experience, the investigator would say, "Nah, this is something we will *not* follow through

on," but after the September 11 attacks, the director has stated that no counter terrorism lead will go uncovered.(emphasis added)[82]

Instead of investigating these leads quietly with a background check or informal questioning, FBI agents located and interviewed Muslim men and detained them as "of interest" to the September 11 investigation if they did not have proper immigration documents. This classification occurred without any evidence of or link to terrorism, especially in the New York area.[83]

Despite the fact that most of the arrests occurred after the 9/11 attacks through racial profiling and bogus tips, the Department of Justice (DOJ) took pride in claiming the success of its intelligence operation and publicized the total number of arrests through media and official press conferences. Initially, the DOJ released a running tally of people detained and in early November 2001 affirmed that it had detained 1,182 "Special Interest" individuals.[84]

Entrapping Undocumented Immigrants

Steven Brill, in his book *After*, notes,

> [The Bush administration] knew that the attacks had come from Muslims.... So without any better leads, why not just question any such men you could, and hold those who it turned out were violating the terms of their visas?... Had they taken jobs... Had they overstayed their visas?... they would then be detained for immigration violation and questioned repeatedly. It didn't matter if the violation were minor transgressions for which immigrants of other nationalities are rarely, if ever, held.... The goal, Ashcroft and Chertoff told the FBI and INS agents, was to prevent more attacks, not prosecute anyone. And the best way to do that was to round up, question, and hold as many people as possible.[85]

Brill's research and interviews with the DOJ administration reveal that young males from the Middle Eastern countries whose immigration papers were out of order became the focus of the intelligence community. My research and interviews with former detainees and the larger Muslim community reveal the implications of this policy on the ground and the way immigration status played a pivotal role in sorting out suspects and detaining them. For example, both my brothers were questioned because law enforcement officers saw them as Muslim immigrants engaging in suspicious activity in the aftermath of 9/11—one was a pilot and the other was a businessman. If they were not citizens, I believe both of them could have been locked up. Of course, there were some special cases in which individuals were arrested even though they did not have any immigration violations. For example, Ansar Mahmood, a young Pakistani man arrested in upstate New York, had a valid green card. However, he was imprisoned even though he had not participated in any terrorist activity. Another example is the arrest of eight men from Evansville, Indiana; six had valid green cards, one was a U.S. citizen, and one had a minor immigration violation.[86] Despite these exceptions, the overwhelming majority of individuals arrested in connection with the 9/11 attacks had immigration violations.[87]

The government's focus on undocumented immigrants with a Muslim background makes very little sense in terms of good intelligence. In Yasser Ebrahim's narrative, I provide an example of four Egyptians in Brooklyn, New York, who were arrested for immigration violations. One of their housemates, a young man from Morocco with a valid green card, was not arrested. Even if we accept that young men from a certain ethnic/religious group tend to be radicalized for certain political reasons and law enforcement officers need to ask them a few questions, immigration status should not be the determining factor in sorting out who is a suspect and who is not. Almost ten years after the 9/11 attacks, immigration status has not helped the government find any real terrorists. Some individuals who have been found guilty of planning a terrorist attack, attending Al-Qaeda training camps, or providing material support to a so-called "terrorist organization" were U.S. citizens. One of these examples is Faisal Shahzad, the car bomber who tried to detonate a bomb in Times Square on May 1, 2010.[88]

Like Michael Welch's *Scapegoats of September 11*, this book argues that undocumented Muslim men were arrested and classified as terrorists because they could be held easily under immigration laws, not because they had actual links to terrorism. The heavy concentration of undocumented immigrants in high-security jails suggests that the government deliberately targeted individuals who were vulnerable because they were visible—most of them worked in public spaces such as taxis, restaurants, and newspaper stands—and easy to detain. Even among the detainees, the individuals subjected to the harshest treatment were the ones who were the most vulnerable, the ones least familiar with immigration laws, or the ones who did not have any family members to support them from outside the jail. Sandra Nicholas, an attorney who worked with several of these detainees, describes the courtroom right after 9/11:

> I was going in for their first hearings [in September 2001]. And it was a mob scene when I got there. There were 40 or 50 prisoners shackled to each other, packed into courtrooms. Relatives, lawyers, court personnel, guards were all just wandering around the halls and trying to get things organized.... It was so chaotic. I said, oh, my God what a mess.... it was like a zoo, a three-ring circus. I have never seen such chaos in the immigration court. Everybody was still very anxious and nervous because of 9/11. The judges did not want to erroneously free someone who might be a terrorist....All of [the detainees] were on [immigration charges]—anyone who would interview them...anybody with

their right mind talking to these guys would know in a minute that they were not terrorists... they were the guys who overstayed the visas.... they just wanted to send money back home.[89]

Undocumented immigrants who lacked political power because they did not have voting rights became the state's scapegoats in the war on terror.[90] They bore the brunt of antiforeign sentiments because they lacked public sympathy and support.[91] The process began with restrictions on immigration and ended with the detention of undocumented immigrants. It was easy for the government to justify their detention because they were already in contravention of U.S. immigration laws. After September 11, immigrants (and specifically undocumented immigrants) were transformed into terrorists because of the general public's hysterical overreaction and consistent labeling by the media. It was easy to do so because immigrants have been blamed for economic, social, and cultural chaos throughout the history of this country.[92]

The Institutionalization of Detentions and Its Impact on Muslims in America

In the first six months after 9/11—while the majority of the arrests were occurring through racial profiling and tips—the executive branch of the government initiated, adopted, and implemented several policies, programs, and laws, which expanded the government's powers to question and detain Muslim males on the suspicion of terrorism. For example, the state initiated a volunteer interview program on November 9, 2001, under which several Muslims were detained.[93] The U.S. PATRIOT Act—unveiled on September 19, 2001, and adopted on October 26, 2001—expanded the state's powers to wiretap, question, and keep individuals under surveillance.[94] The government implemented the Absconder Apprehension Initiative on January 25, 2002, for the purpose of locating 314,000 people who already had a final deportation or removal order against them.[95] The DOJ used the criteria of nationality, age, and gender to prioritize this selective enforcement list,[96] and 6,000 men from Al-Qaeda-harboring countries were the first to be entered into the National Crime Information Center database.

Approximately nine months later, the government initiated the Special Registration program, which required that all males over the age of 16 from certain countries (predominately Muslim countries) who had entered the United States with temporary visas before specific dates had to report to the INS to be photographed, fingerprinted, and interrogated.[97] In January 2004 the Department of Homeland Security (DHS) suspended the Special Registration program and launched the U.S. Visitor and Immigrant Status Indicator Technology (or US-VISIT Program) in its place.[98] Michael Welch reports that over 82,000 foreign nationals registered under the Special Registration program. None of them were found to have any links with terrorism, "yet the Justice Department moved forward with plans to deport as many as 13,000 Arab and Muslim men whose legal immigration status had expired."[99] These mass detentions and deportations sent waves of fear throughout Muslim communities across the nation. Many Muslim families fled and camped out along the Canadian border to escape the Special Registration requirement.[100] Many others took volunteer departures and returned to their home countries. During my visit to Pakistan in early 2003, I was told that many families had moved back to Islamabad, Lahore, and Karachi from New York and New Jersey. The hostility against Muslims in the United States converted the home country into a safety zone.

The following graph shows a sudden increase in the number of deportations to Muslim countries resulting from the Special Registration requirement in 2002.[101] These governmental statistics only include formal removals, and, therefore, volunteer and other 9/11-related departures are not reflected. Although these deportation statistics are not completely accurate and I believe that the deportations were higher than what were recorded (as only 2,218 and 2,416 deportations are recorded for the years 2002 and 2003), the graph still captures a sudden increase in the number of deportations for individuals from Muslim countries.

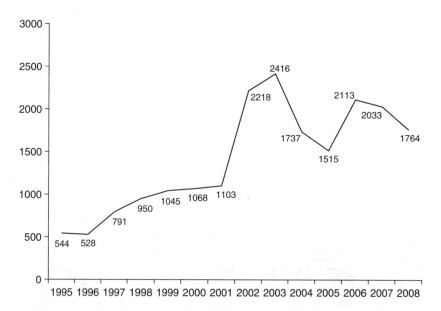

Graph 1 Deportations to Muslim Countries (for explanation see endnote number 101).

Source: U.S. Department of Homeland Security, *Yearbook of Immigration Statistics*, Table 43, 2003 and Table 37, 2008..

The U.S. Government's Justification of the 9/11 Detentions

Overall, the government's response to the 9/11 detentions is that it acted within a legal framework to detain and deport individuals with immigration violations. Even after the publication of documentation, scholarship, and critiques, the government has continued to maintain that long delays in processing, the denial of basic legal access and rights, physical and psychological abuse during detentions, and long delays after the issue of deportation orders resulted from the chaotic situation caused by the tragic events of 9/11. After the release of the OIG report, Barbara Comstock (a DOJ spokeswoman) noted, "We make no apologies for finding every legal way possible to protect the American public from further terrorist attacks."[102]

Soon after 9/11, numerous human rights and legal groups—including Amnesty International, Human Rights Watch, Lawyers for the Protection of Human Rights, Migration Policy Institute, and the American Civil Liberties Union—published reports that documented the disappearances of individuals under suspicion of terrorism and challenged the U.S. government's practice of arbitrary detentions.[103] For example, an Amnesty International memo issued in November 2001 about the post–September 11 investigations stated that over 1,100 people from mainly non-U.S. nations have been taken into custody.[104] A few months later, a March 2002 report by Amnesty International expressed its concerns about "reports of incommunicado detention, harsh custody conditions and a lack of public information on those held.... Keeping detainees for periods of prolonged detention in these circumstances may amount to arbitrary detention in contravention of international law and standards."[105] Human Rights Watch pointed out, "The veil of secrecy the Department of Justice [DOJ] as wrapped around the post–September 11 detainees reflects a stunning disregard for the democratic principles of public transparency and accountability."[106]

Given this criticism and other challenges, on January 9, 2002, the Department of Justice's inspector general announced the creation of a special unit to investigate 9/11 civil rights complaints and in April and December 2003 issued two reports about 9/11 detainees.[107] These reports—which included interviews with then attorney general John Ashcroft, FBI director Robert Mueller, other DOJ officials, and September 11 detainees—confirmed that immigration detainees were erroneously connected with the September 11 attacks and placed in solitary confinement under restrictive conditions for weeks and months. However, both of the reports imply that lack of resources and a failure in coordination and communication among various government agencies caused the detention of hundreds of Muslim men. The report also implied that Ashcroft and Mueller were not aware of the abusive conditions of the confinement and were not told it was taking FBI agents months to clear a detainee designated as "high interest" even after it was evident that he had no connections to terrorism.

As of January 23, 2002, there were at least 53 people held longer than 90 days after getting a removal order by a judge.[108] In some of the cases, INS lawyers were raising concerns through working group meetings, but the associate deputy attorney general of the United States claimed that he did not know there were legal concerns about holding detainees beyond the 90-day limit.[109] The OIG's April 2003 report concludes, "In sum, while the chaotic situation and the uncertainties surrounding the detainee's role in the September 11 attacks and the potential for additional terrorism explain some of these problems, *they do not explain them all*" (emphasis added).[110]

Steven Brill's book *After: The Rebuilding and Defending of America in the September 12 Era* provides interviews with several Department of Justice officials who administrated 9/11 detentions policies, including Attorney General Ashcroft and the assistant attorney general, criminal division, Michael Chertoff.[111] Brill's book criticizes the Bush administration and the DOJ officials for holding Muslim males in prolonged detentions without having any evidence to link them to terrorism. Brill asserts that Ashcroft knew

> from the threat matrixes he sees every day, and from all those wiretaps and other intercepts—and, indeed, from the reality of the September 11 attack itself, which was carried out by nineteen sleepers—that there are lots of elephants out there, and that none were able to pull off a new attack in the year after the first strike.[112]

However, for Ashcroft and his team, these immigration detainees "were not defendants in cases where evidence stemming from an improper search or interrogation might be excluded at a trial .They were potential killers who had to be stopped."[113]

Since 9/11, several scholars have written about the loss of civil liberties, the precarious balance between freedom and security, and the cost of killing dissent during wartime. The leading legal scholar David Cole argues that throughout history, the government has repeatedly targeted noncitizens and manufactured them into "enemy aliens" during wartime emergencies.[114] Although the process starts with noncitizens, the expanding powers of the state eventually entrap citizens as well. Cole suggests that both citizens and noncitizens must challenge this expansion of power. Michael Welch argues in *Scapegoats of September 11* that the "War on Terror" has wrongfully connected thousands of Muslims and South Asians to the September 11 attacks. Through secret detentions, Special Registration programs, and deportations, the state has produced scapegoats to displace blame and deny responsibility for failures in intelligence.[115] In *Silencing Political Dissent: How Post-September 11 Anti-Terrorism Measures Threaten Our Civil Liberties*, Nancy Chang explores the suppression of dissent during wartime and discusses the implications of the U.S. PATRIOT Act.[116] Vijay Prashad finds similarities between the McCarthy era of the 1950s, when fear of "Reds" prevailed, and the targeting and criminalization of Muslims after 9/11.[117] He labels this period the "Green Manic."

Along with these legal and policy critiques, a limited number of scholars have used the voices of former detainees to show the human cost of the loss of civil liberties. Former detainees have also contributed to this discourse by writing first-person narratives. Tram Nguyen provides stories of "suspicious immigrants" living in New Jersey, New York, Minneapolis, Chicago, Los Angeles, Arizona, and Canada and argues that in the aftermath of 9/11, immigrants living all over the United States could become suspects at any time. Her scholarship reveals the severe impacts of state-sponsored terror on real people.[118] Moazzam Begg in his memoir provides horrific details of his three-year imprisonment at Guantanamo Bay, after which he was released without charges in January 2005.[119] Chaplain James Yee wrote an autographical account of his detention at a navy prison after he was labeled an "enemy combatant" for providing services as a chaplain to Muslim detainees at Guantanamo Bay. In his account, he reveals the ignorance and cultural blindness of the U.S. military and government in their war on terror, which has had significant implications for civil liberties.[120]

Using Oral Histories to Refute the Government's Justifications

This book uses the existing scholarship on the 9/11 detentions as a stepping-stone to present the oral histories of former detainees, which powerfully refute the government's position. Through these narratives, former detainees challenge the government's assertion that it acted within its legal framework to detain and deport immigrants who were initially suspected of terrorism because of their religion and ethnicity. One story after another reveals that racial profiling triggered suspicion against individuals and that specific questions about their religion led to their arrests. Even if we accept the government position that these individuals were undocumented and had to be removed, their lengthy detentions in high-security jails where they were physically and psychologically abused and called "terrorists" indicate that they were scapegoated. The narratives explain that when law enforcement agents were unable to find any terrorist connections, charges such as expired visas, credit card fraud, working on a nonauthorized social security card, lying to federal agents, and helping undocumented immigrants were tacked on to the cases as afterthoughts. The government had to charge these detainees with something to save face. The individuals who had been stuck in solitary confinement for months at a time decided to accept immigration and criminal charges in exchange for their freedom.

None of the 1,000-plus individuals classified as "Special Interest Cases" and arrested in connection with the 9/11 attacks have been found guilty or convicted of terrorism.[121] With the exception of Ali Saleh Kahlah Al-Marri, who pled guilty of material support for providing resources to a foreign terrorist organization,[122] all of the "Special Interest Cases" have been released within the United States or deported to their home countries. Some individuals arrested a year or so after the September 11 attacks have been convicted of terrorism. These terrorist convictions are also controversial, and several legal and civil rights organizations have raised civil liberties concerns with them, including the excessive use of the material support statute, secrecy about the evidence, and entrapment through paid informants.[123]

I argue that the state scapegoated the six individuals included in this book, like the 1,000-plus other detainees arrested under similar circumstances after 9/11. The state channeled the aggression created by the war on terror to these individuals and violated their rights.[124] It transformed undocumented immigrants who resembled the 19 hijackers into the "next wave" of terrorists[125] because they could be detained easily under immigration laws. Their arrests also compensated for the state's intelligence failure, enabling officials to avoid taking responsibility for breaches in national security. The oral histories presented in the following chapters illustrate that the 9/11 detainees framed as terrorists by politicians and the media were innocent individuals entrapped by the state's racial and religious profiling practices.

The overwhelming majority of individuals arrested after 9/11, like five of the individuals profiled in this book, had minor immigration violations. However, one of the interviewees (Ansar Mahmood) had a valid visa. In his cases, the state converted him into a criminal and added the charges of harboring illegal immigrants to detain and deport him. This case is not an exception. During my research, I encountered similar examples when state officials closely scrutinized paperwork until they found something for which to detain and deport individuals who had no links to terrorism. The state combined its knowledge of rules and regulations with the power to enforce them to detain and deport individuals.[126] Through oral histories, this book dismantles the false connection between immigration detainees and terrorism and explains how the government used detentions and deportations as a tool to appease the general public's fears about future terrorist attacks.

In *Prison Notebooks*, Anthony Gramsci defines hegemony as a dominating power that the state develops and maintains through force and coercion. Another critical element of this domination is the consent of the subordinate classes.[127] Through the interplay of force and coercion, the state develops an environment in which the subordinate classes find their interests intertwined with advancing the interests of the dominant class. The purpose of hegemony is the promotion of dominant class interests through the conformity of the masses.[128]

Using the concept of hegemony, I explore the time and space after September 11, 2001, as an "exceptional time" in which the state developed a political climate of fear, in part by converting immigration detainees into terrorists. The subordinate classes—in this case, law enforcement officers at various levels and the general public—promoted the state's interests and advanced this hegemonic discourse because they believed that placing Muslim males behind bars would stop additional terrorist attacks.

State policies and strategies deliberately targeted vulnerable Muslim males using the rhetoric of national security. The constant spectacle of Muslims parading in shackles in the local and national news heightened the climate of fear that enabled the abrogation of civil rights. Like the black surplus population in the prison industrial complex,[129] the notions of "terrorist Muslim men among us" and "sleeper cells" contributed to creating a sense of panic and an image of the state as a protector of U.S. citizens. Placing more than 1,000 so-called terrorists behind bars concretely illustrated the state's efficiency in stopping additional attacks. It also served as evidence of potential "sleeper cells" in the United States, justifying increased surveillance and policing of Americans. As a result, the general public relinquished civil and legal rights to stop additional terrorist attacks.

The following oral histories illustrate that many FBI and immigration agents, prison guards, prosecutors, deportation officers, and judges perceived most Muslim-looking men as terrorists. Through these arrests, law enforcement officials wanted to prevent additional terrorist attacks. Every national television news channel and newspaper published stories of ongoing arrests in connection with terrorism without proper fact-checking. Concerned citizens flooded FBI hotlines to report suspicious "Muslim-looking males" living in their neighborhoods. Within days, every Muslim-looking male became a potential terrorist. At airports, racial profiling for Muslims became acceptable. The six personal narratives reveal the mechanisms used to maintain the continuity and reciprocity of the hegemonic discourse of the Muslim terrorist. Arrests, detentions, and deportations helped create a consensus that every Muslim-looking male is suspicious. Through oral histories, this book dismantles the false connection between immigration detainees and terrorism and explains how the government used detentions and deportations as a tool to appease the general public's fears about future terrorist attacks.

Oral History Methodology

Between October 2002 and April 2004, I completed over 40 in-person interviews with individuals arrested and deported after September 11, 2001. All but two were male. These interviews were conducted with individuals detained in jails, individuals released after detentions within the United States, and individuals deported to Pakistan, Egypt, and India. Another 20 interviews were conducted both in the United States and abroad with friends and family members of detainees. I selected Pakistan and Egypt because the largest numbers of "Special Interest Cases" were from these two countries.[130] Two important "Special Interest Cases," those of Mohammed Azmath and Ayub Khan, inspired me to go to India.

To access former detainees, I initially worked with a few community organizations in New York, such as Islamic Circle of North America (ICNA), Desis Rising Up and Moving (DRUM), American Friends Service Committee (AFSC), and Muslim Community Services (MCS). These organizations worked diligently during the 9/11 crisis to provide legal, financial, and emotional support for detainees and their families. Their efforts built name recognition among former detainees and enabled the organizations to gain their trust.

Among these, Adem Carroll of ICNA was my key contact. He provided me with a few connections to individuals who were in jails, released, and/or deported. He also wrote a letter on ICNA letterhead that introduced me to former detainees, explained my project, and encouraged them to talk to me. Without these community connections, I would not have been successful in my research.

Overwhelmingly, the majority of the individuals that I interviewed fit the profile outlined in the section on the demographics of 9/11 detainees, meaning that they came to the United States for better economic opportunities over the last ten years, and after their visas expired, they used community networks to disappear in New York and New Jersey. Most of these individuals also worked in nonprofessional jobs. During my interviews, former detainees pointed out time and again that they did not consider their undocumented status a crime because they observed that the United States was swarming with undocumented immigrants. They also noted that employers liked hiring undocumented immigrants for their hard work and willingness to work for lower wages. For them, getting arrested was like getting pulled over for driving five to ten miles above the speed limit on a highway where all the drivers are doing so. It was the arbitrary and discriminatory nature of the application of laws that agitated former detainees. A common complaint I heard was this: "If you are going to be tough on undocumented immigrants, then arrest everyone. Why only us? Why only Muslims?"

For these former detainees, sharing these stories is a political project. These individuals were kicked out of the country for minor immigration or criminal charges. They saw themselves, therefore, as victims of racial profiling and saw me as a vehicle for carrying their voices back to the country from which they had been deported. They wanted to make sure they told me the truth so that my scholarship could be trusted and their voices could be heard. For example, no one denied that they had an expired visa or an expired immigration application. They knew that I could verify the facts about the cases given that most of the information was available through the court files and public lawyers. However, they never considered their undocumented status or any other minor immigration violation (i.e., working on a visiting visa, marriage fraud to obtain a work permit) to be of any significance because they encountered other individuals with similar situations living and working in the United States.

There were several individuals who did not want to talk to me for numerous reasons, including shame, fear, hesitation, and lack of trust and comfort.[131]

I respected those reasons and decided not to include those individuals in this book. I discuss some of the reasons behind their reluctance to talk to me in an article published in *Amerasia Journal*.[132] Despite having an intimate knowledge of the six cases included in the book, I don't profess to be a complete insider and confirm that, at a certain level, "we are all outsiders."[133]

Six Oral Histories: Rationales for Choosing Them

Even though I conducted more than 40 personal interviews with former detainees, this book focuses on the lives of six individuals who were arrested between September 11, 2001, and December 31, 2001. I selected these particular individuals primarily because I was able to conduct more in-depth interviews with them. Their willingness to share their stories and certain circumstances enabled me to spend more time with these individuals. I discuss my relationship with each individual in the chapters that follow. Along with the recorded interviews, I stayed in touch with them through telephone and e-mail and continued to clarify their stories. After 2004 I made several visits to the Middle East and South Asia, during which I frequently met these individuals informally and cemented our relationship of trust. Along with recording hours of interviews with these six people, I researched and unearthed every possible detail before writing about their cases.

Four of the six individuals were detained on the ninth floor of the MDC in Brooklyn. The details they gave me independently about the conditions of the detention were consistent and corroborated by government sources. In addition to those four included in this book, I personally interviewed another ten individuals housed on the ninth floor of MDC, and they confirmed patterns of abuse, strip searches, and solitary confinement.

I met the four detainees independently for the most part, on an individual basis in New York, Alexandria, Karachi, and Hyderabad. Their stories and the specific details about the MDC's ninth floor that I collected from the interviews were all very consistent. After I listened to multiple stories, the reality of the ninth floor started to emerge and take on a life of its own. I heard the same details over and over about the prison environment from each person interviewed—the six-by-ten-foot cell, solitary confinement, bright lights that never turned off, video surveillance cameras, rectal examinations, cavity and strip searches, the punitive recreation area,[134] the cursing of the prison guards, and physical abuse inflicted by the MDC staff.[135] The two OIG reports issued about September 11 detainees in April and December 2003, referenced earlier, corroborated essentially all of the details I recorded from their interviews.

Mohammed E******, interviewee for one of the narratives in this book, was taken to Passaic County Jail in New Jersey instead of the MDC. After being deported to Egypt, he spent a few months in jail, where he was physically beaten and tortured with electric shocks. Shortly after his release, he fled Egypt and gained political asylum in Switzerland, where he currently lives. One of his attorneys, Steven Watt has confirmed his story and appeared at various human rights conferences with him.[136] The fact that Mohammed could not be safe in his own home country after being labeled as a terrorist inspired me to document his story in depth.

Ansar Mahmood is a close friend who was detained at the Buffalo Detention Center in Batavia, New York. I got involved in his legal case when he was still fighting his deportation and worked closely with his lawyers and community organizers for over three years. Despite our efforts, Ansar was deported to Pakistan.

Part of my motivation in choosing these six narratives was to provide a broad range of detention experiences and to simultaneously highlight the similarities and the differences between cases. I wanted to retell the story of detention and deportation from several angles so that readers can feel the intensity of the experience. I also wanted to provide enough details and depth so that readers develop emotional connections to the individuals. For me, these stories are not only facts and figures but also explorations into the lives of immigrants who came to the United States to realize a dream. Each case presented in this book prompts the reader to take a deeper look into the featured individual's life. If not for 9/11, none of these individuals would have been detained or faced such hardships.

These narratives also include several substories and themes that I felt were important to highlight. For example, I wanted to examine gender, despite the fact that most of the former detainees were males. During my research, I only interviewed two female detainees, and only one of them was arrested between September 11 and December 31. To incorporate a wider perspective on gender, I include the stories of female family members who were devastatingly impacted by the detention of their loved ones, regardless of whether they were living in the United States or abroad. The voices of these female family members also help us to see that the detentions had a far-reaching impact. Entering the homes of former detainees allowed me to see the interviewees as fathers, brothers, and sons who had been framed as terrorists or criminals. One of the primary purposes of this book is to humanize these individuals.

Interviewing Government Officials

In spite of repeated attempts to reach government officials, I often felt as if I was hitting a wall in this aspect of my research. The FBI and immigration officers involved in the cases were not available for interview, even though I located and called them. For example, one of the officers told me on the phone that he did not remember the details and that he would try to get back to me if he had anything to add. He never called back or returned my phone calls. One officer had retired, and even though I left messages for him, he never called back. I got the same lack of response from the immigration officer involved in Ansar Mahmood's case.

Someone told me that FBI officers don't like to discuss cases, and I thought at the time that maybe their reticence was due to the fact that I was not related to the detainees. I decided to test this theory by calling the FBI agent who investigated my brother; I found that regardless of my personal connection to the case, FBI officials chose to remain silent. I left the agent at least ten messages explaining that I was a family member interested in knowing what made my brother appear as a suspect. He never returned my phone calls.

After some persistent efforts, however, two high-ranking FBI officials, one immigration judge, one senior district judge, two prosecutors, and one high-ranking police officer talked to me. One of the FBI officials was Coleen Rowley, a whistle-blower and one of three persons of the year for *Time* magazine in 2002. She critically examined the government's 9/11 detention policies and gave me insights on the government's perspectives. Her office worked on the Zacarias Moussaoui case,[137] but she was not directly involved in any of the cases included in this book.

Compared to the interviews with former detainees, my interviews with government officials were short, guarded, quasi-official, and often off the record. A few critically examined government policies, but the majority defended the government's position and repeated the mainstream argument that the government acted within its legal framework to detain and deport individuals with immigration and/or criminal violations. They blamed the chaotic situation after September 11 for some of the delays that the 9/11 detainees experienced during detentions. For the majority of these officials, I noticed an indifferent attitude; they acted as if they had seen worse and that prolonged detentions were not a cause for concern. The typical attitude was

> Well, it happens. Too bad that it happened, but worse happens. Former detainees should be thankful that they are out. They were out of status or they had done something "illegal,"[138] which made them suspicious and so should they should not be complaining. We followed laws.[139]

Steven Brill's book *After*[140] and the Office of Inspector General reports about September 11 detainees[141] include interviews with DOJ officials. I use both of these publications for reference throughout the book.

Legal Research

For each of the detainees featured in the book, I met at least one defense attorney,[142] who confirmed the legal information independently provided by their clients. For the most part, the defense attorneys felt that their clients were victims of the 9/11 backlash and they were sympathetic toward them. These conversations about the legal aspects of the cases allowed me to understand their situations better given that some of the details were not clear from the legal files or the detainees' narratives. The defense attorneys also described the moods and attitudes of the courts, the judges, and the prosecutors.

Along with these personal interviews, I also reviewed all the legal files that were publicly available for the six cases, including trial or court transcripts.[143] The transcripts reveal that court discussions generally revolved around credit card frauds, expired visas, or some other suspected crime. The transcripts also show that some judges were aware of the conditions of confinement, and in some cases, detainees complained to them (such as Yasser Ebrahim). In most of the situations, either the judges decided to ignore the detainees' complaints or accepted the government's explanations that these detainees were kept in high-security jails in solitary confinement to protect them from other inmates (as with Mohammed Azmath).

Organization of Each Chapter

I begin each oral history by briefly describing the legal case and discussing how and where I met the individual. Details of the surrounding environment, the interview settings, and my interactions with my subjects are provided to give insights into the narrative and to explain how each interview was conducted. These aspects are also important for understanding the power dynamics between me as the interviewer and the detainees as the interviewees. Following that, I present the story of the former detainee in first-person narrative. Subheadings and italic comments in my voice are added to provide clarity to the narrative. All of the interviews were audio recorded.

While writing these narratives, I visualized the former detainees and allowed their voices to run through my mind. Compared to the court trial transcripts and other written archival materials, which are sketchy and for the most part lifeless, my recorded interview and my interactions with the detainees are vivid and have a life of their own. I transcribed all of the interviews and read over them several times to organize them under certain themes. I talked with Yasser Ebrahim, Nabil Ayesh, and Mohammed E****** in English. I spoke Urdu with Mohammed Azmath and his wife, Tasleem Jaweed. I also spoke Urdu with Anser Mehmood, his wife, Uzma Naheed, and their three young children; and I spoke Punjabi with Ansar Mahmood. Many times, the individuals did not share the details of their experiences in a chronological manner, and our conversations did not have a linear nature to them. Furthermore, each narrative includes the voices of several other people, who were recorded separately. I took the liberty of reorganizing parts of the conversation to facilitate the readability, but I tried my best to keep the words, tone, and essence of the interviews intact. During the interview, I focused on my subjects; while editing and writing the interviews, I focused on ensuring that unfamiliar readers would be able to grasp each individual's story, starting from their arrival to the United States and ending with their deportation. During the writing process, I contacted the subjects several times via phone and e-mail to ask additional questions and fill in gaps in the stories.

I have presented these narratives in the first person so readers can feel a direct connection to the individuals who were framed as terrorists or vilified for being undocumented or committing minor crimes. Although I occasionally provide endnotes to indicate the outside sources I used to recount the stories as completely as possible, I deliberately decided not to overburden the narratives with notes and my comments. Doing so would make the cases appear clinical and impair the ability of readers to empathize with the interviewees. The information provided in the narratives is accurate, and much of it is confirmed by outside sources. The remainder of the information is based on what the detainees told me and could not be corroborated by outside sources such as legal files or third parties—either because I could not access them or because the others involved in the case were not willing to discuss it.

I cannot fully describe how these individuals felt about me, but I believe they respected me because they felt that I was doing something meaningful. I started my research before most other researchers had had an opportunity to visit Egypt, Pakistan, and India. The OIG report had not been released yet. At that time, it was their word against the government's. They felt that I trusted them at that emotionally and politically charged time when perhaps others may not have trusted them or believed their stories.

Objectives of the Book

My primary objective in writing this book is to provide a space for these individuals to tell their stories completely. Many media outlets have interviewed almost all of the men included in the book,[144] but to give objectivity to their articles, journalists have tried to provide equal space to government officials. As a result, the voice of the former detainee often was drowned out by the authoritative, powerful voices of government officials, who invoked laws, policies, and the need for national security to dominate the discussion. They also repeatedly used words like "illegals," "criminals," "dangerous," and "suspicious," to obscure the situations and justify the injustices endured by these individuals. I deliberately provide space for these individuals to tell their stories and allow readers to reach their own conclusions about their characters and their cases.

As I write these stories, I follow in the footsteps of prominent scholars who have documented oral histories of victims of social injustice, like the Japanese American internees of World War II.[145] Along with the historic and archival research, the purpose of these oral histories is to reveal the interpretations of the intended or unintended consequences of internment. For example, we already know that Executive Order 9066 was posted throughout neighborhoods and gave instructions to "all persons of Japanese ancestry" to report for relocation. Oral histories reveal how American citizens of Japanese ancestry interpreted those posters as individuals. They provide some answers to questions like these: How did they communicate with their family members and friends about the meanings of these posters? What steps did they take to gather or sell their belongings and line up in the assembly halls? How did they feel about being considered enemies in a country where they were born and worked day and night to build their lives and communities? What explanations did they give to their children about where they were going? How did their impressions about being American change? How were the patterns of family life interrupted as a result of this mass internment?

The 9/11 detentions are analogous to the Japanese American internment in the sense that official sources like legal files, scholarly research, nongovernmental organizations, and government officials have confirmed that these detentions occurred and the detainees did not have any connection with the 9/11 attacks. However, these legal files and governmental and nongovernmental reports don't provide details about the interior lives of the detainees. The oral histories included in this book, much like the oral histories of Japanese American internees, reveal the human cost of those detentions and how they impacted the lives of former detainees and their families. They provide answers to such questions as, What did the former detainees tell themselves about what was happening to them when they were picked up from their homes by law enforcement officers with helmets, bulletproof jackets, and machine guns? How did they interpret the shock of their personal losses, which did not even allow them to join the nation in grieving the loss of human lives in the 9/11 tragedy? What explanations did they provide to their families and friends back home about their sudden return? How did they pass their time in solitary confinement? How did they cope with the physical, psychological, and emotional abuse when they were not allowed any contact with the outside world? How did they feel when they thought that they might die there without seeing their loved ones?

Through these oral histories, I am also exploring the various patterns of power that operated between detainees and government officials. There is no way for me to confirm the specific conversations that occurred between detainees and law enforcement officers, but it is important to recognize the former detainee's memory of such conversations, his interpretation of these memories, and the significance of those experiences to him. Through these oral histories, I hope to

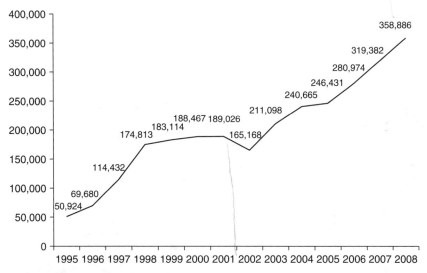

Graph 2 Deportations from the United States 1995–2008.

These numbers are based on an order of removal.

Source: U.S. Department of Homeland Security, *Yearbook of Immigration Statistics*, Table 36, 2008.

present each experience as it registered in the mind of the former detainee when he was helpless, alone, and vulnerable as closely and accurately as possible.

Deportations are not new in U.S. history—Latino and especially Mexican communities have historically experienced deportations. However, scholars estimate that since the passage of the 1996 Anti-Terrorism and Effective Death Penalty Act,[146] deportations have surged (see graph 2). Despite this surge in immigrant deportations, a book featuring the personal narratives of deportees is nonexistent. The narratives included in this book examine the lives of Muslim immigrants in the United States after they have been deported to their home countries. In doing so, it includes their reflections, captures their experiences of uprootedness and family breakups, maps out their psychological frame of mind, and traces their evolving attitudes toward the United States. By compiling personal narratives of deportees from four different countries, this book aims to establish a new field of deportation studies at a global level.

Finally, I wrote this book in the hope that student and progressive lawyers will pick up these cases for discussion and suggest ways to reopen and retry them—so that, at the minimum, the names of these people are cleared. The government also needs to pay reparations to former detainees and issue an apology for violating their civil, legal, and human rights. I hope some of these narratives can be used to influence those decision makers.

Figure 1 Azmath Mohammed with his wife, Tasleem Jaweed, and son, Bilal, in India, March 2003. Photograph by Irum Shiekh.

CHAPTER I

The Transnational Implications of 9/11 Detentions

Mohammed Azmath and Tasleem Jaweed

Mohammed Azmath[1] *and Ayub Ali Khan,*[2] *two friends from India, came to the United States on visiting visas in search of better economic opportunities. Mohammed arrived in the United States in 1991 and rented an apartment in Jersey City, New Jersey. Ayub , joined him in 1994. Their visas expired, but they were able to find employment at grocery stores, warehouses, and newspaper stands. They also sent money back home to help their families. On September 1, 2001, they both lost their jobs at a newspaper stand, which they had been working for some time. Soon after, one of their friends invited them to visit San Antonio, Texas, for a potential new job; on September 11, 2001, they took a flight from the Newark airport to San Antonio with a stopover in Saint Louis, Missouri. After the attacks on the World Trade Center, all flights were grounded. During their layover in Saint Louis, they learned that future flights were uncertain and decided to take an Amtrak train to complete their journey.*

It was during the Amtrak journey that law enforcement officers investigated them. After confirming that their visas were expired, the officers arrested them and classified them as "Special Interest Cases," which meant they were under strong suspicion of involvement in the 9/11 attacks. Within days, they were moved to the ninth floor of the Metropolitan Detention Center (MDC) in Brooklyn. Their names and faces were featured in the headlines of all the major newspapers.[3] *Approximately a month later, the* New York Times *reported,*

> *The Federal Bureau of Investigations interpreted the closely cut hair, and otherwise shaven bodies, as a possible sign that the men, Ayub Ali Khan and Mohammed*

Jaweed Azmath, might have been ready to die in a similar attack, and were "prepared to meet Allah."[4]

Both Azmath and Ayub stayed on the ninth floor in solitary confinement for almost a year.

During Azmath's detention, his wife, Tasleem Jaweed (a Pakistani national living in India), was also subjected to investigation and harassment. Indian intelligence came to her house in Hyderabad, India, and searched it, along with her belongings. She remained under surveillance for a long time. Officials also arrested her for an expired visa and placed her in a local jail. With the help of a local politician, she was able to stop her deportation.

On December 13, 2001, Azmath was charged with credit card fraud. In September 2002, he pled guilty to the charges and was finally deported to India in early 2003. He did not have any connections to terrorism.

Meeting Azmath and Tasleem

On January 9, 2003, I traveled to the Passaic County Jail in New Jersey to meet Mohammed. After undergoing the security and identification checks in the jail, I suddenly felt very exhausted and weary in the face of a large, heartless bureaucracy. In my journal I wrote, "Doing interviews in the jail is the hardest part of the research. It feels like the guards in uniform, the gates and the batons are constantly breaking you down."

I thought about the prisoners living in this situation. If a half hour in the detention center can drain me, what is the psychological impact on individuals who have been living there for days, weeks, months, and years? My train of thought was broken when Azmath's name was called out on the loudspeaker. I approached a glass door and put on a telephone headset to talk to him. I found a pleasant and sweet-mannered person smiling at me on the other side of the glass. At that time, Azmath was waiting for his deportation to India. We talked for about an hour, during which time he told me about his detention and arrest. He expressed his anger with the American government and fear about the future awaiting him in India after his deportation. At the end, he gave me his home address and telephone number and asked me to visit him in India. In March 2003, I traveled to India and met Azmath, his wife, Tasleem, and their young child, Bilal. I stayed for three days in Hyderabad, and every evening, I went to Azmath's clean and simple house. Tasleem cooked delicious food, which we all ate together.

For the most part, I audio-recorded separate interviews with Azmath and Tasleem in Urdu. Azmath was forthcoming in his criticism of the United States and its policies. Tasleem was cautious in her selection of words and held back her criticism of the United States and the Indian government. I translated and transcribed the interviews *and sent a draft version of this narrative to Azmath in August 2007. After reviewing the narrative, he wrote back in an e-mail:*

> *When I read/watch any news about Guantanamo Bay Prison, I feel that there is no difference in MDC Brooklyn 9th floor SHU [Special Housing Unit] and Passaic County Prison in NJ on American soil, the treatment with Prisoners by the guards in Guantanamo Bay Prison.[5]*

Azmath gave me some documents from his FBI file, including sworn and official statements from various intelligence officials. I also reviewed his legal file, which was kept at the Records Department of the U.S. District Court for the Southern District of New York.[6] The following narrative is based on those conversations, legal documents, newspaper articles, and research.

The Arrest

The train ride from Saint Louis was pleasant. Azmath and Ayub had a routine conversation about their trip with the two passengers who were sitting in front of them. They talked about where they were going and coming from, and nothing unusual was mentioned from either side. At one point, Azmath left the cabin and smoked with the train conductor.

Close to Fort Worth, Texas, the train stopped. Drug Enforcement Agents boarded the train and directly approached us. One officer asked where we had come from and where we were going. We told him, and he asked for our identification cards, which we handed over. I was not afraid of their questions. I cooperated because I thought that they were just doing a routine check, but when the questions kept coming, I got a bit uncomfortable.

"Why are you asking these questions?" I asked one of the officers.
"Due to suspicion."
"What kind of suspicion?"
"I can't explain."

I assumed that the law enforcement officers just looked at the passenger list, saw Muslim and Arabic names, and singled us out. I noticed that they did not approach or question anyone else. Initially, they said that a waitress had complained. Later, they said that a passenger had complained about our misbehavior. I couldn't imagine what he was talking about because nothing had happened. The train ride had been pleasant and we had had a normal conversation without any mishaps with the two passengers that were sitting in front of us. We had even chatted and smoked with the conductor.

In a sworn Affidavit in Support of Search Warrant, Kristina E. Sheppard, special agent, Federal Bureau of Investigation, stated,

> On September 12, 2001, Dallas Division received information from Dallas Area Rapid Transit (DART) Police Department that two individuals were causing a disturbance at a train station shared by DART and Amtrak in downtown Dallas. The officer identified the individuals through Amtrak ticket stubs as Ayub Khan and Mohammed Azmath.[7]

Along with this sworn statement, which erroneously records a "disturbance," I found several other official and nonofficial statements recording that Azmath and Ayub bought one-way tickets with cash, making them appear suspicious because that is a common habit among drug dealers.[8] With all these conflicting statements, it is hard to determine exactly why Azmath and Ayub came under suspicion.[9]

After some simple questions, they wanted to search our luggage, but they did not have any search warrants. They could not find anything, and then they told us that they wanted to ask additional questions and arrested us. We traveled back to the local police station in Fort Worth for investigation because there were no facilities near the place where the train had stopped.

I had never had a legal problem before in my life, so I was inexperienced and didn't know that I should have asked for a lawyer. At the time, I thought getting a lawyer would lengthen the investigation, so I decided it would be better to just talk to the FBI and let them finish their questioning. I thought they would be satisfied with my answers, close the case, and release me, but it did not turn out that way.

Immediately after the arrest, CNN started to broadcast stories about the pair along with photographs. The following sensational coverage on September 19, 2001, connects both Azmath and Ayub to the September 11 attacks. It is unclear how CNN determined that both of them had extensive knowledge of "the terrorist network":

> Mohammed Jaweed Azmath and Ayub Ali Khan...authorities believe may have been intent on hijacking another plane last week. The two had been on a flight Tuesday from Newark, New Jersey, to San Antonio, Texas, that was safely diverted to St. Louis. They then headed by train for San Antonio, but were detained in Dallas, sources said.
>
> Sources said the two men had box cutters on them—instruments carried by at least some of the 19 hijackers on the four jets—and had extensive knowledge of the terrorist network.
>
> On Saturday, authorities raided an apartment in Jersey City, New Jersey, where Khan lived. Sources said others on a "watch list" established by the FBI may also have lived at that address.[10]

The FBI special agent Kristina E. Sheppard's sworn statement in front of Magistrate Judge John Primomo, dated September 15, 2001, noted the following:

> *There is a probable cause to believe that: Ayub Khan and Mohammed Azmath (AKA Azmath Jaweed) are involved in the alleged acts of terrorism or associated with individuals believed to be responsible for the alleged acts of terrorism committed at the World Trade Center and the Pentagon on September 11, 2001.*

Sheppard's conclusion was based on the fact that both Azmath and Ayub had expired visas and that they were carrying cash in their briefcases and two box cutters. She also said agents had found a letter "written largely in what appears to be the Urdu language with Arabic characters. Small portions of the letter are written in English, including the statement, 'I look forward to seeing you after my death.'"

A quick investigation by a qualified FBI agent could have provided a rational explanation for all of the suspicious items. Both Azmath and Ayub used to work at a newspaper stand, where workers use box cutters routinely on the job.[11] The $3,000 in cash was intended for relocation from New Jersey to Texas. For many immigrants, opening a bank account can be difficult, and it is not unusual to carry thousands of dollars in cash. As for the Urdu letter, Ayub explained to me in an e-mail dated September 8, 2007, that the text of the letter written by his wife was taken completely out of context:

> *I got married in the year of 2000. Immediately after that I traveled to the U.S.... In the letter, she insisted that I come back to India because we were newly married and she missed me lot. In anger [she wrote] that if you don't come soon you will see my death face.... The FBI went through the letter from my luggage and took wrong meanings.[12]*

Ayub told me that he repeatedly provided explanations for all of these items to the FBI agents, but they refused to trust him.

The DEA took us to the FBI office, where they separated Ayub and I and then interrogated us. I never talked to Ayub after our initial arrest, and I did not know his whereabouts. Even after we arrived at the MDC, they put us in separate areas.

After the initial FBI investigation, they took us to the INS. The immigration authorities confirmed that our visas were expired and ordered our deportation. I signed my deportation papers and prepared to leave the United States, but instead of deporting us, officers took us to San Antonio and picked up a Saudi doctor. They shackled and chained us and then put us on a charter plane to Minnesota, where we picked up Zacarias Moussaoui,[13] who was also being held on some immigration violations. After that, they brought us to the MDC on the evening of September 14, 2001. When we landed at the airport, twenty or thirty officers surrounded us and pointed their guns at us. They told us, "Don't move. If you move, we will not hesitate to shoot at you."

Law enforcement officers put each one of us on a separate truck. Military officers accompanied us, and cars with loud sirens drove in front and in the back. The truck had tinted windows so no one could see us. They had blocked all the roads up to the Brooklyn MDC, and everybody watched us from their homes as we drove through the streets. In the ten to twelve years that I lived in the U.S., I never saw or heard about anything like this.

Some scholars have discussed the theatrical performance that FBI agents put on during raids of Japanese Americans during World War II to create a spectacle for anxious neighbors, outraged politicians, and sensation-hungry journalists.[14] *During my interviews, I heard about similar cases of law enforcement officers staging spectacles by blocking off streets, raiding buildings, and arresting Muslim-looking individuals. My research suggests that through these theatrical performances, officers were appeasing the general public's fears, attracting media attention, and framing Muslims as terrorists.*[15]

Tasleem's Anxiety Over Azmath's Disappearance

Tasleem Jaweed, Azmath's wife, knew about his travel and moving plans. When she did not hear from him, she got worried.

I knew that Azmath was going to Texas. When I heard about the plane crash, I became worried and wanted to find out if he had arrived safely. His friend called and said that Azmath had left Jersey City, but then his friend from Texas called and told us that he had not arrived in San Antonio. A plane had taken off in New Jersey and had crashed. I was very worried and afraid that he might've been on that plane. I also heard about planes being grounded, and I hoped that Azmath's was one of them. I hoped that he was just stuck somewhere and that he would get to Texas once the planes started to fly again.

In Hyderabad, I was living with Azmath's father. We were all anxious because we could not find out what was going on and there was no way to contact him. Fifteen days passed before we found out that Azmath had been arrested. I read it in the local newspaper, and then I heard it on the BBC and CNN. Even though I felt very tense and confused, I was confident that he would be released soon because he had not done anything. I thought that it was going to be a temporary problem.

Reports kept coming from CNN, the BBC, and the local newspapers that he had been arrested under suspicion of terrorism, but I remained optimistic that it would all be over once they found out that they had made a mistake. I continued to wait. One month passed, two months, three months, and then a year. I trusted that God was watching and He knew that Azmath was innocent and that there was no evidence against him. Azmath did not know that his name was publicized worldwide and that his family had learned about his case from the media. I never used to watch the news that much before, but I started to because CNN was constantly reporting on him and airing his photograph. My blood pressure would rise as I watched the reports.

Tasleem was a few months pregnant at the time of Azmath's arrest.

Day and night, it was the same story. It was a big problem at that time especially because I was alone. My mom was not with me. There was no one around to counsel me or comfort me by putting a hand on my head [*she cries*]. I could not do anything except pray because I was in a new country by myself and I did not know what to do or where to go. I was in such a state of mind that I could not see the sky or the earth. I felt that I was stuck deep in quicksand and would never find my way out. I was in such a horrible condition [*close to finishing her crying... takes a deep breath... silence*], and I just prayed to God to please give us justice. It was a very difficult time for me.

Moving to the Ninth Floor of the Metropolitan Detention Center

In New York, Azmath was taken to the MDC in Brooklyn, where he encountered a darker side of the American justice system.

When I arrived at the ninth floor of the MDC on September 14, there were about 10 to 15 individuals there who were suspected of terrorism and connections to the September 11 attacks.

On the way to the MDC, the guards misbehaved a lot. They pushed us and banged us against the walls and the doors. The sides of those doors were pretty hard, and the prison guards wanted us to feel pain. When they put handcuffs on us, they tightened them to the point that they hurt. They also twisted our hands in the back. I think the prison guards were angry with us because they thought we were terrorists.

The Office of the Inspector General's December 2003 report documented similar patterns of abuse for other September 11 detainees at the MDC. The report noted,

> [There is] evidence that some officers slammed detainees against the wall, twisted their arms and hands in painful ways, stepped on their leg restraint chains, and punished them by keeping them restrained for long periods of time.... We determined that the way these MDC officers handled some of the detainees was in many respects unprofessional, inappropriate, and violation of... policy.[16]

The report explained some of the reasons for this abuse:

> Many of the staff members we interviewed described the atmosphere at the MDC immediately after September 11 as emotionally charged. One of the lieutenants

currently at the MDC said the staff "had a great deal of anger" after September 11 and that it was a chaotic time at the MDC. Another lieutenant, one of the lieutenants responsible for escorting detainees, stated that upon entering the institution the detainees were handed over to teams of five to seven officers who were "spiked with adrenaline." He said that there were some officers on the escort teams who were "getting ready for battle" and "talking crazy." Another lieutenant responsible for escorting detainees similarly described the officers as "high on adrenaline."[17]

The ninth floor of the MDC is designed to punish individuals from the general population unit who get involved in fights or misbehave with prison guards. At the maximum, this punishment generally lasts for one week, but I was kept there in solitary confinement for a year. During this time, I was not able to hear any news or watch anything, nothing at all. After a few weeks, they painted the windows so that we could not even look outside. The lights were on 24 hours a day.

In the beginning, I could not fathom what was happening to me or around me. I noticed that some people were talking with each other, but I did not understand how. Later, I realized that people were talking through a small ventilation hole on the top of the cell wall. I did not know any of the other prisoners so I did not talk to anyone for the first eight to ten days. Then I started talking to them, and I learned that one guy was working in a restaurant making sandwiches when he got arrested. Another was driving a taxi, and one was just sleeping in his house. After talking to them, I realized that there were others in situations similar to mine.

There were also five Jewish men on the ninth floor, but they were released much earlier than the Muslims. A few Jewish groups came to meet them, and they also had the ability to call because the counselors brought them phones. We were never given those privileges.[18]

Total Blackout

I wasn't allowed to meet or call anyone until December 13, 2001. During this time, the only people that I talked to were FBI officers, prison guards, prosecutors, and other government officials. I met my lawyer Anthony Ricco on December 13, 2001, in the courtroom, 92 days after my arrest. Sometimes, they would prevent me from meeting my lawyer by lying to him and telling him that I had moved. He complained in the court.

According to the court records, Anthony Ricco, Azmath's lawyer, wrote a letter to Judge Shira Scheindlin dated May 17, 2002. In the letter, Ricco wrote that he went to see his client at the MDC but that the Bureau of Prisons informed Ricco, "Mohammed Azmath has... been transferred, as of today, from the Metropolitan Detention Center, to an undisclosed facility."[19] *Azmath was never transferred.*

They would also record my conversations with my lawyer Steve Legon[20] and told me that it was legal to do that because I was a high-profile case and a terrorist. Prison guards did not permit me to make telephone calls or write letters, so I could not tell my family where I was. I knew that my family members were very worried, but there was nothing I could do about it. Solitary confinement means that it is a no-access facility and I was in lockdown 24 hours a day. I needed money to make a telephone call, but the FBI seized what money I had.

After eight months, I was able to call my family for the first time, and I explained to them that I had not done anything wrong. I tried to console my wife and family members because I knew that they must be very worried after reading all the news. Later, when I started to receive letters, they were already opened and sometimes they were returned to the sender. I often received letters four months after they were mailed.

Transnational Implications

Azmath's wife, Tasleem, also became a suspect and underwent investigation, surveillance, and arrest. She was almost deported during his detention in the United States, and she described the transnational implications of Azmath's detention.

I am originally from Pakistan. I moved to India in February 2001, married Azmath in March, and lived with him for three months. I had a three-month visa, and before leaving, Azmath extended it for a year. I was hoping that he would come back in a year, but legally I don't need him there to extend my visa because I am married to an Indian citizen. Under normal circumstances, it should have been an easy process.

The Indian police came to our house for investigation the day the media reported on Azmath's arrest. Big officials from the Indian police came and blocked the entire road. The house was filled with policemen, and the sight was troubling. I wondered why they were doing this. They did not have any warrants, but they searched all our closets and checked all our papers. They could not find anything. At the end of the search, the Indian police consoled us and told us that Azmath had been caught without any proof and that he would be released very soon.

The press also interviewed me and everyone around the house. They wanted to prove that Azmath was innocent. They were trying to find out whether he had a family or not and whether he had any involvement in the attacks.

Tasleem was also suspected of links to terrorism. On October 7, 2001, the Washington Post *reported on her possible connections to "radical Islamic groups" in Pakistan, but it is unclear how journalists reached that conclusion. Was her Pakistani identity the major reason for this assumed link?*

Indian intelligence is also looking for any possible links between radical Islamic groups and the Pakistani wife of one of the men, who were picked up by federal agents on an Amtrak train in Texas the day after hijacked airliners slammed into the World Trade Center, the Pentagon and the Pennsylvania countryside.[21]

Tasleem had a string of encounters with various law enforcement agencies and reporters after Azmath's arrest.

In the beginning, reporters from both the Indian and the American press questioned me. At that time, they were suspicious of Azmath's identity, and many were wondering if Azmath was really an Indian national. After they confirmed that Azmath was from India and Hyderabad, they stopped questioning his identity, but due to this media publicity, the entire world knew that he was arrested under suspicion of terrorism.

The neighbors did not say anything negative about him because they had known him from childhood. Everyone who knew him from school and college praised him because they knew that he was innocent and that the American government was detaining him without any proof. They would try to comfort me by reminding me that it takes time to get released from prison.

In December, two white male FBI agents from America came to my house with an Indian translator. First they apologized for the interview and then said, "We just want to find out about your husband. We just have a suspicion. We don't have any proof." They asked me questions like, "Does your husband know how to fly planes?" Then they gave me a few names and asked if Azmath had any connections to those people. I told them that I had never heard those names before and that not only does Azmath not know how to fly planes, but that he barely knows how to ride a bike! The interrogation was surprising.

Then they asked me how Azmath felt about the U.S. and the life and people over there. I told them that he really loved America. He had always thought that there was justice in the U.S., and that officials would never give anyone trouble without proof. He felt that if he had the opportunity, he would just stay there because it was like paradise to him. I told the FBI agents, "Injustice is happening to a person who loves America." They told me that this wasn't the case and promised that he would be released very soon.

People would come and tell me stories about torture in prison. After hearing them, I used to get depressed and I wouldn't be able to sleep all night. That period in my life was so terrible that it is hard to describe. During the day it was okay, but it was very difficult at night because bad thoughts used to come to my mind. I felt like a corpse because I did not have any hope and I didn't know who to contact or what to do. At the end, I thought that I should go to the American consulate in Delhi and stage a hunger strike. Perhaps they could help me in some way. The FBI agents had promised me that they would allow Azmath to make a phone call and took my phone number, but no call came.

Occasionally, I received a letter from Azmath, but it went through so many security checks that it took forever to arrive in India and I wasn't even sure that he had written it. After six or seven months, Azmath was able to call us. It was a total surprise and it made me happy. After I heard his voice, I felt renewed. Suddenly, a wave of peace rippled through my body and I found a new world and a new life.

Becoming a Mother

I was four months pregnant when Azmath was arrested. I delivered my son Bilal during a tense time, and it was a very painful pregnancy. Due to the tension, my blood pressure got really high and I had to undergo an operation. Bilal was born without defects but the pregnancy had complications because of my stress. Doctors told me that I had a slim chance of survival. It was destiny that I survived for my child.

During the delivery, my feet swelled up and my water dried out. Since my child was born under such difficult circumstances, he was very weak and fragile. Doctors told me that he suffered a lot due to the tension. I used to pray, "Please give me a healthy child. This child is Azmath's keepsake." I prayed five times a day and read the Koran to ensure the safety of my child. After he was born, I hoped that Azmath would arrive soon. I counted the months, and soon Bilal was one year old. He started to say, "Dad come home. Dad come home."

Bilal also began praying to God. He used to see his father's photos and kiss them. After hearing Bilal pray, I used to plead to God that he listen to the calls of an innocent child, if not my own. Seeing other children with their fathers made me wonder when my child would be able to spend time with his father. I wasn't able to say anything to anyone. I just used to cry and then sit quietly. I started to look older than my age, and my family could not even recognize me. I was in such bad shape.

Tasleem's Deportation Fiasco

Two months before my visa expired, I went to the immigration office to get an extension. First, they refused to accept my application because my husband was not there. I explained to them that everyone knows about the status of his case and that everyone also knows that he has not been convicted of anything. Finally, they agreed to accept the application and sent it to Delhi for a final decision.

After my visa expired, the Delhi office sent me a letter declining the extension. The letter said that I needed to leave India and that they were going to deport me. I was still dealing with Azmath's problem and now I found myself embroiled in another major problem, so I contacted the court. At the first appeal, the court refused and issued deportation orders. Indian officials came to my house and told me to leave. I told them that I couldn't leave because I had an infant who was an Indian citizen. How would the Pakistani officials accept him? One of the inspectors told me to leave Bilal behind, and I said, "How can I leave him behind? Should I put him in an orphanage? Who will take responsibility? Will the home ministry take responsibility?"

The inspector became quiet and said, "We can't do anything." They took me with them to Narka, close to Bansi Bazar, to a police station where they kept me for six to seven hours. They had promised that they would provide me with a nice room where I could stay with Bilal.

When I got there, the place was in such a terrible condition that I was in disbelief. Those six to seven hours felt like *Qiamat* [the final day of judgment in Islam]. They put me in a small dirty storage room swarming with mosquitoes. Policemen came and went repeatedly and gave me strange looks. There was no space for me to feed Bilal when he got hungry. Finally I took off my *chadar* [shawl] and spread it on the floor to make a space for him to sit. It was so shameful. I had to stay all night in that condition, and then they booked a ticket for me on the morning train to Delhi. At that point, Brother Asaduddin Owaisi (our local representative) intervened and called the home ministry officials. They released me so that I could appeal the court decision. As soon as I was released, I appealed and I got the opportunity to stay here. If Azmath had not been in jail, this would not have happened.

During the appeal, I questioned the Indian authorities. "Americans put Azmath in jail but what does it have to do with me? There is no law that says you must also punish the wife." They told me that since Azmath was in jail in the U.S., they didn't know when he would be able to come back here, so I needed to be deported. In response, Azmath's lawyer wrote a long letter in which he stated that Azmath was not involved in any crime and that he could be deported at any time. At the second appeal, the judge read the letter and was very impressed. He was good and helped me by telling the government that he had received a letter from the U.S. and that there was no reason not to believe it.[22]

I often thought about Tasleem and Azmath during my research. Both were immigrants. Tasleem was a Muslim immigrant in India from Pakistan and Azmath was a Muslim immigrant in the United States from India. Both of their cases revolved around expired visas, but the circumstances of their detentions were different. In the beginning, Tasleem had difficulty in getting a visa extension in India, and the court denied her appeal based on suspicion of terrorism.[23] Azmath's family and friends used their connections to contact a local politician, who intervened and stopped her deportation.

For Azmath and many other individuals arrested on similar charges, such access to influential politicians in the United States who could have made calls to decision makers and stopped their deportations was not available. This lack of networks and resources made immigrants and specifically undocumented immigrants more vulnerable.

MDC Guards

The brutal attitude of prison guards was another factor that made life on the ninth floor of the MDC miserable. Azmath recalled:

The guards were always angry. They often said that we were going to die in prison and that we were terrorists. Maybe they thought that we were really terrorists. The government gave false information about us to the media, and the guards trusted that information and did not question if it was accurate. At nights, when we were sleeping, they would come and bang on the metal doors. Sometimes, they gave us the finger. They subjected us to a lot of mental and physical torture. When the guards moved us from the prison to the court, they would twist our hands, put on the handcuffs really tight, or bang us against the walls.

I lost a lot of weight in the jail. We were supposed to have a daily recreation break for an hour. On the ninth floor, there was a cage in the middle of an open-air hallway, and in the winter, the guards purposely left us out in the freezing cold for four to five hours. They were expressing their anger indirectly.

FBI Interrogations

Initially, Azmath underwent intensive FBI investigation. After he was charged with credit card fraud on December 13, 2001, the FBI investigation ended. However, jail administration kept him on the ninth floor of the MDC for eight more months until August 2002.

On the first day of investigation, FBI agents asked me what I knew about New York and the World Trade Center. I told them that I didn't know anything. I didn't even know that the attacks had occurred until the plane stopped in Saint Louis and I watched the news at the airport. They repeated the question, and again, I told them that I didn't know anything, but they remained suspicious.

Then the FBI agents started asking me about my background. They asked me where I was from and refused to believe me when I said India. They insisted that I was from Saudi Arabia and that I went to Afghanistan for the war, even though I've never been to either of those places. They also claimed that I was a pilot and a navigator and showed me a license from a flying institute in Virginia with my name on it. The license indicated that I had taken flying lessons. I've never been to a flying institute in Virginia or any other place, but they insisted that I had.

On September 14, 2001, Daniel D. O'Brien, an FBI agent, made the following statement in a sworn affidavit in support of Azmath's detention: " FAA records from March 1996 reveal that Mohammed Azmath is a certified pilot, engineer, and navigator, with an address listed in Mountain Terrace, [sic] WA. The records identify him as an Indian national."[24] Given that Mohammed Azmath is a common name among Muslims, it is possible another person with the same name lives in Washington. A quick search in the white pages lists over ten individuals with the same name in the United States. It is also possible this person is a pilot or has taken a flight training course. Careful intelligence, however, could have clarified that the Mohammed Azmath in custody had neither visited the West Coast nor taken any flying lessons.

They kept pinning false information on me and told me that everyone in the government was aware that I had taken flying lessons and that I was a pilot. Then they told me that I had traveled to Egypt and Sudan and that they had the pictures to prove it, but they never showed me those pictures. They kept on forcing me to accept that I was a Saudi and told me that they had my birth certificate and passport, which proved my Saudi nationality.

At that point, I was still under the assumption that they would clear and release me after a few days once they realized that I didn't have any connection to the attacks. Instead, they started a lengthy investigation. They interrogated me two to three times a week, eight to ten hours at a time, for three months. Two of the FBI officers were always there, and additional officers would accompany them from time to time. Sometimes, there were officers from other agencies also. All of them insisted that I was definitely involved in the attacks and that I would never be released. They showed me pictures of people who had died in the WTC attacks and said, "You are responsible for the deaths of these people. Do you know the punishment for the deaths of these people? You are going to die." It was mental torture, especially when I couldn't even talk to anyone about it. They kept telling me, "You will die here. You will be killed and your family will be in trouble."

My prosecutor was present during this FBI interrogation, but he never identified himself as a prosecutor. I recognized him later in the court. He had been very angry during the interrogations. Perhaps he thought I was a terrorist and he was frustrated that he could not find any evidence to prove it.

According to the court trial transcripts, Azmath made the following complaint in the court against the prosecutor:

"Your Honor . . . in 92 days I was in SHU and interrogated by the FBI and Eddie Bruce [sic] the prosecutor, but he didn't introduce himself as a prosecutor. I thought maybe is one of the FBI guy[s]. . . .

And one time he came with eight or 10 agents with the video camera and cameraman, took off the clothes—forcibly, by the security guards, and took pictures without clothes. They said they have their orders. And after one week they came with the article of the New York Times.[25] They showed everything, that I was shaved the body while I was traveling. Its totally wrong and false story.[26]

The prosecutor, Eric Bruce, was not present in court on the sentencing date, the day when Azmath had an opportunity to address the court. I called Mr. Bruce for a personal interview, but he refused and referred me to the public records. Karl Metzner, who represented the government on the day of the trial, called Azmath's statement "highly incredible" and commented that "Mr. Azmath may be twisting some of the words that he heard during the period of time that he was being interviewed by Mr. Bruce."[27] After Azmath's encounter with Mr. Bruce, however, the New York Times published a story about how Azmath had shaved his body in preparation for a suicide attack.

Ayub Khan also reported experiencing abusive conditions at the MDC. Ayub and Azmath were not in touch with each other during their detention, but their reports corroborate each other. Mr. Bruce was also Ayub's prosecutor and participated in his investigation. In a sworn statement, Ayub also bitterly complained about prison guards, the long detention, and the awful housing conditions at the MDC. He stated, "I was questioned during this period of time several times by agents and an Assistant United States Attorney (the same one who is now in charge of my criminal prosecution), who did nothing to ensure my rights or to bring me before a magistrate."[28]

In October, the FBI told me that they thought I was lying and that I needed to take a polygraph test. The agent conducting the polygraph test told me that if I passed the test, I would be released. I was not lying about anything, so I agreed to take it. They repeated the test three or four times. In the last session, an FBI agent said the question about whether I had any prior knowledge of the attacks was giving him a problem. He said, "Maybe you were walking on the street and people were talking among themselves. You did not see them. You just heard it and became knowledgeable." I insisted that I didn't have any prior knowledge. At the end, the FBI agent gave me a choice:

If you agree that you had prior knowledge, you will be released. You and your family will receive legal immigration status. Your wife will join you in the U.S. within two to three weeks. You will get enough money that you won't have to work for the rest of your life. The only thing that you have to do is say "yes." Say "yes" and it is an instant release. Say "no" and it could be 30 or 40 years. You will spend the rest of your life in prison.

I repeated that I was not hiding anything. He said, "This is your last chance to make the deal. I am sending this information to Washington, D.C." I could not find any reason to say yes because I really did not know anything. They tried their best to pressure me into agreeing.

FBI officers also constantly asked me questions about my religion. They asked if I was religious and whether I prayed and attended mosque. I told them that I went to the Newark mosque, and they asked if I went to the mosque in Jersey City. I didn't, so I said no. Later, they told me that there was a blind sheikh at the Jersey City mosque who was arrested in connection with the 1993 World Trade Center attacks.[29] I told them that I didn't know that mosque and had never met him nor seen him.

During the interrogations, they were very rough. They tried their best to find something, but they were wasting their time and effort on the wrong person. The way they interrogated and got information from here and there—that's not intelligence. First, they thought I was the twentieth hijacker,[30] and then they changed their statement to say that I had prior knowledge of the attacks.

Impact of the FBI Interrogations

For Azmath, the hardest aspect of his detention was the FBI interrogation. He explains the impact as follows:

The days I had FBI interrogations were the hardest, and I used to get really scared. The long interrogations and the FBI's constant insistence that I was involved in the World Trade Center attacks and that they had proof and so forth drained me completely, and I felt as if I were losing my mind and my consciousness.

There are special rooms designed for FBI interrogations, with space for two or three officers to sit and talk. Legally, this is what is allowed. One officer asks questions and the other one writes down the answers. Unfortunately, six to eight officers interrogated me for eight to ten hours at a time. They asked questions simultaneously in rough and rude language and threatened me. I would get tired of answering their questions and feel completely finished. Sometimes the interrogations were so long that the shift of the guard who brought me to the interrogation room would end, but they would continue to interrogate me. My lawyer told me later that it was illegal for so many FBI agents to simultaneously interrogate me for that long. After two or three hours, you start losing your mind.

I was shackled and handcuffed during the interrogations. My throat would get dry, I would not have the energy to even talk, and my body would shiver. There were so many questions, and because they scared me, sometimes I used to feel that maybe I had been involved in this attack unknowingly.

When I would go back to the cell, I would not feel anything for hours. Prison guards would bring my dinner and leave it in the cell, but I had no appetite, and I could not sleep at night. It was mental torture. Sometimes, I felt that

I might just die there. They threatened to harm my family, and I felt that they were serious. They had shown me this fake pilot license with my name on it, and I felt that they could do and prove anything in court.[31]

Azmath's Evaluation of the FBI

The FBI try to present themselves as having excellent intelligence capabilities, but in reality, they lied a lot and handled my case very unprofessionally. They are the worst government department, and the agents are cruel. They asked me stupid questions as if I didn't have a brain, and then they forced me to agree with them. They insisted that I had spent five years at a flight institute in Virginia and that I was a navigator. One FBI agent even made a false statement under oath and claimed that I was a pilot. Later, I asked them to give me a copy of the license, but they never gave it to me. Why did they fabricate this license and claim that I was a pilot? They could not find any proof or evidence, but they continued to search for it.

Intelligence officials also told the media that we had shaved our bodies, which was completely wrong.[32] I have never shaved my body because there is no reason for me to do that. They tried to make the case that I was part of some cult and was on a suicide mission. A simple check with any Islamic organization would reveal that shaving the body is prohibited, but the general public believed it. In discussions, people were also saying that I had the eyes of a terrorist, and the general public believed that also.

Azmath said that he naturally does not have a lot of hair on his body and, therefore, he believes that intelligence agents jumped to the conclusion that he had shaved. Many Islamic scholars were surprised to hear that the September 11 hijackers shaved their bodies and offered their criticism of connecting Islam with the ritual of body shaving. Traditionally, in Islam, shaving of body hair is not recommended for Muslim men. Examples can be found from the appearances of many traditional Muslim scholars, who generally wear long beards. According to government statements, hijackers who belonged to Al-Qaeda practiced the Sunni or Wahabi traditions of Islam, in which shaving of the body hair is not preferable for men.[33]

Courtroom Drama

Azmath was arrested on September 12, 2001, for an expired visa, and criminal charges of credit card fraud were added on December 13, 2001, while he was in custody. Several FBI reports documented Azmath's statements in which he admitted to committing the credit card fraud. In September 2002, Azmath pled guilty to credit card fraud and was finally deported to India in early 2003. Azmath believed that he could have fought those credit card charges, but it meant staying in jail longer. His wife was facing deportation from India, and he wanted to escape the anguish of solitary confinement.

The court experience was very strange and painful. In the court, the judge had been following my case, and I assumed that she knew about my terrorist charges because the media had reported it. However, when we went to the court, there were no terrorism charges, only the credit card fraud charges. Initially, they were treating it like a terrorist case, but when they could not find any evidence, they were forced to tack on the charges of credit card fraud.

Even after they charged me with credit card fraud, the marshal guards in the court and the prison guards claimed that I was a part of Al-Qaeda. When they moved me from the ninth floor to the first floor, they announced loudly, "Moving a terrorist. Moving a special package." Prison guards also announced that when they handed me over to the court marshal and when they were taking me back to the prison from the court. All the guards used to call me things like "Al-Qaeda," "terrorist," and "bin Laden" in front of all the other prisoners.

When the courts were discussing my credit card fraud charges, I wrote a letter to the warden requesting a move to the general population unit. In response, the MDC warden told me that I was connected to terrorist activity and that they couldn't move me.

Azmath made several requests to the jail warden to move him to the General Population Unit. In one of his requests dated July 17, 2002, Azmath wrote,

> *I want to be removed from SHU into general population for my mental and physical well-being. I strongly believe and feel that I am being put under undue pressure both mental and physical in order to affect my court proceedings. I am being held in SHU for over 10 months, not allowed to use the law library, make legal and social calls, receive or send any mail, and proper food to eat. I am being physically assaulted constantly by the security guards and extremely discriminatively treated and not provided anything to read. Therefore, I would like to bring this to your attention hoping you would do something about it. I kindly and respectfully request that you do immediately move [me] from SHU into general population because I feel this [is]... the limit of psychological and physical torture. I have not received any replies to my previous complaints. Thank you in anticipation.*[34]

In response to this request, on August 9, 2002, Michael Zenk (the jail warden) wrote:

> *A review of your situation in light of the... policies revealed that you are appropriately housed in the Special Housing Unit. The Bureau of Prisons has been informed*

by other law enforcement agencies that you are currently under investigation for a potential affiliation to terrorists and/or terrorist activities. You will continue to receive 7 day and 30 day SHU Reviews and 30 day Psychological Reviews. If during this review process, it is determined that general population would be more appropriate, you will be transferred to such a housing unit. Your allegations of abuse by staff have been referred to the appropriate Bureau of Prisons component for investigation. You can be assured that staff abuse of any inmate will not be tolerated. Based on the above, your request is denied.[35]

My lawyer, Anthony Ricco, was a professional man who had fought terrorism-related cases in the past. When I asked him what happened to all his cases, he told me that all of them got life sentences. He fought the case of Yousef Ramsey, who was arrested for the first World Trade Center attacks.[36] For my case, he challenged the solitary confinement and pointed out that in other terrorist cases, defendants were not placed in solitary confinement. He said that even prisoners with life sentences are kept in general population, including individuals with credit card fraud charges. It didn't make a difference. The judge said that according to the written documents, I was placed in solitary confinement for my own safety, which was threatened by bad media publicity.

It was just an excuse. If they were doing it for my safety and not for punishment, they should have given me some amenities, but there were none whatsoever. There were no pillows to sleep on, no reading materials, nothing. The food was cold and tasted terrible. It was clear that it was a punishment, but in the court they claimed that it was for my safety.

After I pled guilty, the judge issued the final decision and said, "Time served." At that time, they could have released or deported me, but then they started immigration proceedings and placed me in the immigration jail. They don't have any mercy.

A Year of Solitary Confinement

Solitary confinement is a very painful experience and can cause mental disorders. It is not a regular prison; it is a punishment where you are totally isolated from the world. No phone, no sunlight, no concept of time, nothing at all. Some people tried to commit suicide in solitary confinement. I thought about committing suicide many times but didn't because it is prohibited in my religion. Human beings are social animals, and interaction with others is necessary. In solitary confinement, there is no one around except for the guards, and you can't even talk to them. They are not allowed to even open the window.

Solitary confinement was very difficult mentally because I did not know what was happening to my family. I don't think there is anything worse in the world than solitary confinement at the MDC. All the false accusations—the flying license, connections to terrorism, my Saudi nationality—were torture. These were not elements in my life, and suddenly without an opportunity to disprove anything, I was submerged in those accusations.

All the threats from the guards—that I would die at MDC, that my family would be in trouble—were also torture. The eight- to ten-hour interrogations were not investigations; they were torture, and they made me feel like committing suicide.

In the cell, there were only two things to do—praying and reciting the Koran, or sleeping. How many hours a day could I sleep? I spent most of my time reading the Koran and praying. I did not talk to the other inmates because there was nothing to talk about, and they didn't have any outside information either. The only thing we could talk about was our cases.

Tasleem felt the impact of solitary confinement on Azmath as well:

Keeping him in jail for 15 months, mostly in solitary confinement, was torture. Even big criminals don't have to suffer the way Azmath had to suffer. It was illegal for them to keep him like this. I did not expect that U.S. officials would treat him the way they did and for that long. They destroyed his life and his career.

Moving to the General Population Unit

Azmath was moved to the general population unit in August 2002.

Three weeks before I moved from the MDC to the immigration jail, the jail administration put me in the general population unit. Criminals wait in this unit while the court makes its final decision. The general population section was a hundred times better than solitary confinement. It was still a prison, but at least I had some freedom and could see and talk to people.

After I moved to the general population unit, I began seeing a psychologist, and he told me that I had a mental disorder. I used to talk to him for hours, and he explained that the conditions that I had lived in—the long interrogations and the isolation—had caused it. I could not sleep, so he gave me sleeping pills and said that it would take time to resume a normal sleeping pattern. He said that after spending 30 days in solitary confinement, normal human beings become suicidal. I had spent a year in that prison, in that hole. He was surprised that I had spent that much time there.

The psychologist told me to interact with people, but I did not want to talk to the other prisoners. I just wanted to be left alone. After having lived in solitary confinement for a year, it was strange to be surrounded suddenly by a lot of inmates. The prisoners around me had followed my story and were suspicious of me. I was in general population when the media reported the story about those three Miami doctors who became suspects right after 9/11.[37] At that time, everyone was watching the shocking news and saying that I was involved in a similar case. Some prisoners asked me if I knew those doctors. The situation made me feel very uncomfortable because all eyes were on me. Everyone thought that those Miami doctors were terrorists and that I was like them.

It was very difficult to trust anyone. The prisoners in the general population unit believed the news that they had watched about me, and they thought that I was a terrorist. The warden had told me that the FBI was still investigating me, and I continued to feel the effects of surveillance. In the beginning, even though I was surrounded by inmates, I still felt that I was in solitary confinement to some degree. I did not feel comfortable talking about my case, so I did not talk to the other inmates. I only prayed with them and that was it.

After staying in the general population unit, I was moved to Passaic County Jail, and I met a prisoner who was a doctor. His wife used to visit, and he gave me her phone number so that I could make a three-way call to Tasleem through her phone. The doctor's wife started visiting me also on a regular basis, which helped a lot. She put some money in my account so that I could buy a few items from the jail commissary. Another prisoner's sister helped me to get some clothes so that I wouldn't have to be deported in prison clothes.[38]

The Deportation, At Last

Tasleem describes how she felt when she heard about Azmath's release and reunited with him in India.

I had no idea when Azmath would arrive. I wasn't even sure that he would come at all. Ayub arrived first and suddenly I felt a big sense of relief. I had been completely broken inside, and when Azmath finally returned home, I felt revived suddenly. It felt like I had just seen the moon indicating that it was *Eid* [a day of religious celebration for Muslims]. When I heard that he was in Mumbai, I was so anxious that I could not sleep the entire night. I celebrated for three days and when my mother called, I told her that it felt like *Eid*.

Azmath provides some of the additional details of his deportation experience:

They drove me from Passaic County Jail to John F. Kennedy airport in New York, without handcuffs. The MDC had used some terrorism regulation to hold all of my property, including the money that I was traveling with, and my lawyer did not try to get it back. They gave my travel documents to the pilot, who eventually gave them to the Indian government officials.

They did not arrest me in Mumbai but kept me under surveillance so that I couldn't leave the airport. I traveled alone from Mumbai to Hyderabad. I wasn't afraid in Mumbai, but things changed in Hyderabad. Government agencies investigated me from 2:30 a.m. to 12:30 p.m. the next afternoon. One department after another came and asked me questions like: What were you doing there? Where were you? Who was living with you? What kind of work were you doing? When did you go there? What was the last time you visited back home? Who was your employer? It made me afraid.

I had called my family from Mumbai, but when I came to Hyderabad, they did not allow me to make any telephone calls. My family was sitting outside the airport. After the interrogation, they took me to the court and charged me with providing wrong information on my passport. My name and age were slightly different.[39] I paid a small fine for that, and then they let me go. I was a bit scared to deal with the Indian government because physical torture and misbehavior towards prisoners is common here. Fortunately, nothing happened to me.

The Lingering Effects of Bad Publicity

Before my release, I was depressed because I was afraid of harassment from the Indian government authorities. My wife, my father, and entire family had suffered from police harassment in Hyderabad because of my detention. Police authorities searched my home and interrogated my family, neighbors, and friends. They tapped the phone lines and monitored who came in and out of the house. Friends, relatives, and acquaintances are still very afraid to come here; they think something bad might happen and they will have to face the police.

Due to these investigations and the bad publicity, everyone thinks that I was involved in the September 11 attacks. I feel a bit uncomfortable that people are aware of all the bad publicity about me, even though most of them don't believe it and know that the American government was arresting Muslims under false charges. In their view, I am a victim of the American system. However, I still feel a bit uncomfortable with this attitude, and it impacts my personal and family life. I don't have any privacy anymore because everything is in the news and out in the open. Pictures of my family—my father, my child, everyone—are in the newspaper.

America is creating a new environment in which they are giving Islam a bad name. The way they falsely connected me with terrorism shows that anything is possible. So far, the Indian government is behaving well, but you never know what can happen. They can use anything against you because the justice system is weak and there are no human rights. For example, look at what happened in Gujarat.[40] A lot of people were killed and raped, but nothing happened to the perpetrators. As you know, Muslims are a minority in India, and every day horrible things happen to them. The government uses the excuse of the war on terrorism to do whatever it wants. When I see a military or a police officer on the street, I don't make eye contact because I don't have the same level of confidence anymore. Since American intelligence has made me notorious, I don't know what the officers think of me. I live in fear.[41]

Tasleem talks about the lingering impact of Azmath's detention:

The U.S. officials put a bad stamp on his character by falsely arresting him in connection with the September 11 attacks. It is impossible to explain to everyone that he is innocent. Due to the bad publicity, the first thing people are going to say is that he was arrested in connection with September 11.

American intelligence bad-mouthed his name to the whole world. However, after they found out that he was innocent, they should have used the same level of publicity to clear his name. Azmath was an innocent person who went to the U.S. to make a living. He was traveling with some money so that he could start a new business, and the government snatched that money away from him. After the American officials finished the investigation, they should have returned everything that they confiscated. If they can't compensate for the wrongs that they did to him over 15 months, they need to at least return everything that they took. He worked hard for that money.

Changes in Attitude Toward the United States

Before 9/11, Azmath's experience in the United States was pleasant. Even after his terrible experience on the ninth floor of the MDC, he makes a distinction between the American public and the government. However, he does not want to go back to the United States.

Overall, American people are very nice and open minded, and I have had really friendly encounters with them. The government system and departments like the FBI and the DEA, however, have problems. After I got arrested, my perspective on the government changed because I saw that it was a system filled with discrimination and racism.

Outside the prison, you feel that you have freedom, that there is a respect for humanity, and that America is the guardian of human rights. Inside the prison, it is the opposite. The way they arrested innocent people and put them in jails with no evidence shocked me.

Law enforcement officers are still arresting more people in the U.S. When I was in jail, I heard about the arrest of three young male doctors in Florida.[42] Someone complained, the FBI got suspicious, and it became big and shocking news. CNN covered it live, and the drama lasted for ten hours. Officers only arrested them because they were Muslims but later they found out that they were doctors and not terrorists. These kinds of incidents are happening to Muslims all the time in the U.S.

When I read articles about individuals arrested in connection with terrorism, I don't trust the information because those individuals might be completely innocent like me. They might be undergoing a similar experience and dealing with false charges. I know about several other individuals who were arrested from the streets, their homes, and their jobs and who were classified as terrorists. After the FBI could not prove anything, they were released or deported. All of these individuals were arrested only because they were Arabic or Asian.

I don't think that Muslims even carried out the attacks because Islam does not allow the killing of innocent people. There is a possibility that some American did it.[43] When the Oklahoma bombing happened, they arrested many Muslims in that area.[44] Later they found out that Timothy McVeigh did it. I believe that someone else did the attacks and that the U.S. government is using Muslims for political purposes.

The FBI assumed that Muslims were responsible for the 9/11 attacks, and as a result, all Muslims became suspicious. For example, when I was traveling from New York to Saint Louis on September 11, there were only two Muslims (Ayub and I) traveling on that plane. Let us assume that there was a problem with the plane and it crashed. The FBI would go over the passenger list, see our names, and claim that two Muslims did it on purpose. The entire world would believe that Muslims did it because we had box cutters on us. There is a possibility that the people who have been classified as hijackers were just passengers with Muslim names. They are dead now and can't prove their innocence, so they have been classified as terrorists. If I had been on that plane, my name, Mohammed Azmath, would've been next to Mohammad Atta's.[45] I would have been labeled a terrorist, even though I was innocent. Just because a Muslim is on a plane does not mean that he is a terrorist.

I don't trust any information that the FBI provides because agents lie. They claim that the air-hostess called to describe the hijackers.[46] But the FBI also told the *New York Times* that I had shaved my body when I hadn't, along with other lies.[47] My lawyer told me that if the FBI wants, they could prove that I was Osama bin Ladin's brother. He also told me that the FBI has the right to lie during interrogations.

In jail, I learned about a few individuals who were working with the FBI. Some of them were from Pakistan, and some were from Arabic countries. They claimed to know about suspicious people in their communities so that the FBI would drop their charges and release them. They were supposed to provide the FBI with names of suspects, and sometimes, these informants would purposely give the names of innocent people so that the FBI wouldn't think that they had lied.

These informants are only working for their own freedom and immigration status. I saw people who were caught because of these informants. This is wrong but it is happening. Eight Yemeni individuals were arrested because of an informant in the community.[48] Generally, people who are outside the jail don't want to work with the FBI as informants. The individuals who are in jail with lengthy sentences, however, are more likely to make a deal with the FBI to spy on their own communities.

In Lodi, California, an informant was instrumental in the arrest of a group of Pakistanis in June 2005. A Frontline *documentary prepared about this case reveals that in the aftermath of these arrests, the Lodi community has stopped trusting jour-nalists and newcomers.*[49] *During my research, I found that a sense of mistrust per-vaded larger Muslim communities, especially those that had been stung by some of these intelligence operations.*[50]

Before this incident, I used to believe that the American justice system was the best in terms of respect for human rights and values. I had many friends who were police officers. After I got arrested, I noticed that this was not the case. Inside the prison, officers violate human rights and values and treat people like animals by putting them in solitary confinement and serving cold food. They don't care whether you eat or not. The picture is completely different on the inside as compared to the outside, especially if you are a Muslim.

A lot of mistakes occur in the American justice system, but the government ignores them. A few mistakes leak out, and the public becomes aware of them, but most of them stay hidden. America is a good country, but its federal system has problems, and American institutions are not good for Muslims. I went to the U.S. 12 years ago for better opportunities, but I don't have the desire to go back there.

Tasleem's attitudes toward the United States have also changed because of this experience.

Before this incident, I was hoping to migrate to the U.S., but I don't have any inclination to do that anymore. I've had a change of heart because they put Azmath in jail for 15 months. America did a big injustice to him, and I have never heard of anything like this happening before. People used to say that there is justice in America, but I did not find it. My heart is spoiled now.

The Government's Response

James Comey, the U.S. attorney whose office prosecuted the case, justified the govern-ment's position in May 2003 in a CNN report. His comments fail to explain why Azmath's detention was so lengthy, why he suffered abuse, or why he was placed in solitary confinement for almost a year:

> They were flying on September 11, 2001. They carried box cutters and had shaved their bodies like some of the hijackers. They had numerous passport photos and a lot of cash. They even lived in Jersey City, New Jersey—a base in the past for terrorists plotting against the U.S.
>
> "I don't think anyone would say the government acted unreasonably," said U.S. Attorney James Comey, whose office prosecuted their cases. "It could be that they were victims of extraordinarily bad fortune, that they were flying in the air during the time of the 9/11 attacks, had one-way tickets, and were carrying their devices," Comey continued. "There were a lot of circumstances that warranted the govern-ment taking a very, very close look at them."[51]

Not only does Comey fail to express regret about the injustices that Azmath endured, but he also fails to distinguish between a "very close look" and the violation of legal, civil, and human rights.

Detention: Afterthoughts

Azmath reflects upon the reasons for his detention and his prison experience.

Sometimes when I think about what happened to me, it feels like a huge nightmare. It is sad that from the highest to the lowest levels, everyone from the FBI administration to the prison guards was involved in this injustice. Even officials in third-world countries don't behave the way the FBI did. Despite all the technology and the professional training, the FBI picked up innocent individuals from the streets and called them terrorists. They did not have any proof or evidence, and it took them months to clear an individual.

From their attitude, it was very clear that they were using me for their own benefit. The government wanted to appease the concerns of the general public by saying that they had arrested someone within 24 hours.

Initially, they arrested Muslims in connection with terrorism. When they could not find any evidence, they tacked on an immigration violation or some other kind of charge and either released or deported them. The government wasn't able to connect these individuals with any terrorist activities or the September 11 attacks. They also did not arrest anyone that was actually connected with the September 11 attacks.[52]

Tasleem, living in India, has started to recognize the pattern of racial profiling that triggered Azmath's arrest.

I don't know why it happened to Azmath or why they kept him in jail and tortured him for such a long time. The only thing that I can think of is that he is a Muslim. If he were an American, it would not have happened. I suffered because of what America did to my husband and... [*she is reluctant to say anything bad toward the United States*], but at the end, they did justice to my husband. They took a long time though, and they destroyed our lives. They kept him away from his family for so long.

(Azmath) I am angry, and I have the right to be angry because they involved me in a crime that I was not a part of. Many other individuals like us have had to suffer because they are Muslims or have Asian/Arabic names and looks. The government should apologize and pay for its mistake because it destroyed thousands of lives. If we make a mistake, we have to pay for it. Now the government has made a huge mistake, and it must compensate these individuals and their families. I am interested in suing the American government so that it won't hurt an innocent person like me in the future. I heard about the Japanese Americans who were arrested during World War II. The U.S. government paid reparations only after a good majority of them had died.[53]

Since the government makes the same mistake over and over, it is not a mistake; it is intentional. They know what they are doing, and they do it repeatedly. I want to stop it. Americans should practice at home what they preach abroad about human rights. They talk about violations of human rights in other countries, but they must first stop the violations in their own country. The way they religiously profile Muslims is wrong and should stop. The general public deserves to know the real truth, and I hope that others won't have to suffer the way I suffered.

I want to tell the American public that there is racial profiling and discrimination going on in the United States. The government is targeting Muslims, even though it is not even clear that Muslims were responsible for the attack. Even if they were, it does not mean that every Muslim is like the hijackers. If a white American like Timothy McVeigh destroys a building, it does not mean that all white Americans are like him. You can't treat all Muslims as terrorists and claim that Islam teaches terrorism. This is completely wrong and needs to stop.

Life Today: Today Azmath lives in Hyderabad with his family. He is the proud father of Bilal and a newborn daughter named Safia. The family lives with Azmath's aunt, father, uncle, and younger brother. Azmath manages a truck transportation business and hopes that soon the U.S. government will accept its mistakes, pay reparations, and formally apologize for its actions.

Azmath's narrative illustrates that detentions in the United States have significant transnational implications because families living continents apart also suffer pain and anguish from the detentions of their loved ones. In some situations, their emotional pain is more severe than that of the detainees because they even don't know what the detention conditions are like. Not being able to communicate with detainees, they imagine the worst: torture, beatings, and death. Perhaps the worst aspect of being on the other side and so far away is that they are powerless to do anything because they can't come to the United States. The visa restrictions, expenses, distance, and unfamiliarity with the culture and the legal system exacerbate the pain of detentions for loved ones.

In some exceptional situations, families of detainees experience more than just pain and agony. In Azmath's case, his wife, Tasleem, became a suspect and subject to arrest and deportation in India simply because she was married to him. Her expired visa gave the Indian officials an opportunity to replicate the process of detention and deportation that Azmath experienced in the United States. Ayub Khan's family also underwent major investigation, questioning, and surveillance by both the Indian and American governments. Although many other families of detainees did not experience such questioning, surveillance, and detentions, they experienced mental distress. This chapter attests to some of those unquantifiable impacts of U.S. policies.

Figure 2   Ansar Mahmood, Pakistan, 2008. Photograph by Irum Shiekh.

CHAPTER 2

Lifelong Deportation: The Punishment for Helping a Friend

Ansar Mahmood

Ansar Mahmood was arrested in October 2001 when someone witnessed him photographing a scenic view of a water treatment plant in Hudson, New York. Ansar's Pakistani and Muslim looks aroused suspicion, and the observer reported him to law enforcement officers. FBI agents performed a thorough search of his house and belongings. Although they did not find anything relating to terrorism, they found that he had helped his undocumented childhood friends Yusuf (a pseudonym) and Fatima (a pseudonym) get an apartment. He had also registered their car under his name to save them car insurance expenses. Ansar had a green card, but his friends had expired visas. He never knew about their immigration status.

During an intense investigation, Ansar signed a document stating that he knew about his friend's expired visas that made him subject to detention. On October 16, Ansar pled guilty to the charges and was temporarily released on a bond. However, by pleading guilty, Ansar became a criminal, which made him subject to deportation under the 1996 immigration laws. He was arrested again in January 2002, and after fighting a long, hard legal battle and spending approximately three years in prison, Ansar was deported to Pakistan in mid-2005. He is one of the few individuals among the 9/11 detainees barred from ever reentering the United States.

Meeting Ansar

I first met Ansar in January 2003 at the Buffalo Detention Center in Batavia, New York. I had read about him in the Human Rights Watch report prepared about September 11 detainees and had called his immigration attorney, Rolando Velasquez, to inquire further about his case. After the attorney learned that I spoke Punjabi, Ansar's native language, he encouraged me to visit him. I drove to Batavia during a blizzard, stayed in a local motel, and went to the detention center around 10 a.m. to visit him. We talked for the next two hours through a glass window using a telephone headset. At that time, he was fighting his legal battle. I was hoping that the government would release Ansar because he had a valid green card, a strong moral character, and significant community support.

In May 2003, Ansar lost his legal battle, and the judge ordered his deportation. Frustrated with the legal system, I began working closely with Susan Davies, a community organizer in Hudson, New York. Susan, in collaboration with a few other individuals, had formed the Free Ansar Mahmood Committee to stop his deportation. Unfortunately, despite our efforts, Ansar was deported for life back to Pakistan in April 2005.

After his deportation, Susan and I traveled to Pakistan to meet him, and both of us conducted interviews during this visit. Susan worked with Ansar in the morning, asking him questions and typing up his detailed responses. I worked with him in the evening and recorded over 20 hours of interviews in Punjabi. We continued with this process for about two weeks. After a week and a half, Ansar was exhausted and protested, "You guys get to take a break, but I am working nonstop. I need a vacation." Ansar confessed that speaking about his prison experience for more than eight hours a day was emotionally and physically draining for him. His lips would dry out, and his body seemed to be overtaken by heaviness. Even though the interview process was painful, he wanted to go through with it because he found it therapeutic at a certain level. He once stated, "I have deep sadness in my heart. I want to be able to share it with someone who can understand me. It is also difficult to think about those memories but after talking, I feel lighter."

The following narrative presents the essence of my recorded interviews with Ansar, Susan's detailed written notes,[1] legal files,[2] and media articles.[3] I interviewed Fatima, Yusuf, and Majeed (a pseudonym)—the two other individuals arrested with Ansar and his employer. Susan and I also had a brief meeting with Ansar's public defender, Kent Sprotbery. In this meeting, Kent stated that he fully informed Ansar of the consequences of pleading guilty to harboring illegal immigrants—meaning that after pleading guilty, Ansar would be released on a bond for a short duration and later would be subject to deportation under the 1996 immigration laws. Kent stated that Ansar wanted to be released as quickly as possible and make quick money for his family before his deportation to Pakistan.[4] Last but not least, I met with Ansar's prosecutor, Tina Sciocchetti. In the meeting, Ms. Sciocchetti stated that the investigating officers did not use racial profiling, followed standard legal procedures, and read Ansar his Miranda rights. She also stated that the government informed Ansar of his rights during the trial and that Ansar understood the significance of pleading guilty.[5] I also held telephone conversations with his immigration lawyer, Rolando Velasquez. Without going into the legal details, I try to capture the gist of these statements in the narrative.

I am telling Ansar's story as a participant-observer and an oral historian. My visit to his house in Gujarat gave me insights into his deep relationships with his family and community. His two-week stay in my family house in Islamabad, Pakistan, allowed me to capture his spirit.

More specifically, this methodology has allowed me to independently judge Ansar's character. The court transcripts, hearings, and other written archival materials are sketchy and only depict the partial truth—they don't reveal the anxiety that Ansar felt in not being able to work and send money to his family. They don't capture the pressure he felt to be out or the desire to save money. If he had not trusted the American legal system and had used shrewd strategies for his defense, Ansar might still be living in the United States.

Through his narrative, Ansar reveals what he was thinking when he answered legal questions in the courtroom. Ansar explained to me not only what he told the court but also the reasoning behind his answers. Factors such as being a new immigrant, his unfamiliarity with complicated immigration laws, and his trust in the American legal system influenced his responses. The government's archival records called him a "criminal, liar, and perjurer." I found him to be an honest and committed friend, son, and brother. The following narrative is not only his story; it is a testimony to his character.

Growing Up in Pakistan

I grew up in Lahore, Pakistan, in the late 1970s. My father was a suborder [noncommissioned officer] in the Pakistani military. Each month when he got his paycheck, he gave me a rupee for pocket money. I would buy *samosas* [appetizers] and then go over to a small ditch close to my house. There I would eat and talk with my friends. Some school nights, I watched television late into the night and could not get up in time to catch the school bus. On the days I missed school, I went with my brothers to the airport close to my house and watched the planes landing and taking off.

I did well in my studies and enjoyed them except when we had to write with *thaties* [a piece of wood used for writing]. One of my teachers insisted on practicing with *thaties* on a daily basis and would get angry about my sloppy writing. I got a lot of beatings for not writing well with *thaties*. Sometimes during the prayer break, my friends and I would go outside the school to pick berries from trees, or the teachers would ask us to pick radishes from the fields outside. The teachers would then wash and peel them, and we would all eat them with salt. Life was full of fun and lightness.

After my father retired, he bought a piece of land in Muhammadi Pura, a small village close to Gujarat, and built a small house. My mother was not in favor of moving to Muhammadi Pura, but my father wanted to be close to his father, siblings, and other relatives who were already established in the village. My father had a high school degree and so was able to get a job easily in the local vegetable market as an *arti* [accountant]. He also bought some land to harvest wheat. With nine children at home, it was difficult to make ends meet, but with his pension, his *arti*'s salary and the harvest, we had enough to eat. I liked working with my father in the fields, and I always insisted on joining him, but he felt that I should pay attention to my studies. One day, I cried so hard that he gave in and let me help him cut the greens in the fields.

My parents worked very hard to provide for us. My father would give his monthly pay to my mother, and she would manage the entire household. Along with paying bills, she took care of the nine children and all the animals. She worked very hard but hardly complained. To supplement the household income, she raised chickens to sell eggs and a buffalo to sell milk and manure. She was also an excellent tailor and made some extra money sewing clothes for local villagers.

My parents have a great loving relationship. Whenever they fight, my mother prepares sweet rice, which is my father's weakness. Initially, he resists and says, "I don't want to eat it, take it away," but later, he changes his mind and finishes the entire plate. Afterwards, we all gather and talk with each other.

Growing up, I spent most of my time with my younger sisters and mother and was very close to them. My mother would join us in playing jump rope and would win most of the time. My sisters liked to cheat by pretending that they had just stopped to take a breath when their feet got caught in the rope. We enjoyed playing board games all through the summer afternoons. Whenever I was losing, I would cheat and all of us would get into a fight. My mother would get angry at us for fighting and then beat all of us. By nighttime, however, we would have forgotten all about the afternoon fights. I would bring home some biscuits, cakes, Pepsi, or something that my sisters requested, and we would all eat and drink together peacefully in front of the television.

I could talk to my mother about anything. She loved me the most. Every morning, my mother prepared *paratha* [bread cooked with butter] and tea, gave me pocket money, and told me to do well in school. When I returned home, my mother had the lunch prepared. She would inquire about my studies and made sure that I finished my homework each day. After finishing my homework, I would go out to play cricket, football, and billiards with my friends and also to fly kites.

Flying kites was an obsession. One hot summer day, I was on the roof wearing clean new clothes when I saw a kite falling from the sky. Chasing the kite from the roof to the ground, I ended up running into a dirty pond, and came out drenched, holding a wet and broken kite. When I showed up at my house, dripping and soiled, my mother ripped the already torn kite into pieces. Then, she turned her anger on my body, but I continued to fly kites.

I did well in school. I had asked my parents to send me to City School, which was a private English medium school, but they could not afford it, so I went to the local public school. Muhammadi Pura had only one high school. Many of the students came from the *Syed* families who owned large tracts of land in the village. These *Syed* kids were not interested in their studies and went to school to hang out, pick fights, and tease the teachers. Often, they would get angry with me for doing well and would hit me. Once they hit me on the head with their *thaties* and it bled, so I tried my best to stay away from them.

I had two close friends who also liked studying, and we would hang out together. At the end of high school, I was the only student who passed the state government examination. Everyone else failed. The entire village gossiped and said, "Look, the tailor's son passed." My family and I took immense pride in my results.

The village of Muhammadi Pura was established before Pakistan's independence in 1947, and most of its residents were from the *Syed* caste. These *Syeds* considered themselves superior to the rest of the people in the village because of their lineage to the Prophet Mohammad.[6] No one could stand up to them, and everyone had to behave like their subordinate. The other castes in the village were cooks, household cleaners, laborers, and so forth, and most of the *Syeds* called them *Kamis*.

My family comes from the tailor caste and has never worked for the *Syeds* because we have been able to be self-sufficient. My grandfather and uncles owned a tailor shop. My father had a job in the city, and he leased land to harvest instead of working on someone else's land. The *Syeds* did not like my family's independence and were always looking for opportunities to undermine us. Sometimes, the *Syeds* would get their clothes tailored at my uncle's shop and then would not pay him. My uncle would either get the money through negotiations by involving an elder, a wise person of the village, or would make an excuse to avoid tailoring jobs in the future. But the *Syeds* continued to use other methods to harass and threaten us. I can never forget the day when the *Syeds* burned my father's harvest.

It was the summer of 1992. My father had leased the land for two years from a local landowner. This land was uneven and did not have good access to water. My father was proud of the agricultural knowledge that he had picked up from my grandfather and perfected with his education and hard work. He cleared the land, installed a tube well to irrigate it, sowed high-quality seeds, and spread fertilizers at the right time. A few months later, the wheat fields, tall and golden, waved in the wind and the harvest was plentiful. He paid 10,000 rupees for the lease from the first year of the harvest, got wheat for the house, and made a profit of 10,000 to 15,000 rupees.

He was very optimistic for the second year's yield and was hoping to reap a bigger profit. In the summer, I worked hard with my father in the fields. The golden wheat leaves were large and full in the heat. One late evening, after finalizing the details for hiring a tractor to cut and collect the wheat, I was returning home and saw a large fire in the distance. I ran towards the fire and noticed that the flames were blazing in our field. The dryness of the wheat combined with the dry heat and strong wind allowed the fire to spread quickly and swallow the entire field in a matter of minutes. There was nothing that could be done now. Local villagers were standing next to the field watching it burn. I picked up a large brush and jumped inside the fields to try to quench the fire. Local villagers grabbed me and held me back from trying to stop the uncontrollable fire. Some of my hair got burnt.

I watched the gigantic flames consume the golden wheat, and I fell on my knees, crying and screaming. The pain of the loss drained me. I stayed in front of the field watching it burn to ashes along with all our family's hopes. How was I going to tell my family that all of our hopes and yearlong labor had been lost in a few minutes? I walked home and fell sobbing into my mother's arms, but my parents were strong. They said, "Why are you crying? We will get a better harvest next year. You did not have to enter the fire and put your life in danger." That day I cried and cried. Although we knew that the *Syeds* had ignited the fire, there was no one who could bring them to justice.

The harassment did not end with the burning of the wheat. The *Syeds* also made serious threats to our lives. One day, my younger brother Asghar was walking home when some of the *Syed* kids started taunting him. Asghar got angry and fought with them. In the evening, all of us were sitting at home when we heard a loud noise outside the door. I went outside with my father and older brothers and saw some *Syeds* firing guns in the air. They were angry that Asghar had stood up to them and wanted to teach him a lesson. I watched my father and older brothers trying to calm them down and tell them politely, "We are sorry. Asghar won't do it in the future. Please go back to your home." Asghar, meanwhile, was hiding in the back of the house.

In response, the *Syeds* waved their guns, cursed and yelled, and demanded that Asghar come out of hiding. They just wanted to kill him that day. At one point, they got on top of the adjoining wall to our house and fired inside our yard. We were all very scared. I don't remember how we finally convinced the *Syeds* to leave. I am sure that some wise people of the village must have intervened. The next day, my father went to the house of the *Syeds* with some wise men of the village and requested that they stop this harassment. My father also promised that Asghar wouldn't repeat any such actions in the future.

I felt so powerless and vulnerable at that time. We could not contact the local police. We did not have the guns or a stronghold in the village to confront them. The only solution was to escape from Muhammadi Pura to a place where we could live in peace and dignity, but we did not have another house to go to. I wanted to be able to leave, and I made a personal vow to take my family away from Muhammadi Pura.

America's Pull

I wanted to become a military officer from an early age. A military job is the only way for lower- to middle-class families to climb out of poverty without resorting to bribery and family connections. Of course, a military officer's job does not achieve upper-class status, but it promises some dignity and security. For me, it was a beam of hope, an escape from the daily harassment by the *Syed* families.

After high school, I went to Zimidar College in Gujarat, which is one of the best colleges in the city. After completing two years in college, I took an examination for a military officer's position. It was around 5:00 p.m. in Rawalpindi when military officials told me that I had passed both the written and medical examinations. I was so excited to hear the news that I could not wait to share it with my family. Taking the next available bus, I arrived in Gujarat seven hours later, at midnight. I did not have any money for local transportation, so I walked for about an hour before I finally reached my home around 1:00 a.m. I woke up my sisters, mother and brothers and told them that I had just passed my examination. Everyone was so happy. We all got up and talked late into the night. It was a memorable night.

A month later, I was sitting at home when the postmaster delivered a rejection letter from the military. I still don't know the reasons for the rejection. I thought that my interview went well, and I had already passed my physical and written examinations. All of my dreams of moving my family out of Muhammadi Pura died with that rejection. There was no hope left, and I cried for days. Within the same week, the postmaster returned with another letter. This time, the postmaster took 500 rupees from my mother before handing her the letter from the U.S. consulate.

During my early college years, I had looked into an advertisement for the diversity lottery that allotted a certain number of U.S. visas each year to Pakistanis on a random basis. Every year, all the bookstores in Gujarat would hang large banners advertising the lottery. The price ranged from five to ten rupees. Normally, I would just look at the advertisement and turn away. But the previous year, my friend Rana and I had decided to apply for the lottery together. Rana was a close friend, and we used to hang out at a local bicycle shop. I trusted him.

The procedure was simple and required filling out a form and mailing the application with the required fees. After filling it out, I had put it out of my mind until now. That week, nothing could have lifted my spirits except for a note from the American consulate saying that I had won the lottery. It was like a dream come true. I could not believe that destiny could be so merciful to me, and I couldn't sleep that night. Winning a lottery in Pakistan for a U.S. visa is like winning a million dollars. I was afraid to share this information with the village because I feared that someone might steal the winning letter.

For days, I did not even touch the papers, thinking that they could be fraudulent. My father was angry because he felt that my mother had wasted the 500 rupees that she had given to the postmaster. One day, finally, I got the courage to show the papers to a neighbor who had won the lottery the previous year. He had not been able to go because of some technical reasons, and he said, "What are you waiting for? These are real. Hurry up." I sent the completed papers to the consulate but held on to the processing fee. I did not have that much money in my pocket, and I wanted to make sure that it was not a fraud.

My dream was to support my parents, who had worked so hard all their lives. Now they were getting old, and I wanted to be able to take care of them in return. My father wanted to provide the best education available for my sisters who wanted to study science. A degree from a private English medium school was kind of a necessity for pursuing science, but our family couldn't afford it. I wanted my sisters to be able to go to the English medium school and have the kinds of opportunities that are only available to upper-class kids.

At the end of 1999, I got a call from the American consulate for an interview. By that time, I had collected everything that was required for the interview, including the affidavit of support, my college diploma, birth certificate, police clearance, and the application processing fee. I was nervous about speaking English and began practicing my college English in my head.

When I entered the consulate, the cashier told me that I had to pay a 17,000-rupee nonrefundable interview fee. It was a large amount of money for me, but I thought that many people pay hundreds of thousands of rupees for a green card, so I should take a chance. Another guy who was standing next to me got scared, refused to pay the interview fee, and left.

A few hours later, a young white American woman called me for the interview. When I approached the window, she greeted me, "As-Salaam-Alaikum." As soon as I heard that expression, half of my fear disappeared and I relaxed. I replied, "Wa-Alaikum-As-Salaam." A Pakistani translator was standing next to her, and the entire interview was conducted in Urdu. The American woman asked me questions about my family, my education, and my background. As we got deeper into the conversation, I relaxed more. The interview went smoothly, and at the end, she congratulated me. I left the consulate and felt as if I was walking on air. Tears were trickling through my eyes. I never imagined that I could get a visa for the U.S. I was in a state of ecstasy.

Traveling back to Gujarat on the bus, I remained in a strange state of disbelief for the next four hours. I dreamt about going to the U.S., working hard, and sending money back to my family. People had told me about the limitless economic opportunities in the U.S. I was hoping that I could use them to take my family away from Muhammadi Pura. As Gujarat approached, my next concern was where to keep my visa packet because I had heard of people stealing visas. When I received the winning lottery papers, someone offered me ten hundred thousand rupees for them. They were expensive papers, and the environment in the village was dangerous. I did not want to take a chance on someone stealing those papers or creating any problems for me.

I knew that I could trust Rana. I went to his house and told him that I wanted to keep the packet there. Both of us had applied together, and even though he did not win, he was very excited for me and congratulated me. He took the packet and assured me that it would be safe with him. Later, I came back home and told my parents that the consulate had postponed the interview, but it was hard to lie to my mom. She was on to me quickly and said, "You got the visa. You are just lying to us." I could not continue the lie and gave them the news but strictly explained to everyone not to tell anyone in the village until I had bought the airline ticket.

At that time, I was working for a travel agency. It was a small office, and the owner, the son of my high school headmaster, admired my hard work. After I got the visa, I told my boss that I needed an airline ticket for myself. He was happy for me and organized a farewell party. He also paid for half of the ticket.

On April 20, 2000, my entire family came to Islamabad with me for the farewell. We spent a day in Islamabad, visited the Faisal Mosque, which is the largest mosque in Pakistan, and had a picnic at a park. The next day, I left for the U.S. The hardest thing was saying goodbye to my mother. This was the first time that I was going to be away from my family for a long period of time. I promised all of them that I would pray five times a day and lead a pious life in the U.S.

I flew on Emirates Airlines, and my heart pounded as I sat for the first time on a plane. Am I really going to the U.S.? It was like a dream come true, and I felt numb with disbelief. The next leg of my flight was from Amsterdam to New York. During the four-hour transit, I saw young American girls wearing pants and hanging out with boys. I had seen this kind of mingling on films and television, but seeing it in person was strange. I began preparing myself for new experiences.

Arriving in the United States

My plane landed late at night at the John F. Kennedy airport in April 2000. Going through the immigration process was simple. I gave my packet to an immigration agent, and he stamped my passport for a yearlong visa. I walked outside with my luggage and saw a man holding a sign with my name on it. The man belonged to a community of Pakistanis who had immigrated from Gujarat, and he worked as a limo driver in New York. He had brought his big Lincoln Continental limo, and I exclaimed, "This big car to pick me up!" He replied, "The same car came when I arrived." We drove to his two-bedroom apartment, which was next to a grocery store in Coney Island. He shared the apartment with six or seven other Pakistani men, and I was surprised to see so many people living together. He explained that New York is expensive and most of the working men live in large groups to save money.

I enjoyed my first few weeks in Coney Island. I would get up, eat breakfast, go out for a few hours, and return back to the apartment in the afternoon. Later in the evening, my friend would take me out to show me around New York. I really liked the U.S. There was nothing to fear, no one to bother you, no one to harass you about anything. I asked my friend about work, and he said, "Everybody works like a machine here. If you start working now, you will never get an opportunity to see New York. Enjoy the time that you have." Later, I discovered that he was right.

Approximately two weeks later, I got a job at a pizza store in Salisbury, Maryland, through an acquaintance from Gujarat. I moved to Salisbury and stayed in a two-bedroom apartment with another Pakistani guy. The pizza store was about a half-hour walking distance from the apartment, and I enjoyed walking to work. The tree-lined path was beautiful, and there was a small zoo with lots of birds and animals on the way. Sometimes, I stopped at the zoo and watched the birds. I enjoyed walking, observing, and experiencing Salisbury.

At the pizza store, I quickly moved from sweeping the floor and washing dishes to preparing pizzas. Most of the workers at the store were Pakistanis, and they taught me to make dough and bake pizza. A young American woman helped me to take and write down orders, which improved my English. She also taught me how to drive and took me to the local DMV for the written and driving tests. Soon, I bought my first car, which gave me more freedom.

At the store, I worked from 10:00 a.m. until 1:00 or 2:00 a.m. and made about $400 to $500 per week. I returned home exhausted after working over 12 hours a day. Now more than ever, I missed my mother's cooking and love, and life in Muhammadi Pura seemed more attractive. I remembered my mother's attentions, long chats with my sisters, and days hanging out with friends. The work-sleep-work cycle was making me feel lonely.

A few months later, Majeed, a neighbor from Gujarat who owned a pizza store in Hudson, New York, called and offered me a higher-paying job. I decided to take a quick drive up to Hudson. The deer sprinting in the tall, serene Catskill Mountains, the meandering Hudson River, the miles of trees, and the fresh air quickly convinced me to relocate. I came back and told my boss in Salisbury that

I was quitting. He was unhappy that I was leaving so quickly and offered me a raise, but the charm of Hudson was more attractive. A few weeks later, a friend gave me a ride to Hudson. On the way, he advised me not to go upstate and to stay in New York City, but I was determined to go to Hudson.

Work at the pizza store in Hudson was easier than my work in Salisbury because most of the stuff came prepackaged. For the first few weeks, I accompanied other drivers during deliveries and learned about the areas surrounding Hudson. One of the drivers drove a taxi during the day, and he taught me several shortcuts. Majeed and I were the only Pakistanis at the store, so I got lots of opportunities to speak English with the other employees and the customers. Soon my language skills improved and I was delivering pizza. Tips from delivering pizza were lucrative, and some days I made over $100 per day. Life started to become a bit more relaxed.

I shared an apartment with Majeed, the owner of the pizza store. He often left early to cook at home, and I would close the store and come home to an excellent Pakistani meal. After dinner, we hung out, played cards, listened to music, and talked. In the morning, he made omelets and heated the bread from the pizza store; it was a perfect combination. Another Pakistani family also lived in the same apartment complex. Sometimes, we shared the pizza bread with them and they brought us delicious homemade curry in return.

I called home once or twice a week, and everyone was eager to talk to me. I would be chatting with my sister Marium, and my other sister Sara would grab the phone and run away. In the background, my mother would scold the girls for not giving her the opportunity to talk to her son. After a long day of work, talking with my sisters would melt away the tiredness of the day, leaving me relaxed and comfortable. I would make them jealous by telling them that I owned a cell phone and a car and lived in a nicely furnished apartment in a beautiful place with trees, a river, and snow.

My sisters' education was very important to me. After I sent money back home, they were able to enroll in an English medium school in Gujarat and pay for tuition, books, and transportation. After I heard that they were admitted in the school, a sense of relief went through my body. I knew that they were intelligent and driven, and I wanted them to have more opportunities. Often I would hang up the phone and continue to talk to them in my sleep. Their happiness encouraged me to work on my goal—to take them away from Muhammadi Pura to a place where the *Syeds* did not dominate. I also started to save some money for emergency purposes.

Working for the pizza store, I could make about $3,000 per month. Every month, I sent about $500 to my family back home, spent about $1,500 on rent and utilities, and saved about $1,000 per month. I was very happy with my income. The money that I was sending to my family was not a large sum by U.S. standards, but it amounted to 20,000 to 30,000 rupees in Pakistan. When I was in Pakistan working for the travel agency, I could make up to 3,000 rupees a month. The second time I sent the money home, my sisters went to the market and bought a 24-inch, flat-screen color television. No one in the village had that.

I wanted to work hard to make money and to save, so I worked at the store from open to close. Some weeks I worked 80 to 90 hours. The other American drivers worked 20 to 30 hours per week and spent their money on their girl-friends, on going to clubs, and on buying brand-name clothes. Some areas in Hudson were considered dangerous and the other drivers would refuse to deliver there, but I always accepted the jobs and got good tips in return. All of the things that I used to enjoy doing, like wearing nice clothes or taking vacations up in the hills, stopped after I moved to the U.S. My only dream now was to work hard so that I could save money to support my family.

Growing up under the domination of the *Syeds* had created a fear inside of me. After arriving in the U.S., I started to discover and enjoy my freedom. Everyone treated me respectfully. I was nice to the people at my job, and they were very nice to me in return. I also noticed that there was not that much differ-ence between the laborers and the owners. The pizza owner in Salisbury used to work harder than most of the workers. Similarly, I hardly felt any class difference between Majeed, the pizza store owner, and myself. We both worked together and respected each other. This sense of equality and freedom started to erase the fear that I had carried within myself since I was young. A new sense of joy, free-dom, and dignity started to fill me, and the change made me happy.

One day, Yusuf, a friend from Pakistan, called me from New York. I knew Yusuf from Gujarat, where we had grown up together. Yusuf's wife, Fatima, was my best friend's sister. Fatima and Yusuf had gotten married recently and were in the U.S. for a visit. Currently, they were sharing a one-bedroom apartment in New York with another married couple and lacked privacy. During the call, Yusuf asked me about work and housing opportunities in Hudson. I told him about the possibility of getting a job with the local pizza store and also that the rent was cheap in Hudson.

A week later, Yusuf and Fatima arrived in Hudson. I knew the apartment manager of my building and an apartment was available, but the manager needed a credit check. He asked me to cosign the rental application for Yusuf. There was no reason to hesitate because Yusuf belonged to an upper-middle-class family in Gujarat and I knew his father and brothers. Both of us signed the lease, and Yusuf and Fatima moved in next door.

I felt elated to have them both in Hudson. It was like building a community. Majeed was a good friend, but he was also my boss and sometimes he acted like one. Now I had a friend from childhood and a family that I cared about. Fatima cooked, and we often ate together after work. Later, we would hang out, play cards, and just talk. Life suddenly became more interesting and filled with fun and laughter. One day, Yusuf told me that he was paying a high insurance rate for the car he had bought in New York and that it would be much cheaper if I registered it under my name. The next day, both of us went to the local DMV office and transferred the registration from Yusuf's name to mine. Later I insured his car under my name and I paid $150 for my car and $50 for his car. If we hadn't moved his car to my insurance, Yusuf would've been paying $200 per month for his car alone. I wanted to help them as much as possible because they were recent immigrants and had a lot of expenses. I was happy that I could help my childhood friends.

It had been over a year since my arrival in the U.S. As soon as I got my green card and travel documents, I called home. My mother and sisters were excited, but then Marium suddenly got quiet.

"Is everything okay?" I asked.
"Yes, everything is okay," she replied.

I had grown up with Marium, and so I could decipher that something was wrong by the tone of her voice. I probed deeper, and Marium confessed that last month our father had had a stroke and that he was in the hospital recovering.

"Why didn't you call me?" I yelled, unable to stay calm.

Marium was quiet for a few seconds and then said, "We did not want to make you upset." After I hung up the phone, my head was spinning. The image of my strong father flashed in front of my eyes, and the thought of him lying in a hospital was painful and disturbing. Although I had been contemplating a trip to see my mother before the news, now I knew I had to visit—it was my responsibility as a son. I went straight to a travel agent and booked a ticket for Pakistan. Later, I showed my airline ticket to Majeed and packed my luggage. Majeed was also contemplating a trip to Pakistan at that time to get married, but he postponed his trip because of the seriousness of my situation.

Without informing my family, I arrived in Lahore on August 18, 2001. It was late evening, and I felt completely exhausted from my flight from New York, but I continued my trip and arrived late at night in Muhammadi Pura. My mother opened the door, gave me a tight hug, and kissed my face. My father had moved back home from the hospital and was recovering. A sense of relief came over me. We all got together and stayed up late into the night talking.

My sisters were curious about my life in the United States. What did I do there? What was it like working there? How did I deal with my customers? What did I mean when I said that I delivered pizza in the snow? How could the pizza stay warm? Who cooked? What did I eat? How was the weather? What were the people like? There were so many questions. I spent the entire night satisfying their curiosities, distributing gifts, and catching up on the town gossip. I heard the cock crowing and realized that it was dawn. Smiling at my sisters' curious faces, I promised them more stories for tomorrow night. I slept through the entire next day.

August is a summer month in Gujarat, so I tried to spend most of my time inside the house. The people in the village complained, "Look at this *gora* [white man] who can't leave the house." I just wanted to be with my family, but I noticed that the attitude of the villagers towards me had changed. People who would never even talk to me before began visiting my house. I watched their attitude change, but I knew that these people were fake and were being nice to me only because I had a connection to the U.S. This trip convinced me more than ever that I wanted my family to move out of Muhammadi Pura, away from the *Syeds* who still dominated the local economy and politics.

I had brought about $5,000 with me. I used that money to buy a water heater for my father's frail body and a washer and a refrigerator to reduce the housework for my mother. My sisters were still in college. Marium was going to be the first girl in our family to receive her BA, and I was proud of her. I told my mother that the sisters had to finish their education regardless of what happened.

I was supposed to return on September 22, but Majeed called and asked me to come back sooner because labor was short at the pizza store. I got frustrated with being unable to spend even a month with my family after not having seen them for a year. Those 10 to 12 days passed in a flash, and I was back delivering pizza again in Hudson. The trip to Pakistan had cost me a lot of money. Also, now I had witnessed that my family needed my support more than ever. The bills in the U.S. had piled up during my short absence, and I decided to work harder so that I could save some money.

I was sleeping when the September 11 attacks happened. Later when I woke up, I watched the towers fall on television in horror. No religion could allow such merciless killing of innocent people. There were many Muslims working in those buildings also. What were those hijackers thinking? Some people in Hudson gave Yusuf, Majeed, and I strange looks, but besides that, little else changed after the attacks. Orders continued to come in from customers for the pizza store.

Becoming a Terrorist by Taking a Photograph

In the beginning of October 2001, I delivered a pizza to a man on Roseman Avenue. Standing in his living room, I saw the most amazing sunset. The owner of the house smiled at my mesmerized face and told me, "You should go a bit farther up the road and then you will experience the most marvelous view. Go there close to sunset time."

Last month in Pakistan, I had told my sisters about the beauty of the Catskill Mountains and the Hudson River and promised them that I would send photos. Majeed was leaving for Pakistan to get married next month, and I was planning to send some photos with him. I borrowed a camera from a friend, took half a day off, and started taking pictures. At the end of Roseman Avenue, there was an empty area where I stopped my car. The blue and green water of the Hudson River to the east of the Catskill Mountains reminded me of the Safal Moluk Mountains in northern Pakistan, and a smile spread over my face. I knew that these pictures would impress my sisters. I took out my camera and started snapping pictures of the water, the mountains, the road, and everything.

Next to the empty area, there was a building, and two guys were working outside. I approached them and asked one of them if they would take my photo with the scenic backdrop. I was still wearing my pizza delivery uniform. There were a few other shirts in the car, so I decided to change into a dark T-shirt. The guy who took the photographs asked me to move a bit to the right and then to the left to get a better shot. I was happy, and I thanked him and left. I put the camera back in my car and went to pick up more pizzas to deliver. At around 8:00 p.m. Yusuf called from the pizza store, sounding concerned.

> "There are police asking about you and waiting at the store. What have you done?"
> I had never had any trouble with the police, so I did not think much of the call.
> "Alright, I'll just make my delivery and will come straight there," I told him.
> It was dark when I arrived in the parking lot. Two Hudson police cars were parked outside. One local officer came up and asked, "Your name is Ansar Mahmood?"
> "Yes."
> "Did you take the photograph of the water treatment plant?"
> "No, I did not." I was surprised by the question.

The officer repeated the same question several times, and I kept saying no. Eventually the officer pointed to the police car and said, "Why don't you come to the station with us and if everything is okay, you can go home." I went in the car and saw that Yusuf was already sitting in the back. He looked stern. "Don't talk with each other," the officer said.

Ansar did not know that there was a water reservoir at the end of Roseman Avenue.

At the time, I did not think anything of it. The only thing that I could think of was that maybe I had been speeding and someone had complained. I was not scared. The officers turned on the sirens and the flashing lights and drove very fast through traffic lights to the Hudson Police Station. They took the longest, most populated route to the station.

After we arrived at the station, the officers put Yusuf and me in separate rooms. They handcuffed me and tied me to the bench in the room. Fear started to creep inside my body. I had heard recently that the immigration authorities were arresting Muslim men with minor immigration violations, but I had a green card. After the officer locked me up, I lost my patience. "Why are you locking me up in the jail? Why are you doing this to me? What have I done?" I asked them repeatedly.

One of them finally answered, "Just sit down and wait. The FBI is coming to ask you a few questions."

"What have I done? What have I got to do with the FBI?" I felt helpless. No one had told me that I had the right to remain silent or ask for a lawyer. I was a new immigrant, and I did not know that I had those rights.

It was late in the night when I met 10 to 12 officers at the Hudson police station. One introduced himself as a special agent, another as an immigration officer, and yet another one as an FBI agent. It was difficult to understand who was who. A few sat on the right side and a few on the left, while the rest stood in front of me. The wall was behind my back. It was a confusing and threatening situation. Again, no one read me any of my rights. They were all asking questions: "What were you going to do with the photographs? Did anyone give you any money to take the photos? Why did you take pictures?"

"It was a beautiful scene," I responded.

"Did you have any intention of throwing anthrax in the water?"

"What is anthrax?" The officers' tones were getting scarier and so were their questions. "Have you traveled to Afghanistan? Did you travel to the northern part of Pakistan? How many times do you pray? Where do you go to pray? Do you know Osama bin Laden? Do you belong to Al-Qaeda?" Now, I started to feel scared. I had not done anything, and I couldn't understand why they were asking me all these questions. I kept repeating no, insisting that I had nothing to do with what they were talking about and asked them to stop interrogating me. They said, "We have a lie detector machine. We can find out if you lied."

"Go and get the machine." I replied. I could not predict what they were going to do with me from the way they were asking those questions. Were they going to frame me for a crime I hadn't committed? I did not have anyone in the U.S. who could help me. I got the uneasy feeling that I was getting into trouble.

After the question, they wanted to search my house and car. "If you don't give us the permission, we will still search," an officer said. I did not have anything to hide and I wanted the questioning to end, so I signed the search form.

Majeed, the pizza store owner, came to the police station to inquire about his employees. He was sitting on a chair when the officers cuffed his leg and detained him. Majeed had a green card and had been living in the United States for a long time. He took note of the mood in the room and prepared a defense plan in his head. Initially, the law enforcement officers asked him about Osama bin Laden, Al-Qaeda, and anthrax. Then they searched his store and apartment. At the end, they asked him about Yusuf's immigration status. Majeed told them that Yusuf had a social security number, which he had used to get a job at the pizza store. He did not have any other information about Yusuf. The immigration officer tried to sway him, but Majeed stuck to his statement.[7]

A few hours later, officers returned after searching my apartment. Now their questioning shifted in a different direction. They asked me about Yusuf and Fatima. "What do you know about them? Why was Yusuf driving a car registered under your name, and why did you cosign the apartment lease? Did you know about their immigration status?" I told them about my long-term friendship with Yusuf and Fatima and explained that I had signed the lease and the registration to help them. I did not have any information about their immigration status, but one of the immigration officers insisted that I knew that they had expired visas. I did not accept this.

In the other room, immigration officers were talking to Yusuf and Fatima, who had already admitted that they had come to the United States on a visiting visa. After the visa expired, Yusuf had bought a fake ID from someone in Coney Island to find a job. However, he never told Ansar or anyone else about his and Fatima's immigration status. The immigration officer told Yusuf that he had found some of his immigration documents in Ansar's briefcase, and Yusuf explained that he had kept personal papers in Ansar's briefcase for security reasons. He believed that Ansar had never read them because the briefcase was in Yusuf's possession.[8]

The night was getting long. All the FBI officers left after they realized that none of us had any connections with terrorism, but three immigration officers remained and I overheard their conversation. One officer said, "The young man has a green card. He has not really done anything. We should let him go."

Another officer responded, "We came all the way from Albany. This guy bothered us all night. We have to do something about it." He was the same immigration officer who had been assigned to me and was forcing me to admit that I knew about Yusuf's and Fatima's expired visas. Close to dawn, he came to me with a piece of paper and said that he was writing a statement. He wrote down my name, date of birth, and green card number. At the end, he wrote that I knew that Yusuf and Fatima were undocumented. My eyes filled with tears, and I screamed, "I didn't know about their status."

"Yusuf told me that you knew about his immigration status."

"No, I don't know anything about their immigration status," I yelled back. The only thing that I knew was that Yusuf had a driver's license. He must have prepared it with some legal documents. I never asked them about their immigration status because it never felt right to do so.

The officer pushed the paper towards me and said, "It doesn't matter whether you knew or not. Yusuf has signed the papers saying that you knew. Fatima and Yusuf are illegal and they will be deported. You have a green card. Nothing is going to happen to you. Sign the statement and we will release you in the morning."

I looked at him. After over ten hours of intense investigation, I was mentally and physically exhausted. I just wanted to get out and go back to work so that

I could send money back to my family. The officer was promising me freedom. "You will release me in the morning?" I asked. The officer replied affirmatively. I signed the statement and started sobbing.

Ansar's investigation is a typical example of how Attorney General Ashcroft and his assistants had crafted the art of exerting maximum pressure on individuals arrested after 9/11. The agents were told,

> *If [detainees] were not citizens, the FBI and INS would look for something that they had done wrong in terms of their immigration status. Had they taken jobs, even though they only had tourist visas? Had they overstayed their visas? Such violations usually were easy to find, especially since INS's enforcement of these conditions over the year had been almost nonexistent They would then be detained for immigration violations and questioned repeatedly. It didn't matter if the violation were minor transgressions for which immigrants of other nationalities are rarely, if ever, held. Ostensibly, they were being held pending a hearing in which the government would move to deport them for the visa violation.*[9]

The agents were following the orders.

In the morning, when the officers released Majeed, he inquired about Ansar. The officers promised him that Ansar would be released shortly, but they didn't release him. It is not clear why his detention continued. Susan and I tried to interview the immigration officer who had arrested Ansar, but he refused.

In the morning, the officer drove me to the Albany federal court. They put chains around my waist and leg irons on my ankles. At the court, I saw Yusuf and Fatima shackled in front of the judge with the sworn statements and charges— statements that they were forced to sign the previous night in return for freedom. I was charged with an aggravated felony for "harboring illegal aliens" and helping them obtain a vehicle and housing. Yusuf and Fatima were charged for having expired visas and fake IDs. The judge gave me a court hearing for October 16, and Fatima and Yusuf got one for October 25. Afterwards, the marshals took me back to the Albany jail. On the way, I saw the immigration officer who had forced me to sign the sworn statement the night before, and I confronted him.

"You first promised that I would be released in Hudson. Then you said in Albany. After that you said the court and now nothing is happening." The officer smiled and walked away.

I came back to Albany County Jail and waited in the processing area. This was one of the worst areas that I saw during my detention. It was dirty, crowded, and filled with criminals and people from the street. A few hours later, someone called my name. There were three or four officers sitting in the area processing detainees. My processing officer was nice. He started to ask me questions like my name, social security number, and background. When I said, "I am from Pakistan and I am a Muslim," one of the other officers said, "He is a terrorist."

My processing officer said, "Don't pay attention to him. There are a lot of good people over there and the U.S. is still a good place to live." He gave me a prison jumpsuit and asked me to change. Afterwards, they gave me a very dirty blanket with a lot of holes and hair in it, a sheet, and no pillow. They offered me a phone call, and I called Majeed and told him that I was in the Albany County Jail.

He said, "I know. I will try to get an attorney for you." Five days passed and I still didn't have an attorney. I started to think about my family. What would happen to them if they heard about this arrest? I was worried that they would worry. I had made a lot of promises to my family last month about sending more money. My sisters were dreaming of a house and a car. I was going to find a place to live in Gujarat far from the curse of the *Syeds*. My internal fear of the *Syeds* began to resurface again. I cried day and night and wondered why it had happened to me. I had not done anything wrong. The only thing that I wanted was to be out. I was a new immigrant and did not know the American legal and immigration system. No one tried to get a good lawyer for me or provide me any legal counseling.

The time I spent in Albany jail was horrible, and I felt like a bird that had suddenly been trapped inside a cage. I stayed in a small cell, with a toilet, a metal bed, and a sink. It was extremely cold in Albany, and the cells were not heated well. Yusuf was in the cell next to me, and I could talk to him by speaking very loud. He was also very terrified and worried about Fatima. She was alone in an unknown location. How would she handle this situation? Both of us did nothing but cry. He would call out and ask me what I was worried about.

I told him, "I am worried about Fatima and you."

He replied, "I am worried about her also." After two or three days, when they started letting us out of the cell for an hour each day, I would hang out close to Yusuf's cell and talk to him. He did the same when he got his hour of recreation. At least we were together and could talk to each other. We wondered what must be happening to Fatima. She was alone, young, and had never experienced anything like this in her life.

Marshals took Fatima to Schenectady County Jail, where she underwent a cavity search. She says that during her processing, an officer asked her to marry him to stop her deportation. Later, after she arrived in her cell, fellow inmates asked, "Did you put anything in the water?" Fatima was confused. They told her to watch the news on the television, which reported that Fatima, Yusuf, and Ansar were taken into custody under suspicion of throwing anthrax into the water at the water treatment plant.[10] The women continued to tease, "You wanted to kill us? You wanted to throw anthrax in the water. All you Muslims want to do this?" Hurt and teary-eyed, Fatima replied, "I have not done anything." Up until then, she thought that she was there for her expired visa.

A few days later, I met the public defender briefly. He was a criminal attorney with no background in immigration law, but he had been working in the court for over a decade. I told him that I had signed a statement affirming that I knew about my friends' expired visas, and he said, "It is not a big deal. Everything will be okay." I conveyed my desire to get out of jail as soon as possible. The public defender was sympathetic and suggested a plea bargain to end the case quickly and secure a release. I trusted my lawyer's judgment. He said, "I will talk to you more about the case," but he never explained that I could be subject to deportation. Initially, he asked me if I needed a translator. After talking to me for half an hour, he concluded that I didn't need one. I did not see my lawyer until I went to court, five days later.

On October 16, I appeared in front of the judge. Right before my hearing, my lawyer approached me and told me to say that I had helped Yusuf and Fatima find an apartment, a car, and a job. "Just say that in front of the judge and he will release you on a bond for $10,000 or less." I shook my head. The lawyer suggested a video hearing, which would allow for faster processing of the case, and I agreed. In the courtroom, the judge appeared on the television.

The October 16, 2001, court trial transcripts state clearly that the judge got Ansar's consent for a video hearing and that Ansar understood the significance of pleading guilty. However, the judge never told Ansar that after pleading guilty to a criminal charge, he could be subject to deportation. The prosecutor told the judge about the "collateral consequences connected with his admission to a felony and his felony conviction, not the least of which, your Honor, would be some consequences regarding his immigration status, and he may face removal from the United States." However, the judge never explained the exact meaning of "collateral consequences" to Ansar. As a new immigrant with limited English skills, he did not understand the complicated legal language.[11] The public defender claims that he explained to Ansar the implications of pleading guilty and that Ansar was aware that after a temporary release he would be deported eventually.[12]

At one point, the judge asked me, "Has your lawyer or anyone else made any other promises outside of the plea agreement that you would be treated leniently in order to induce you to plead guilty? Do you understand the question?"

I replied, "Yes." At that moment, my lawyer intervened.

"Just a moment, Your Honor." He took me aside and said, "Just say that nobody promised you anything."

Even though the lawyer had told me that after the guilty plea I would be released on a $10,000 bond, I said, "No." The rest of the proceedings consisted of me saying yes and no. I just did everything my lawyer told me to do and said yes and no even when I did not understand. The only thing that I wanted was to get out of the jail. At the time, I did not think that I could be deported because I had a green card and I had not committed any crime.

At the end of the court hearing, I was released on a bond with a five-year probation, and the judge set the next court date for January 25 to announce the final sentence. Majeed paid for the bond and came to pick me up. I came home, prayed, and thanked God for this freedom. The next day, I was back to work.

When Ansar returned to the store, the work was slow. The people in the area had heard about the arrests at the store from the local newspapers and television station and had started to boycott it. Children would shout and yell at some of the drivers. One night after closing the store, Majeed went to the local grocery store to buy some soda. He was still in his pizza delivery uniform, and only a store clerk and the night manager were on duty. Suddenly, he heard on the microphone, "There is a Pakistani terrorist in the store... A Pakistani terrorist..." and then laughter. Majeed's blood was boiling, but he tried to control himself. The store clerk was embarrassed and told Majeed that he could file a complaint and that she would give witness. Majeed did not want to make a scene, so he left. His business continued to suffer setbacks and took years to recover.

A few people came to the store to support us and to inquire if we needed anything. Most of the people working in the plaza were friendly. One of the women used to come on a regular basis to support us. After the incident, some locals came to my apartment building manager and asked him to kick us out. The manager replied, "You can leave the building. They are staying."

Sometimes Yusuf would call me from the jail. He was worried about Fatima, who was staying in a different prison. They couldn't talk to each other, so they wrote letters instead. Many times, I wished that I could take Fatima's place in the jail. She also used to call me from the jail.

Fatima liked talking to Ansar because he made her laugh, which lifted her spirits. Soon, however, Ansar's attorney suggested that he should not talk with Fatima because he was a codefendant in her case. When Ansar reluctantly told her that, she felt hurt and lonely. Later, she tried to find other ways to keep herself busy. She received a Koran from a Christian priest who visited the jail. Reading the Koran gave her the strength to pass the time. She also joined the school in the jail; she did very well and enjoyed it. Everyone, including fellow prisoners and guards, were nice and respectful to her. Their interactions with her changed their attitudes toward Muslims. Many of the women suggested that she should fight her deportation case and stay in the United States. She was happy to receive such kind responses. After being transferred to five different jails, Fatima got her deportation orders for January 2002 and was deported shortly after that. She was barred from returning to the United States for ten years.

The Court Hearing, the Legal Battle, and Community Support

I was anxious about my court hearing on January 25. Between mid-October and January 25, I talked with several lawyers, including an immigration one. One lawyer suggested that I should create some strong ties to the U.S. by getting married or starting a business. Another lawyer reviewed the case and asked me for $1,200 to get me out on bail. She said, "You don't have a criminal history and you have a valid green card. Your bail could be high, but I will try to get you out." The public defender expressed his concerns about a possible deportation.

On January 25, 2002, I appeared before the judge through a video conference. As the public defender had explained, the judge gave the final sentence of time to be served and five years on probation. However, there was some discussion in the court about immigration laws that I could not understand. The judge asked me to wait for the immigration authorities, and feeling uncertain, I went to the public defender's office. A few hours later, two immigration officers appeared and took me aside. One said, "Work with us and tell us who are the people talking against the U.S.? Work with us; otherwise, you will be deported and you will regret it for the rest of your life. This is your last chance."

"I don't know any of these people," I replied truthfully.

"Tell us about Majeed. What is his history? What does he know?" I felt that they were trying to pit me against Majeed as they had done with Yusuf and that they were making false promises to me. They wanted excuses to get rid of Muslims and Pakistani people. They had not kept any of their previous promises, and I wondered if they would keep any of their new promises. I told them that I didn't know anything about Majeed, and they arrested me shortly after that.

Under the 1996 Anti-Terrorism and Effective Death Penalty Act, legal residents convicted of an aggravated felony could become subject to deportation. Harboring illegal aliens is one of the identified felonies, among many others, like shoplifting. When Ansar pled guilty to helping Yusuf and his wife, he was not aware of these consequences. Immigration officers arrested Ansar for harboring illegal immigrants and later moved him to the Buffalo Detention Center in Batavia, New York.

Ansar's public defender claimed that he explained to Ansar before he pled guilty that he would be subject to deportation under the immigration laws.

I was in shock. Could the justice system be so cruel? The immigration officer knew that I did not know Yusuf's and Fatima's status and had coerced me into signing the statement in return for my freedom. Didn't the immigration officers owe me an apology for the wrong done to my name and character? I felt like a little bird in the hands of a murderous butcher. What about my rights as a resident in the United States? After September 11, my crime was that I was a Muslim man from Pakistan. Law enforcement officers needed a certain number of Muslim-looking bodies behind bars, and I helped fill that quota. Would this happen to a young, white American man initially caught under suspicion of terrorism? It wouldn't because one of the white officers would see his/her own son or brother in that man, empathize with him, and find a way to get him out. I did not have anyone in the justice system who would do that for me. That is one of the reasons that there are so many people of color stuck in prisons—no one empathizes with them.

I thought about the 1996 immigration laws under which I had become subject to deportation. "Harboring illegal aliens" is a complicated phrase. I was just helping my childhood friend. When I came to the U.S., people had helped me in the same way. They had provided me with a place to stay, connections, networks, and jobs. They did not ask me about my immigration status. When I was building my community and helping Fatima and Yusuf, who were in a similar situation, I did not ask them about their immigration status either. Yusuf had come with his wife, and I figured that they both had some kind of papers. I did not need to see his green card. How awkward is it to ask someone about their immigration status? Many people told me stories of politicians who hire undocumented nannies, caretakers, and day laborers. Since they have citizenship and are rich and influential, nothing happens to them. They can get away with it. Why are only immigrants subject to deportations? A new immigrant like me can get crushed like a wheat kernel under the milling stone. I dwelled on the injustice of the American justice system, and tears continued to trickle from my eyes.

It was late evening when I arrived at the Buffalo Detention Center. Yusuf was still in jail waiting for his deportation. Finding him there gave me a sense of solace. Yusuf prepared a clean bed, hot oatmeal, and tea for me. Compared to Albany, where there was nothing, Batavia was like a five-star hotel. It was clean and had a television and a recreation area. I was amazed.

After I arrived in Batavia, FBI agents interviewed me. They asked me questions about Islam like, "Do you pray? Where? Which mosque?" Later, I talked to other Muslims in Batavia and learned that the FBI had asked them all the same questions. The non-Muslim detainees did not have to undergo this interview. I am not sure why the FBI investigated us. Maybe they were trying to see if any of us had any connections with Al-Qaeda, or maybe they were trying to gain knowledge about Muslims.

After I settled in, Yusuf suggested that I should hire a good attorney and fight for my rights because I had a valid green card. Before he left, he suggested a reputable immigration attorney for my case. A few months later, he accepted deportation and left. He was barred from returning for the next ten years.

Hanna Rosin from the *Washington Post* had attended my court hearings in Albany. She wrote several articles challenging the technicality of the immigration violation and asking for a sympathetic review of my case.[13] The *Hudson [NY] Register-Star*, a local Hudson newspaper, published over eight editorials in support of my case.[14] The Muslim League, a local Muslim organization, hired a criminal attorney to fight for my case. I was optimistic because I had not done anything wrong.

However, I soon realized that the legal battle was not going anywhere. In my plea-bargaining, I had signed that I would not appeal the decision. One of the lawyers tried to reopen the trial, but his motion was denied.

The government claimed that Ansar was aware of the immigration status of his friends. For evidence, they submitted Ansar's sworn statement, which he signed under duress from the immigration officer in return for a release; the signed statements of Fatima, Yusuf, and Majeed, also made under the insistence of immigration officers; Fatima and Yusuf's passports and immigration documents, which Ansar never looked at but which were stored in his briefcase; the rental apartment lease agreement with Ansar's signature; and the guilty plea statement that he gave in court on October 16, 2001, with no understanding of the consequences.[15] On paper, government evidence against Ansar's claimed innocence is strong, but it does not reveal the complexity of the circumstances under which Ansar signed the documents and pled guilty.

Later I hired an immigration lawyer, but the U.S. District Court had already ordered my deportation. In the middle of 2003, I was one of the few remaining detainees arrested in the aftermath of 9/11. I was hoping that someone within the justice system would recognize that I was a hardworking immigrant and that I did everything I could to help others. As a new immigrant, I could not keep up with the ever-changing maze of immigration regulations. I was hoping that someone would recognize that I was coerced by the immigration officer into signing a false statement and that nobody read me my Miranda rights.

My long-term detention and story inspired many media outlets and activists. Everyone who heard about the details of the case felt that I had been caught in an unfortunate situation. Susan Davies was among the many from Columbia County who learned about the case through her husband, John Davies. John was an editor for the local Columbia County newspaper and wrote several articles. Initially, she trusted the court system and hoped that I would be released, but when she noticed that the legal battle was not going anywhere, she brought the case to a Chatham Peace Initiative meeting.

Susan told me that all members expressed their strong support for Ansar. All the members, especially Bob Elmendorf and Nancy Rothman, saw the alarming similarities between the failings of the justice system in Nazi Germany and the U.S. in the aftermath of 9/11.

Susan, Nancy, and Azim [a local community organizer] came to visit me in jail in August 2003. That meeting was a bonding moment and gave them the energy and passion to fight for my case. They established a Free Ansar Mahmood Committee, which included local citizens and community members, and started collecting signatures to stop my deportation.[16]

Through Susan, Bob, Nancy, and others, I started to have a community of friends and supporters. I called them frequently from the jail, and we started to establish a friendship. On my birthday, they came to see me and sang me the happy birthday song. Their support made me see that there were many individuals within the American public who cared about the plight of others. Many other media representatives also got interested and published articles.[17] This sustained effort around my case kept me alive.

Passing Time in the Jail

I waited and waited for my freedom—freedom to get up, to sleep, to have privacy, and to be able to go and meet with my friends and family. Waiting generated anxiety, and I was hospitalized briefly. The doctors told me that there was nothing wrong with me except that I suffered from anxiety of the unknown. I stayed on medication for a long time. Occasionally I called home, and I told my sisters fake stories about getting excellent food and people taking care of me. I tried to paint a bright picture by telling them that there was a recreation room and that I could still work and make a dollar a day. I did not want to talk to my mother because whenever we talked we would end up crying.

In the jail, I spent my time reading the Koran, and I understood its primary message, which is that no one should hurt another. I tried to live my life consciously so that my actions wouldn't hurt others. I also learned patience. Sometimes I led the Friday prayer, and I prayed five times daily. This experience brought me close to Islam.

The jail handbook lists approximately ten paid jobs for prisoners, like cleaning chairs, cleaning tables, mopping the floor, cleaning the bathrooms, changing trash bags, distributing the food, and stuff like that. Prisoners earn $1 per day or $5 per week. Even though these jobs are supposed to be voluntary, jail administrators force people to do them. If the prisoners assigned to do these jobs are deported or moved, the correctional officers [COs] announce that they have a job open and that they need a volunteer. If no one signs up, they punish everyone by shutting down the recreation area, or the juice bar, or making inmates stay in bed until someone agrees to sign up. So it is not volunteer work after all. I volunteered to do the kitchen work under similar circumstances.

Most of the Pakistanis liked hanging out with other Pakistanis, just like the Indians preferred to hang out with the Indians, blacks with other blacks, and Mexicans with Mexicans. When a new person would enter the dorm with his blankets and clothes, the Pakistanis would look at him from a distance and try to determine whether or not he was a Pakistani. One would say, "He is Pakistani," and another would say, "No, he is Indian." Then they would talk loudly in Urdu/Punjabi and say, "How are you?" If the new person answered, it meant that he was Pakistani. Then all of them would go down and introduce themselves, find out his whereabouts, and make a bed or food for him. Later, they would inquire about his case and start giving legal advice. Those who had stayed there longer understood the law better than the newcomers.

Sometimes when there was a large number of Pakistanis in the jail, we would get together and talk for a long time or sing songs. One guy from Lahore had a good voice, and he used to sing Punjabi film songs. The other inmates would look at us and were surprised by our behavior.

One of the Afghanis, who had a restaurant and a family in Albany, was always in a good mood. He would sing, whistle, and tell jokes. He would often say, "What is the worst that is going to happen? They will deport us. We are vacationing in a Holiday Inn." Another Pakistani was smart, educated, and knew about the law. He had a German passport, and he was there for alleged involvement in a billion-dollar fraud. He often helped other inmates with their legal cases or helped them type up letters.

Most of the individuals, however, experienced major psychological problems. One guy from Karachi was arrested at the Canadian border, and initially he was fine, but then I watched him gradually becoming mentally ill. He started getting into arguments with everyone, including the guards and the other inmates. He called me after he was deported to Pakistan.

I saw a lot of cases with mistakes in the jail. Once, I talked to a young Mexican man who was arrested for illegal entry. A few weeks later, the judge found out that he was a U.S. citizen, so he released him quickly. I also heard a lot of horror stories of immigration lawyers who gave the wrong advice, did not file papers on time, or were just lazy. Every year, the immigration laws were becoming more stringent, and keeping up with them required diligence. I remembered one immigration attorney who came to see his client, and the jail authorities arrested him for some technical glitch with his own visa. The immigration attorney spent the entire night talking to detainees and giving them free consultations.

In jail, I missed my freedom and the summer in Hudson. Driving on the streets of Hudson and its neighboring towns was like being on a vacation. Seeing the tree-lined streets, cows grazing along the roads, and the homes dotting the mountains gave me a feeling of satisfaction in my heart. I especially liked the long delivery trips. After making deliveries for a year, I had my favorite customers who gave good tips. Sometimes, they would have $100 orders and would tip me $20 or more. Many times, I would stop by the Hudson River and watch the water running by. I hardly went to the shopping malls. The rivers and mountains were my hangouts. If I had stayed out of jail, I could have become a citizen and gotten married.

Inside the jail, there were several head counts on a daily basis and so many other rules. I tried to follow most of the rules because I did not want to create an argument with the COs. I remember that in the beginning, I was a bit scared of them, but then I started to see that the COs were human beings also and that they were a mixed group, with some good and some bad. Some were power hungry and wanted to give everyone a hard time.

One officer especially was problematic, and everyone tried to avoid talking to him. Muslims and Christians tried to respect each other's prayer schedules and observed silence during those times in the jail. One day, this officer watched the Christians praying and singing together. He told them that from now on, religious practice was not allowed in the jail. Many of them were offended and complained. Some days later, some of the Muslims were praying together, and he said the same thing to us. We also complained to the director, and he suggested that we pray in smaller groups of five to seven at three or four different locations instead of in one large group. We tried to make small groups, and the officer said, "You can't pray in these areas. More than five can't pray." We continued to pray.

One day, the officer got angry and brought 20 to 30 guards with him and said, "Take them to SHU [Special Housing Unit]." He arrested about six of us and took us to the director. He was trying to make a case against us by claiming that we were conspiring against him and had threatened him. The director asked him if he had a witness, but he could not get one and had to let everyone go. Then the director told the officer that prisoners are allowed to pray and came down and wrote in the rules book that group prayer is allowed.

The officer was unable to do anything after the director's order, but he was angry. He came and told the guards to conduct an intensive search. They searched our beds, made us strip down to our underwear, and told us to leave the dorm for ten minutes. Outside it was snowing, and we had to wait in our underwear. All of us knew what was going on. The officer's ego was bruised, and he was taking it out on us. We just let him do it. He did not try to stop us from praying again, but we all avoided talking to him.

There were a few guards who were very good, and they used to support and encourage us or try to reduce our pain. I especially remember one 55-year-old white guard who tried to relax everyone. We used to play handball outside, and he would come and watch us. If the ball fell outside the wall, he would go and get it for us. Sometimes he told us jokes about his family. When I worked in the kitchen, I would often see him, and he would ask me how I was. Sometimes, he would buy things for us like balls, Ping-Pong rackets, or shoes. Then he would tell us, "I especially bought shoes for you from Wal-Mart." Once he tried to get a promotion, but he did not get it even though he was qualified.

I could not understand the operation of the jail. The jail administration was spending about $100 to $200 per day on each of us, which did not make any sense because everyone was willing to pay bail to get out. The only people profiting were the private companies that ran the jail, and the immigration officials were just providing the bodies of immigrants. The situation was especially bad for Pakistanis and Muslims. Either there was no bail or if there was bail, it was too high. Non-Muslims, however, even those who had committed crimes like smuggling people, were able to get out on bail. I was just accused of a crime, not even charged with anything, and I still could not get out on bail. Whether or not an inmate got bail depended on the knowledge and experience of lawyers.

Before 9/11, the administration was thinking about closing the Batavia facility, but after 9/11, they wanted to expand it. The number of law enforcement officers along the Canadian border had increased after 9/11, and so had the number of detainees inside the jail. Specifically, the number of Muslims inside Batavia had doubled and tripled. Many of the Pakistanis were flocking to Canada to escape law enforcement officers in New York and New Jersey. At the Canadian border, they would get caught and sent back to the port of entry, and so they would come under U.S. custody.[18] When I came to Batavia in February 2002, there were about 25 to 30 Muslims. When I left, the number had increased to 50 or 60.

This number does not include the people that were brought to Batavia periodically for deportation flights. During those weeks, the number sometimes went up to 200. Most of the Pakistanis on these deportation flights were laborers working at a gas station or a store.[19] On rare occasions, I saw a store owner or a gas station owner. Once I met this old man from Peshawar who had sold all his possessions, including his house, to come to the U.S. Then he got caught and was sent back without being able to make any money for his young daughters to get married. He had tried hard to get bail but wasn't able to.

Sometimes, we watched the news on the television and saw government officials giving statements about 9/11 detainees. They insisted that they were following laws and that all of the detainees were arrested under a legal framework. They implied that the government had arrested many dangerous terrorists and that the country was safer because of these arrests. We would hear these statements, laugh, and say to each other, "Who is the most dangerous terrorist here? We are the most dangerous terrorists." One of the detainees was very bold, and he said loudly, "Bush is the most dangerous terrorist."

After losing my legal battle, my attorney suggested that I accept deportation. However, members of the Free Ansar Mahmood Committee told me about the Administrative Discretionary Process that allows the immigration administration to consider unusual circumstances and hardships on a case-by-case basis for deportation cases. I had been sitting in jail for over two years, and it was difficult to wait longer, but I wanted to test the American justice system one last time. Also, there were so many individuals that had organized for me for over the past two years. They spent their time and resources to find alternatives for my release. I felt that if they could do this much, I can at least make a small sacrifice by waiting inside the jail a bit longer. Most of the people in my organizing committee were Americans who didn't know me before this incident. I felt that if my case could inspire someone from the community, it could also inspire someone within the immigration administration. After all, they were also human beings.

I filed the application for Administrative Discretionary Review on January 6, 2004. The Free Ansar Mahmood Committee worked on a petition drive, held community meetings, talked to politicians and the media, and networked with other organizations and individuals across the country. Within months, the committee obtained 16 signatures from senators, Congress people, and local politicians.[20] I was continuously interviewed on international and national television and radio and by print media outlets. The jail administration did not like this media publicity and tried different measures to stop it. One day, I had a television interview with Indymedia. The guards called me early in the morning to wait in the waiting area, where it was freezing cold. Around lunchtime, they took me to the cell, and a half hour later, they brought me to the waiting area again. Finally, I met the Indymedia representatives, and they told me that they had been waiting outside since 11:00 a.m. The guards had told them that I was taking my lunch. Despite this waiting around, I had one of the best interviews.

I knew that the guards wanted me to refuse the interviews. I understood their tactics and resisted them politely but persistently. When the protests and vigils started outside, they caused a lot of commotion and the guards went on a power trip. They subjected me to cavity searches before and after each interview. Interviewers had to follow specific guidelines to conduct interviews with me. They moved me from immigration to criminal dorms. During this time, the BBC and CNN also wanted to interview me. The chief came and asked, "Do you still want to be interviewed?" I felt that he was surprised that I was determined to talk even after they had given me such a hard time. I made an excuse that my lawyer wanted me to talk.

It felt good that people outside cared about my case and about me. One man who had been there for nine years told me, "Ansar, if you wait a bit, it is not only going to help you but many other people also. Maybe you won't benefit, but other people in the future might." I also noticed that other inmates got interested in sharing their stories with the media because of my willingness to talk, which created more awareness.

I knew that without this publicity, I would be forgotten. One day, Irum Shiekh, one of the Free Ansar Mahmood Committee members, told me that Amy Goodman, of the radio show *Democracy Now*, was interested in doing a live interview with me. I called Irum, and within minutes, I was talking live on the show via a three-way call. Susan and some other members of my committee met personally with Bill Cleary, the head of U.S. Customs and Immigration Enforcement in Buffalo, and requested a sympathetic review of my application. Inside the jail, I waited. I was still optimistic.

In March 2005, Bill Cleary, using the buzzword of "national security," denied my application on the grounds that I was a "convicted criminal" with an "aggravated felony." In his decision, Mr. Cleary wrote,

It is without dispute that you were convicted of an aggravated felony having pled guilty to have knowingly concealed, harbored and shielded from detection two illegal aliens This is an egregious factor that I find disappointing for a new immigrant to this country to have been arrested and convicted for harboring illegal aliens. Further, it is noted in your testimony before the immigration judge that you lied to the federal court, under oath, during your plea hearing when you admitted your guilt.... After reviewing all pertinent correspondence, it has been determined that the safety and security of the United States far outweighs the amount of publicity that has been generated in this case. The harboring and smuggling of illegal aliens continues to pose a serious threat to national security. Congress has mandated that the Department of Homeland Security enforce the Immigration and Nationality Act. The removal of criminal aliens has become a priority. By law, your conviction has defined you as an "aggravated felon" and your removal is in the best interests of national security.[21]

Susan, Rajesh Barnabas from Rochester, and Aarti Shahani and Subhash Kateel from Freedom for Families set up a camp outside the Buffalo Detention Center and held a vigil for two nights to challenge the decision. However, after reading Mr. Cleary's decision, I lost the last bit of faith and trust I had in the American government system. I signed my deportation papers and went to sleep.

I was disappointed that after all the education and advanced knowledge, the American legal system could not make the distinction between a smuggler and a person who tried to help his friends. This 1996 immigration law must change because immigration agents abuse their power in the field. It is a crime to lie in front of a federal agent, but it is not illegal for federal agents to lie. My immigration agent lied to me. What is his punishment? There is no equality. The government just has too much power, and they abuse it with vulnerable people.

Getting Deported

After signing the deportation papers, I stayed in Batavia for two more months. One day, I heard that the Pakistani Embassy wanted to talk to me. The immigration authorities took me to the Pakistani consulate in Washington, D.C., where I had a fabulous and tasty Pakistani lunch with the acting Pakistani ambassador. He briefly inquired about my case, but I could not understand the significance of this meeting. Maybe the Pakistanis wanted to do a public relations effort to convince me that they cared about me, but that meeting cemented my decision to leave the jail. Getting out of the jail, sitting in a car, and moving around with the general public made me remember the importance of freedom. I just could not see myself sitting in the jail anymore and wanted to go back to Pakistan as soon as possible. During this meeting, I also met briefly with Bill Cleary. He shook hands with me and said, "You have been an exemplary prisoner." I was really surprised at this schizophrenic attitude. On the one hand, he was writing a rejection letter saying that I was a "dangerous criminal," and on the other hand, he was complimenting me.

I felt that my case had created bad publicity for them, and it was their highest desire to deport me. Maybe they felt insulted by the protests. The media representatives used to call the Department of Homeland Security to inquire about my case. I don't think the jail administration wanted to release me, but the bad publicity they were receiving motivated them to close my case.

A week after the meeting, I got my travel documents and the deportation officers got my airline ticket. At the airport, I called Susan and said my final good-bye. The deportation officers asked me what I wanted to eat, and I ordered pizza. I surprised myself because I was not that fond of eating pizza, but I enjoyed that last meal.

I did not have any problems at the Islamabad airport. I took a bus to Gujarat and then a noisy rickshaw to my house in the middle of the night. Everyone in the house was waiting for me. Susan had called my home several times before my arrival to inquire about me, so my family was expecting me. My mother opened the door and hugged me. I came inside the house with mixed emotions. I was happy to be with them, but this is not how I wanted to come back—empty-handed. I thought about the last time I had visited Pakistan. At that time, I had been optimistic. I had plans and hopes to make changes, to buy a new house in the city. Now, those opportunities to change things are gone.

We all got together and we started talking. My mother had cooked my favorite dishes: *karati* lamb and *kheer*. I enjoyed that homemade food and stayed up till the dawn and slept through the day. I stayed inside the house for the next four or five days just talking and sharing with my family. My mother was happy. She told me, "You are my wealth. I am glad that you are back." My father cried sometimes when talking to me. My sisters were a bit quiet. One day, I called Yusuf, who was managing a cell phone store, and he asked me to come and see him. A week later, I went to see him and we hugged and talked.

I am happy to be back with my family and loved ones. I still miss my freedom in the U.S., the people that I worked with, and the community members who organized for me. My impressions about the U.S. and its people have improved after this incident. All the people who helped me were Americans. They did not even know me, but they worked so hard to organize for me. My internal fears, which had resurfaced after the arrest, started to subside again with the love and support that I received from the people around me. Whatever happened to me was terrible, but at least the American public stood up and supported me. I found a lot of love in the U.S. There were many people, Muslims and non-Muslims, who were stuck in the jail with me. By helping me, the Americans were trying to help everyone who was stuck in a similar situation.

Opportunities are not as great in Pakistan as they are in the U.S. There is a lot of corruption, and the rich people with power like to maintain the status quo. However, Pakistan is my country, a place I believe that I won't be kicked out of for helping a close friend. Maybe this is the difference between the U.S. and Pakistan. The United States is a nation of immigrants, but discriminatory laws force immigrants to walk on a long path filled with thorns.

Looking back, I wonder why I was targeted. I looked at my deportation papers, and I am forbidden from ever entering the U.S. again. I don't know anyone else who has been barred for life. I have seen people committing worse crimes and getting barred for only ten years, which is usually the maximum. Why me? Maybe the immigration officials were afraid that if I had stayed, I would have sued the American government. The U.S. government was protecting itself by trying to get rid of me. Sometimes, I think about the immigration officer on the night of October 9 who insisted on my arrest. Was he thinking that by arresting me, he would get a big promotion? Was he trying to be patriotic? Was he taking revenge on me for the tragic deaths of the 3,000 Americans in the World Trade Center? Did I remind him of someone whom he wanted to confront but could not? Was he against Muslims? I don't know. I may not know for a while.

However, I am optimistic that with a change in the political climate, after the global war on terror is over, people will start to see each other as individuals again and not necessarily as terrorists. Maybe something will change then. Documents will be declassified, and I will get to see what was happening. Until then, I have to wait. I have a desire to reopen the trial. I hope someone can reopen the case and see the injustice that has happened to me. I am optimistic that one of these days, something will happen...and I am going to wait.

Life Today: Today Ansar drives a van and transports school children between their homes and their schools. He makes approximately 15,000 to 20,000 rupees per month, which is approximately $400 to $500. It is difficult to live on this income, but he manages to do it by living with his family. He is still unsure about his future and hopes that with a change in the political climate, he might be able to change his destiny. The government continues to claim that Ansar had knowledge of the illegal immigration status of his friends, and if he did not know about the immigration status of his friends, then he lied in a courtroom when he pled guilty to the charges of "harboring illegal aliens."

Ansar's narrative attests to the government's abuse of power and its lack of accountability for its actions. First, he was accused of being a terrorist. When law enforcement officials could not connect him to any terrorist activity, they criminalized him so that he could be deported easily under the current immigration laws.

Crime is a dynamic concept that takes on different meanings in different places and time periods. Helping a childhood friend—a moral responsibility in Pakistani culture—was manufactured into a crime after the U.S. Congress adopted the 1996 immigration act,[22] *and law enforcement officers decided to enforce it strictly after the attacks of September 11, 2001. Ansar's narrative shows that the United States' current immigration laws can transform an honest young man with aspirations into a terrorist or a criminal.*

Figure 3 Anser Mehmood, Uzma Naheed, and their son Hassan Anser, early 2003, Pakistan. Courtesy of Todd Drew and Wendy Sherman of ACLU.

CHAPTER 3

Uprooting Immigrants, Uprooting Families

Anser Mehmood, Uzma Naheed, and Family

Anser Mehmood, his wife, Uzma Naheed, and their four children—Umair (15), Uzair (14), Harris (12), and Hassan (1)—used to live in Bayonne, New Jersey. They had moved as a family from Pakistan in 1994, and Hassan was born in the United States in 2000.

On October 3, 2001, FBI and immigration officers raided their home and detained Anser for an expired visa. His wife and three children who also had expired visas were spared.[1] Immediately after the arrest, Anser was classified as a "High Interest Case" and was taken to the ninth floor of the Metropolitan Detention Center in New York, where he spent months in solitary confinement. During this time, Uzma and his children fought fiercely against the prevailing atmosphere of suspicion and worked extensively with media and nonprofit organizations for Anser's release. Because of these efforts, Anser was moved from solitary confinement to the general population unit in the MDC.

With the breadwinner of her family in jail, Uzma was unable to support herself financially and decided to go back to Pakistan with her children in February 2002. Anser was deported to Pakistan in May 2002 for using his nonauthorized social security card to gain employment.

Meeting Uzma, Anser, and the Family

I met Uzma Naheed in Lahore, Pakistan, in late February 2003. She was visiting her younger brother with her youngest child, Hassan. During this visit, I also met Ahmar

Abaysi, Uzma's brother, who was arrested two weeks prior to her husband in New York. I asked him for an interview, and he assented.

After recording an interview with Uzma and Ahmar, I visited Karachi and met Anser, his three young children, and his father. I recorded interviews with all of them. After returning to the United States, I interviewed Martin Stolar, Anser's defense lawyer in New York, who provided me some contextual information about the case. I also reviewed Anser's legal files[2] and numerous newspaper articles and documentaries about his case.[3]

I translated and transcribed the interviews from Urdu. The following is a compilation of all seven personal interviews along with some archival materials that I found during my research. Anser, Uzma, Anser's father, and the children speak in their own voices. Ahmar's story and my archival research are presented in italics.

The interview with Anser's three children was a group interview. The children often spoke simultaneously and finished each other's sentences and stories. After listening to the recording, it was difficult to tell them apart. Therefore, I refer to them simply as "Children" in the narrative. In certain portions, when I am able to identify the child speaking, I use his individual name.

The Pull of the United States

Before moving to the United States, Anser Mehmood, his wife, Uzma Naheed, and their three children lived in Karachi, Pakistan. Political and violent clashes in the 1980s between the Mohajir Quami Movement (MQM)[4] and the government deeply impacted Anser and his family on a personal level. In 1988 someone set fire to Anser's successful business. Later, someone shot his nephew in the leg. To ensure his family's safety, he sold what was left of his business and moved his family to the United States in 1994 on visiting visas. At the time, they hoped to return to Karachi after the political situation improved.

The family decided to make the United States their home soon after they moved because they noticed that Karachi's political situation was not improving. Anser used his business savings to establish himself and drove a taxi for a while. Eventually, he bought a truck and worked a double driving shift, seven days a week. His hard work paid off, and he was able to make a good living. He provided for his family, bought a house, and sent money to his family in Pakistan. His children started school and began to settle in.

In the late 1990s, Anser decided to establish a trucking company under the name Unique Trucking Company. He registered the company and began negotiating a deal for the trucks. Because the family's visas had expired, Anser explored various options to legalize their immigration status.

Life and Attitudes Toward the United States Before 9/11

(Anser) My life was great before September 11. My family did not have any problems with anyone and never felt any discrimination. I especially liked that people respected laws. I felt that many races lived together peacefully in the U.S.

(Uzma) I felt so relaxed and enjoyed my time there because people treated each other like human beings. The best thing that we found in America was people's respect for each other regardless of race. I felt that was the main reason that everyone around the world wants to settle in the U.S. I never felt that the American people tried to degrade us because we were immigrants. I have lived in the U.K., Saudi Arabia, and Canada, and compared to all those countries, I liked the U.S. the most. I told my husband that I didn't feel like an immigrant in the U.S. because I could access whatever I wanted. It was just that kind of environment because everyone in the U.S. has immigrant origins. They treated us like equals and my children also felt equal to others. I learned about human rights in the U.S. and found so many supporters of those rights there.

(Anser's father) Before 9/11, I had a very high opinion of the American justice system. I thought that it was democratic and had high values. In my personal experience, people treated me with respect. There is respect and dignity for labor, and people don't interfere with your privacy. Law and justice prevail.

Uzma and Anser's three young children—Umair, Uzair, and Harris—were also happy with their new house, the surroundings, and their life.

(Children) Before 9/11, everyone was friendly and nice and our life was very good. We had a big house, a nice car, and everyone had their own room with everything we wanted. Our mom and dad were with us, and we were living the American dream. Initially when we bought the house, it did not look very good. We changed everything—the kitchen tiles, carpets, etc.—and after that it was very nice. We rode bikes and had a lot of friends—whites, blacks, and Muslims, all kinds of friends. Our middle school was one of the best public schools in the U.S. Nobody knew about Osama bin Laden, Muslims, or mosques before 9/11. Now everyone knows about things like terrorism and Al-Qaeda.

Anser had tried many approaches to legalize his immigration status in the United States. After he decided to make the United States his home, he talked to a few lawyers and people that he trusted about his legal situation.

Attempts to Legalize the Family's Immigration Status

(Anser) Uzma's brother Mauzam Ali came to the U.S. in the early 1980s.[5] At that time, the government had an immigration program, which allowed him to legalize his status. We were hoping that the government would start something like that again soon. We talked to an immigration lawyer, who told us that every ten years the government introduces schemes that allow tax-paying immigrants to legalize their status on hardship grounds. The lawyer advised us to wait for seven years so that we wouldn't have to change our names or lie. We liked that strategy and had seen it work for Uzma's brother. Seven years later, we went back to the lawyer, and he said, "The rules have changed. Now it is ten years. Just wait for a couple more years." We listened to him and continued to pay taxes.

After Uzma's brother got citizenship, he put in applications for our visas. The immigration officials told us that it was going to take a few years, and we hoped that this process would grant us legal status.

Uzma's older brother, a U.S. citizen, submitted an Immigration Petition for Relatives for the entire family in May 2001.[6] *However, Uzma felt that her undocumented status was not a crime, especially because her experiences of living in the United States without papers had been positive.*

(Uzma) We were not doing anything illegal. We were doing what thousands of other people were doing around us. If it were a crime, somebody would have warned us. Whenever we dealt with government officials in hospitals or schools, they asked for our social security number, and I always told them that I didn't have one. We never had a problem. If we had felt that there was strict enforcement of immigration laws, we might have tried to get Canadian residency or made a more serious effort to get papers. Some people suggested that we make fake papers, but we did not want to lie or change our names.

Initially, we thought that our stay in the U.S. was temporary, and I had planned to move back to Pakistan for my parents and extended family. But after living in the U.S. for about ten years, I felt that we had settled in. My children were attending school and had started to make friends. We felt that we could settle peacefully in the U.S., especially after my older brother became a citizen and submitted immigration papers for my family.

After looking at many houses, we bought a very beautiful house in Bayonne, New Jersey. We were looking for a neighborhood with good schools and parks, and Bayonne had everything. The middle school, which all my children attended, was across the street from our house. It was comforting to be able to watch my kids from my kitchen window whenever they played outside. We had a very good life with great surroundings.

Life After 9/11

Even before the arrest, Anser and his family had started to feel a shift in the attitudes of the people around them.

(Anser) Everything changed after 9/11, especially the way people looked at us. We lived in a white neighborhood, and our neighbors started looking at us suspiciously. The kids started feeling uncomfortable at school because the other kids called them "Muslim terrorists." They could not believe what was happening, but the fact is that 9/11 changed people.

My wife, who wears a headscarf, was taunted in our peaceful neighborhood. At the time, we thought that animosity from our neighbors was a temporary response to 9/11. We believed that the founding fathers of America had established a strong legal constitution and that it would not be forgotten so quickly. Americans are always talking about human rights, and I never thought that they would be so quick to violate them.

Whenever my wife and children complained, I told them, "It is temporary and things will change." I thought that if a country had already developed its roots, lawlessness could not prevail. I thought that the American public would soon realize that only a few Muslims were involved, not the entire community. If 10 or 20 members of a community do something wrong, it does not mean that the entire community is corrupt. I never thought that Muslims would experience difficult times in the U.S., and I was especially not expecting twisted logic from the U.S. government. After 9/11, it was as if person B got punished for the crime that person A committed. If I had known that the U.S. government was going to respond this way, I would never have brought my family to the U.S.

(**Children**) People started to call us terrorists when they realized that the Muslims did it and that we are also Muslims. After school in the evening, we used to play football with our friends in a field that was across the street from our house. After 9/11, the kids changed completely. They would not allow us to play and would put us on the sidelines. They would throw the ball to the side and call over the big kids to come scare us or start a fight.

(**Harris**) One day, when I sat down at a table with other kids in the classroom, everyone moved to the other side of the table.

(**Uzma**) After 9/11, people started hating Muslims. One day, I was standing outside the house and some children walked by saying, "They did it. They did it." These comments made us feel as if we had killed the people in the World Trade Center or that we were responsible for its destruction. Our neighbors didn't recognize that we felt as sorry and hurt about the loss as any other American. We cried like other Americans when we visited Ground Zero. When my children saw me crying, they said, "Mom, don't worry, we will build a new tower."

There was a lot of discrimination, and people stopped talking to us simply because we were Muslim. I used to wear *shalwar kameez* [traditional Pakistani clothes] but never felt discrimination based on my appearance before 9/11. I felt it afterwards.

Anser's father was visiting the United States from Pakistan on a visiting visa when 9/11 happened. He also noticed a change in American attitudes.

(**Anser's father**) I was there on 9/11 and saw how bad the conditions were for Muslims. The Friday after 9/11, I went to pray at the mosque and I noticed that people were starting to feel fearful. Outside the mosque, a police car was parked for protection. The imam [religious leader] informed the public that the Muslim leaders had met with several people, including the governor and FBI officials. He said to contact the government if we experienced any harassment or hate crimes. I came home and told Anser and Uzma about it. I was thinking that if anything happened, the general public would be the perpetrators. I never expected any harassment from the government.

Anser's father left for Pakistan on September 14, 2001, to attend a wedding in the family.

The Arrest

Anser, Uzma, and their year-old son, Hassan, were at home on the morning of October 3. Hassan, born in April 2000, was sleeping with them. Anser had helped the three young children get ready for school, and he was waiting for a call from his trucking company for work when he heard the doorbell ring around 9:00 a.m.

(**Anser**) I peeped through the window and saw approximately 20 to 30 FBI agents at the door. I was surprised and wondered what they were doing at my house, so I went downstairs and opened the door.

"Why are you here?" I asked.

"We are from the FBI."

"I can see that. Do you have any search warrants?"

"We have everything in the car. Just sit down over here and answer our questions." I sat down in the living room, and the FBI agents went directly to Uzma's bedroom without my permission.

(**Uzma**) I was sleeping in the bedroom. Suddenly I heard some noise and I opened my eyes. I saw a man in my bedroom wearing a jacket with FBI written on it. I was completely shocked to see him in my room. I rushed outside the room and saw my husband standing in the living room. I went and stood with him.

(**Anser**) They told us to sit in one side of the room and inquired about our passports. We told them where everything was, and they started to search the house.

(**Uzma**) The FBI and INS agents were all over my house. Some were really big and tall and made me feel scared. They searched everywhere—the first and second floor, the basement, the attic—and started to throw things around all over the place.

(**Anser**) On the news, I had heard that the FBI was checking the licenses of truck drivers, so I thought that they had come to check my license and after confirming that it was valid they would leave. I did not worry that much. After a long search, seven to eight agents took Uzma to another room and started questioning her. I sat in a separate room with my son, while an FBI officer watched me.

(Uzma) The FBI agents called me into the living room and started to interrogate me. The head detective asked me my name and I replied, "Uzma Naheed." He opened my passport and saw that my name was listed as Uzma Naheed Abaysi. He said, "We caught you from the very beginning. You told us a big lie and you will be punished heavily."

"What did I do?" I asked.

"You said your name was Uzma Naheed, and in your passport it is listed as Uzma Naheed Abaysi."

"So what if I don't tell people my last name? Abaysi is my family name and I don't use it. It does not mean that I have two names. You can check all of my identification cards. My name is listed the same on all of them."

After I expressed my anger, he became quiet and said, "Oh, okay. This is exactly like when people call me by my nickname." I think that from the very beginning, they were trying to threaten and harass me by saying that I had given them the wrong name. However, I was not scared because I knew that I had not done anything wrong.

Then they started asking me questions about my brother Ahmar. I told them that my brother visited us sometimes and that he also used our address to receive packages. I trust my brother, and I am not suspicious of him. They showed me some photos, and I recognized my brother and his friends. There were also some people with beards in the photos, but I did not know them. At that time, I did not even know what Osama bin Laden looked like, and if they had shown me his photos, I would not have recognized him. I was just a housewife taking care of children. I was not working and did not have any interest in or connections with any organizations.

I knew that the FBI had arrested my younger brother Ahmar in late September. I thought the FBI had found our home address from my brother's computer and had come here to ask us a few questions. My brother worked very hard as a cab driver to make his living. He did not have any connections with terrorism and was arrested only because of his friend Amjad.

The FBI arrested Ahmar Abaysi, Uzma's brother, on September 25 with his friend Amjad,[7] a Pakistani national who had come to the United States via Germany. Officials at the Department of Motor Vehicles reported Amjad to the immigration authorities when he tried to make a fake driver's license. Amjad and Ahmar were sharing an apartment, and authorities arrested Ahmar because he had an expired visa.

After the initial investigation, law enforcement officers took them to the MDC in Brooklyn, where they locked them in solitary confinement on the ninth floor, an area designated for individuals suspected of having connections with 9/11. Ahmar recalled his arrival at the MDC:

When they brought me, everyone in the jail stared at me. Ten to 15 officers surrounded me and took me to a small room. At that time, I felt that they had taken me to the very top floor. They asked me to turn my face to the wall and do as they said. There was a window next to the wall. At that time, I recalled images of people jumping from the windows of the World Trade Center. I thought that they were going to tell me to jump now and suffer for those deaths. I lost my mind and started to cry.

Later, when he learned that he was placed on the ninth floor under suspicion of terrorism, he felt somewhat relaxed. He thought that law enforcement officers would release him once they realized that he had no connections to 9/11. Amjad was placed in a separate cell in the same area. Ahmar stayed in the MDC for over six months.[8]

After arresting Ahmar and Amjad, FBI agents started investigating all of their contacts. FBI agents found Uzma's address through Ahmar and came to investigate them. After the officers were finished with Uzma, they questioned Anser in a separate room.

(Anser) The head investigator continued to ask me questions about Uzma's brothers. I told them that I had no information. They continued to insist that I knew something, but I really did not know anything. Meanwhile, they called the immigration agents and told them that I had overstayed my visa. Then I showed them the social security card that I had been using to work.

Anser had removed the "not for employment sticker" from his social security card and used it to gain employment.

The immigration officials already had my information in their records and called to reconfirm. At the end, they said, "You have a very minor violation. We don't have any problem with you. You also have a pending application with us. If the FBI clears you, you are cleared."

The FBI said, "You are clear from our side. We have completed our investigation and we don't have any problem with you. We only have a problem with your wife."

"What is the problem?"

"This is not her personal problem. We need information about her brothers, but she is not telling us anything. We want to take her."

(Uzma) The FBI agents told me that I had to go with them. "Why?" I asked, "What is the reason? What have I done? Even if we are illegal, we have submitted papers." I showed them the receipt of our pending application, which we had received from the immigration office.[9] I started to cry, and Anser pleaded with them not to take me, especially because I was taking care of the children. The FBI agents told him that they didn't have any other options, and Anser asked them to take him instead. When Anser offered to go in my place, I told him, "You have to go to work, you can't go. It is important for the children to be with their father. What is the worst that will happen? I will come back."

(Anser) I told Uzma, "No, you can't go. We don't like our women to go to jail so you should stay home and I will deal with it. We have a small baby and you have to take care of him. If they need to investigate anything, they can do it with me."

When the FBI agent heard that, he said, "We don't have any problem with you, so how can we take you with us? We want to take your wife." The agent asked Uzma to get ready. She went into shock and started to cry. They repeated that they didn't have a problem with her, only with her brother, and that they would let her go in a few days.

I said, "If you want to take Uzma then take my younger son also." My youngest son was about a year old. He was on a calcium diet and could not live without his mom.

"We can't take him. He does not have anything to do with it. Also, he is a U.S. citizen."

"How can he live without her? He is very sick."

"You are the father. You can take care of him."

"I am not home most of the time, so I can't take care of him." They did not care. They asked Uzma to get ready and gave my son Hassan to me. When I took Hassan, he started to cry because he was not familiar with me, and the officer noticed that I was not able to stop him from crying. Uzma came out then, and I gave Hassan back to her. He became quiet suddenly, and when the chief investigator realized that Hassan's separation from Uzma was going to impact him badly, he went outside to call his office to see if I could go instead.

After a few minutes, he came back and said,
I talked to the office and because the child is sick, we can't take the mother. But we have to take someone from here. You can go with the immigration officers and they will charge you for overstaying. Tomorrow they will present you in front of the judge, and by 10:00 a.m., you will be out on bail because it is a very minor violation. The most you will have to pay is $1,000 or $1,500, and they will release you. Things are good for you since your son is a U.S. citizen. You also have a house, family, and a business, and you pay taxes regularly. You will get your papers easily. We don't have any problems with you.

After explaining all this to us, the FBI agents left.

I trusted the FBI at that time. I never thought that they would arrest me, put me in a high-security jail, and abuse me. We did not have any connection with terrorism and we'd never dealt with the FBI or police, so we trusted them.

(Uzma) I did not know where they were taking Anser and why. My husband was not directly related to my brother. We only showed up on their radar because we are Muslims. The FBI had arrested my brother two weeks before and had not found any terrorist connections. Yet they continued to arrest more people like him. They are crazy people.

The chief investigating officer gave me his number and told me to call him. He also promised me that Anser would call me that night and that he would be released the next day. When my children came home, everything—pictures, cushions, books—was scattered everywhere and nothing was in its original place. My kids were very confused and asked, "What happened? Was there a robbery or did the FBI come here?"

"Why do you think the FBI was here?"

"We have seen stuff like this in the films. This is how places look after the FBI searches and scatters things around. Where is dad?"

"Your dad left for a job." I did not tell them where he was because I did not want to destroy their image of their father. I did not want to tell them that the FBI had taken Anser because they might start thinking that he had done something wrong or illegal. I was not crying anymore, but I was still in shock and felt confused. They had taken my husband suddenly, and I hadn't been able to do anything about it. My kids are smart, so they quickly figured out the situation. They started to call their father, but his phone was turned off. They called him over and over.

Then they tried to call him again at night. There was no answer, and they started to ask, "What is the matter? Why is dad not picking up the phone? Why has he not called us?" I was worried also, and I continued to wait for the phone call.

(Children) The day of our dad's arrest, one of our friends, Ricardo, had been at home. We saw him before we went in the house and he said, "Twenty to thirty FBI agents came and took your dad." We did not believe him, but when we went inside and saw that the door hinge was broken and that the computer was gone, we understood immediately that the FBI had been in the house. We tried to confirm it with our mom, but she told us a different story. Everything was gone, including our pictures, passports, books, and the clock and the poster with the World Trade Center on them. We asked our mom about it, and she said, "Your dad has taken the stuff to Brooklyn." We knew that she was lying.

We did not think that our dad had done anything illegal because he was such a law-abiding person. He always told us to obey the law and to never disrespect or hurt anyone. He paid all his taxes, and he would even get angry when we got detention in school.

(Anser) Immigration officers handcuffed me, and I sat with them in the car. I was pretty calm at that time. I had already told them my immigration status, and they had assured me that the arrest would expedite the immigration process. I thought I was going to the police station for a night and would return home the next day. They told me, "You don't have to inform anyone. We are taking you to 201 Varick Street in downtown Manhattan. Just call your wife after you get there and tell her to prepare the bail documents." On the way, one of the officers said,

"Why don't you tell the FBI everything that you know about Uzma's brother in Pakistan?"

"I already told you what I know about him. How can I tell you anything that I don't know?"

"If you tell us those things, we will let you go." I stayed quiet because I did not have any additional information.

Finally they said, "You don't have a big problem and will be released tomorrow." On the way to the Varick Street station, we all joked and laughed together, and when I got there, they put me in a cell with seven or eight Pakistanis and Arabs who had also overstayed their visas. We talked and got to know each other. The guards gave us food and allowed us to go to the bathroom. Immigration officers interviewed everyone but me.

At 9:00 p.m., the immigration officer who had arrested me came to the cell. "You are not going to interview me?" I asked.

"We already have all the information we need about you from the computer. Immigration is charging you with an overstayed visa and we will present you to the judge in the morning. Don't worry."

An affidavit dated October 3, 2001, indicates that Anser Mehmood had been arrested for an expired visa.[10]

I reminded the immigration officials that they had promised me a phone call to my wife, and they told me to ask the jail administration. When I asked the guards about a phone call, they said that they I wasn't allowed to make one. At that time, I wasn't even thinking about contacting a lawyer and went back to the cell.

Later that day, about 10 to 12 FBI and other law enforcement officers came and put me in chains and shackles. "What are you doing? Why are you taking me to the court like this?" I asked.

"Shut up. You keep your mouth shut." They did the same to the other guys in the cell.

One of the Pakistani men exclaimed, "Maybe they are making a mistake!" I did not have any idea what they were doing. They put four of us—two Tunisians, one Pakistani, and I—in a border patrol van. Two FBI cars drove in the front and two in the back. They blocked the entire road, and as we drove, I watched the reactions of the bystanders from the window. They turned their heads as we went by and looked at us as if we were the 9/11 terrorists.[11]

Ahmar, Uzma's brother, said he was brought to the MDC in a motorcade of police cars with sirens blaring. He felt that the FBI used this motorcade to show the public that they were doing their job.[12]

Up until that point, I was still under the impression that they were taking me to court to see the judge. I did not know anything about the MDC yet. First, they took us inside a garage. Big guards who were approximately six to seven feet tall dragged the guys out from the van and started banging them against the walls. Later, they dragged me from the van, banged me against the wall, took me upstairs, and threw me against the wall again. The guards threw me seven or eight times, and I broke my hand. I did not realize that my hand was broken at the time, but I noticed the next day after it swelled up.

Then they put me in front of a camera and took a picture. Since they had beat me up pretty bad, my shirt was pulled up and my mouth was bleeding. The officer taking the photograph wanted to take the photo again. Another officer cleaned my mouth, and pulled my shirt down before they retook my photo. Afterwards, they pushed my shoulder and head against the wall. They told me, "Don't ask any questions. Otherwise, you will be dead." I did not ask any questions, but I wondered if this is how they normally treat people with expired visas.

They took me to another room, unlocked my handcuffs, and gave me an orange suit to wear. One of them asked, "Do you know why you are here?"

"I am here for an overstayed visa," I said.

"No, you are here for the World Trade Center attack." After I heard that, I felt relaxed. I thought they would investigate me for a day or two, find out that I had nothing to do with it, and let me go.

The guards took me directly to the ninth floor and put me in a small cell with another guy named Asraf. "Are you waiting for the court also?" I asked.

"I have been here for three days and they have not taken me to court. They also don't allow you to make phone calls." He consoled me a lot, however, and cleaned and took care of my hand. After that, they did not physically torture me again.

There were about 60 cells on the ninth floor which held either one or two people. Each cell had a solid door with a small glass window and a small window that allowed us to look outside. In late December, they put a thick coat of paint on the window and we could not see outside anymore. We could not tell if it was sunny or dark outside. Compared to the ninth floor, there were large windows in the general population unit.

The ninth floor was designated for terrorists, and all the prisoners there were Muslims.[13] Zacarias Moussaoui[14] was there for a while. No one from the FBI or the INS came to ask me any questions. They knew from the first day that I did not have any connections with terrorism and that I was just waiting for my release.

The Family's Search for Anser

Uzma and her children were shocked at the disappearance of their loved one. Uzma felt that the world around her had collapsed.

(**Uzma**) The night of the arrest ended and I still hadn't heard from Anser. The chief investigator had told me that they would let my husband call me. I waited and kept thinking that the phone would ring any minute, and I could not sleep. The morning came and still there was no phone call. I sent the kids to school and continued waiting for the phone to ring. In the afternoon, I called the chief investigator and asked him about Anser's whereabouts. He wouldn't tell me anything.

Then the kids returned from school and started asking about their father. They were all very attached to him because he took an interest in their lives, knew their daily routines, and would always ask them about their day. Now, two days had passed and the children still had not heard anything from him. Slowly, I started to tell them that the FBI had taken him. The kids were very surprised and then worried. They asked, "What has our dad done? Our dad taught us that we should always respect U.S. laws." He had always taught them that if they respected the law, they would never have to fear anything.

On the third day, I could not take it anymore. I told my kids that they were not going to school and took them with me to the Bayonne police station. When I reached the station, I could not speak. I just cried and cried. I tried to tell them that FBI and immigration officers had taken my husband. They would not even listen and said very coldly, "We don't know about your husband. If the FBI took your husband we can't do anything about it. We don't know where they took him." Nobody listened to us or helped us, so I just returned home crying.

My kids told me, "Don't cry like this. Become a strong lady." They were scared about what would happen to them. Their dad had disappeared, their mom couldn't stop crying, and no one was being sympathetic. They said, "Ask them strongly. Tell them that he has not done anything." How could I have told anyone anything when I was crying like that? I was crying at my helplessness. I was crying about how they came to my home and took my husband for no reason. I was crying because no one would tell me where he was [*crying*].

(**Children**) When we went to the police station with our mom, it was filled with cops. At the information section, we told them that the FBI had come to our house and asked them if they knew anything about it. The police officers in the station said, "We don't know." They were lying. Approximately 20 to 30 FBI officers had visited us, and there is no way that the local police station did not know about it.

(**Uzma**) I called the chief investigator for three days and begged him to tell me where they had taken Anser. He would not tell me anything at first, but eventually he told me that he was with the INS and gave me a phone number to call. When I called the number, the INS wouldn't tell me anything either. I hired a lawyer, and he charged me $300 just to find out that Anser was at the MDC. At that time, I did not know anything about the MDC.

Living With the Stigma of Terrorism

(Uzma) In the beginning, I was scared and did not speak with anyone. Slowly when I started talking, my friends and relatives were surprised that the FBI could be suspicious of a person like Anser. Nobody believed me. People in our community knew and respected us, and we had shared our joys and sorrows with them. Now those same community members were acting indifferently. They would not even pick up the phone. Whenever I called, they said that they didn't want to talk about it. "We can't discuss this issue with you. This is your problem. You go and resolve it for yourself."[15]

They were afraid that they might get into trouble with the FBI like Anser if they talked to us. They wanted to be able to say that they did not have any relationship or affiliations with us. Even his best friends refused to help us. All of my neighbors also became very suspicious. We had just bought the house last year and didn't know everyone in the neighborhood yet because people don't develop friendships very easily in the U.S. They started to hate us and couldn't believe that the FBI would be stupid enough to arrest innocent people. They thought that Anser must have done something wrong. We had no one to turn to. All Americans believed that the FBI was doing the right thing.

(Children) Kids in the school found out about our dad's arrest through the media. One of the kid's uncles read a newspaper article and sent it to him. The kid brought the newspaper to school and started showing it to everyone.[16] Then the entire school started bothering us.

The teachers did not bother us, but they did not protect us either. Whenever I got in trouble, the teacher would take me to the vice principal, and they would blame me for everything. There was another Pakistani kid called Usama, and the school administration would call both of us into the vice principal's office even though we had not done anything. Most of the students were Polish Jews, and they were anti-Muslim. One day at school, I told them that the Jews were responsible for 9/11, which started a fight.[17]

White kids started throwing stones at our house and broke the glass doors. They had so much hatred against us. We knew these two big and tall black kids through other friends, and they wanted to be our friends. After we became friends, everybody stopped bothering us. The black kids told me, "If anyone asks about you, don't say that you are a Muslim or a Pakistani; otherwise they will beat you up." After we came under their protection, everyone left us alone. We used to call them to come and beat up the white kids. When they came, the white kids would run like mice from a cat.

The white kids threatened us a lot. They would come after us when we were walking and say, "Don't look behind you or we will beat you up." Whenever we looked back, they would run away. In the beginning, we were scared but then we got tough. We felt that if we didn't stand up for ourselves, they would continue to abuse us. We learned that to stop them, we had to beat them up. One day, all of us beat up those white kids.

(Uzair) Older people and police officers treated us badly, too. Our dad's absence created some tension and anger in the house. One day, my older brother and I were fighting. He threw the phone at the wall, and I threw the other phone on the floor. Our mom got really angry and called the police. When the police came, I got scared and hid in the room. Later, our mom did not want any of us to go with the police so she explained the situation to the officer. The officer asked, "Where is your father?"

"He is in the detention center."

"It is a good place for him," he said. I got so angry when he said that. We are still very angry at the police officer for talking like that. Our neighbor used to be very friendly before our dad was arrested. She used to come to our house to take care of the trees and clean the yard. Afterwards, she would not even talk to us or come over. Instead, she started to curse at us.

Uzma Finds Her Voice as an Organizer and an Activist

Uzma became active in organizing and speaking out about her husband's case.

(Uzma) For two weeks after Anser's arrest, I received his salary because he had worked for various companies. After that I ran out of money. I did not have any relatives who could help me. The only family I had in the U.S. was my brother, and he was in jail. Someone told me about ICNA and they provided me financial support. Adem Carroll from ICNA also connected me to various organizers and guided me through the legal process.

Monami Maulik from DRUM[18] called to tell me about a protest at Union Square and asked me to participate.[19] I agreed, but I had no idea that there would be so many people and media outlets over there. They asked me to talk about Anser's case, and at first I did not have the words to describe what we were going through. I started to tell our story the best I could, however. This was the first time that I had spoken publicly about the case, and when I told my story, everyone became interested. I could see that they were moved by it. After I finished speaking, the journalists formed a line, and everyone inquired about my case. Adem Carroll appreciated that I was talking because he believed it would help a lot of other people in similar situations.

There were so many innocent people arrested for 9/11, but nobody was talking about it. I was the first one to come out publicly and tell everyone that my husband was arrested for an expired visa and not for connections to terrorism.

A lot of people told me not to talk about my illegal status. They thought that the FBI would detain and deport me because I was illegal and speaking out. Even a lawyer advised me not to talk about it. I told him that I didn't think being illegal was a crime,[20] and even if it were, I wouldn't have any problem admitting it. We had submitted our papers, our immigration status was pending, and I was not ashamed of it. There were millions of illegals living around us. Anyhow, my husband was already in jail and I didn't care if I ended up there also. Whatever the truth was, I had to tell the world.

I believe that my decision to talk publicly about my case allowed many people to know about and understand what was happening. Many Americans sympathized with my situation and told me that what was happening was wrong. My children also spoke out boldly and challenged the fact that they were not allowed to meet with their father. They questioned why he was in jail, talked in front of the media, and attended protests.[21]

The American people were angry about the attacks, so the FBI put on a spectacle for them. They would report arrests of Muslim men and claim that the operation was a big success. They were just trying to appease the fears of the public. It did not matter whether they were arresting innocent or guilty people. They did not arrest even one terrorist.[22] The American government is itself becoming a terrorist. It is terrorism when you arrest people, hide them away, and abuse them. Why are they hunting for terrorists outside the country when all they have to do is take a look at themselves? In the U.S., there are so many large organizations working on the 9/11 investigations. They should get proper detective training so that they can learn how to distinguish between the real terrorists and the innocent people.

Fighting Legal Battles

(**Anser**) The first court hearing with the immigration judge was on October 16, 2001, on the fifth floor of the MDC, and I appeared wearing shackles and cuffs. I did not have a lawyer to represent me.

Anser was charged with an expired visa, although his wife and three children who had similar immigration violations remained free. Anser explained to the judge that it was difficult to contact a lawyer from the MDC, and the judge moved the hearing to October 25, 2001. At the second hearing, Anser appeared with a lawyer. Since Uzma had a pending immigration application and Anser had a labor certification, the attorney argued that Anser should qualify for a stay. The judge responded that it could take years for the approval of the application.[23] An FBI report dated October 31, 2001, sensationalized the fact that Anser had a hazardous material license and stated,

Mehmood is licensed as a hazardous materials driver and is employed as such. The employer indicated that Mehmood refused to carry two shipments on September

11, 2001. One of the shipments was a high paying one, and the employer described Mehmood's refusal of the shipment to be very unusual.[24]

Uzma's interview with ABC provided the following explanation:

Naheed said her husband was loading his truck on the morning of Sept. 11 when she switched on the television and heard the news. "I called him on his cell phone and told him to watch TV," she said. "He went to some place to see TV and heard that the Pentagon was attacked. So he called work and said he was not making the delivery. The company canceled the load because of the emergency and the company said they would pay him for the dry run," she said, referring to cases when deliveries are not made.[25]

Mehmood's employer, Panther 2 Transportation, has refused to comment on the case.

"Why do you have a license for hazardous materials?" the judge asked.

"My company has a rule that all of the 400 drivers that work for the company must be able to carry hazardous materials. You can call the trucking company to confirm."

Before the court hearing, my lawyer had suggested that I apply for asylum. He collected all the paperwork from my wife, which explained why we came to the United States and discussed the burning of my business. The hearing lasted three hours, and after reviewing everything, the judge denied my bail and asylum application on the basis of "danger to flight" and "hazard to community." My lawyer was very surprised and said, "My client does not have any criminal history or record."

The judge responded, "You can challenge my decision."[26] The lawyer met after the decision and expressed his surprise again.

"I am not going to challenge it. I am going to leave," I told my lawyer. I was completely disappointed with the justice system. I knew that this was not the judge's decision. How could he have made such a decision without any evidence? I had a business, a property, a family, and a son who was a U.S. citizen. Moreover, I did not have any criminal background.

Later I learned that immigration judges don't have any power. They only enforce the decisions. I believe that someone from the top told the judge to give such a decision and he just followed directions. Attorney General Aschroft decided that Muslims had to be kept in detention and could not be released on bail. Later, at the time of release, they had to be charged with something because they had been detained for so long.

The Office of the Inspector General's report on the September 11 detainees explains the procedures that were implemented right after September 11 to ensure that Special Interest Cases were not released under any circumstances. In chapter 5 of the report, which is titled "The Department's Policy of No Bond Hearing," the following paragraph summarizes a variety of steps that were instituted at various levels of the immigration court to ensure continuous custody of 9/11 detainees:

> *The INS took a variety of steps to ensure that aliens arrested in connection with the PENTTBOM[27] investigation would not be released until the FBI had determined that they posed no danger to the United States. INS District Directors made an initial custody determination of "no bond" for all September 11 detainees (since granting bond could have resulted in the release of aliens not yet cleared by the FBI). Second, INS Executive Associate Commissioner for Field Operations Michael Pearson issued a directive two days after the terrorist attacks instructing INS field offices that no September 11 detainee could be released without Pearson's written authorization. Third, officials at INS Headquarters created a bond unit to handle the September 11 detainees' cases. Fourth, INS attorneys requested multiple continuances in bond hearings for September 11 detainees in an effort to keep the detainees in custody as long as possible.[28]*

The report implies that immigration judges were unable to release any of the September 11 detainees on bail. Judges accepted government orders without any opposition because of the fear of additional terrorist attacks. Even though the judge gave Anser a deportation order on December 5, 2001, Anser was sent back to the ninth floor and stayed there until Uzma hired the attorney Martin Stolar.

(Uzma) With the joint help of Adem from Islamic Circle of North America and Monami from Desis Rising Up and Moving, I got a very good lawyer named Martin Stolar. Both ICNA and DRUM helped pay for him. Before Martin, lawyers would run away because they thought that it was a terrorist case.[29] When I hired Martin, he said, "The charges placed on your husband's case are nothing."

(Anser) Martin came to see me and told me, "I am your lawyer. First, I want to apologize as an American and say that I'm ashamed about what has been happening to you. I am confident that you will be out of this situation very soon."

"This is America. I thought this does not happen in America," I said.

Martin responded, "If your name today was Philip, Peter, or Mike, I could have taken you out so easily. But your name is Mehmood, and you can't change that." He also told me that he was going to challenge the judge's decision, but I told him that if one judge can issue a racist decision, the next judge would also do the same. I wanted to return to Pakistan because living here was becoming torturous. I had never seen a police jail in my life and now I was sitting in a high-security jail in solitary confinement. It was painful, and I did not want to stay in the U.S. anymore.

Back home in Pakistan, Anser's father had become worried when he heard about Anser's arrest. He trusted that his son was innocent, but he had observed the changing environment and laws in the United States. He wanted his son and his family to return to Pakistan also.

(Anser's father) I was very concerned by the atmosphere over there. They were making new laws, which allowed them to search and detain people without any warrants.[30] I was worried that U.S. intelligence officials might physically torture Anser for information. Anser did not know anything, and it could have been hard for him. It was torture to keep him in solitary confinement.

I was also worried about Uzma and the children. In the school, other kids might be taunting them. There was no one there to guide Uzma, but she handled the household, the media, everything. She is a very strong woman. I told her that she should receive a badge of courage.

The first time, when I heard Anser's voice over the phone, I was in tears. It was an unexpected call. His older brother was also in tears. Whether those were tears of happiness or sadness, I don't know. I had not heard from him for four or five months. It is very difficult to describe the condition that I was in.

Attempts to Visit Anser in the MDC

Uzma and her children made several attempts to visit Anser in the MDC, but the jail administration gave them a constant runaround. The children have a vivid memory of their attempted visit.

(Children) We went to the MDC on *Eid* day [December 17, 2001, a Muslim holiday], but the guards would not let us in. Our dad had written us a letter and told us that he was on the ninth floor of the MDC. He had given us his PIN, ID, cell, and floor number. When we asked for him, we knew that his name showed up on the computer, but the guards lied to us and told us he wasn't there. Our mom pleaded with them to tell us the truth.

Adem was with us, and he had brought a prayer rug because the cells were not clean and a rug would've helped. He told them that he wanted to send a gift. One guard said, "We don't allow gifts." Our mom had also brought some chicken for my dad, but they just refused everything and insulted us. All of them were screaming and yelling at us. Who did they think they were? We were so furious and really wanted to beat them up. We were not scared of them. The woman sitting in the front was especially mean, and she screamed at us to shut up and get out. We wanted to break the glass and hit her in the face. No adult had ever talked to us like that before, especially not to our mom. Then they called down five or six officers to kick us out. There was this huge black officer who came out wearing a bulletproof jacket. He told us to get out, and we felt that he was going to beat us up, so we decided to leave.

Finally, a Prison Visit

(Anser) On January 11, I met Uzma for the first time since my arrest. At first I was hesitant about meeting my wife and children in shackles because I did not want them to see me like that. Later, I realized that my family trusted me. I had taught my children to always respect the law and tell the truth. It was a big shock for them to get up one day and find out that their father had gone to jail, but they were confident that I had not done anything wrong. Uzma had the same confidence. That was why she stood up for me, talked to the media, and organized. At that time, speaking out publicly was hard. People perceived her as the wife and sister of terrorists and could have said anything. She believed in my innocence.

Uzma became a lot more independent after my arrest. In the past, whenever she had to go to the bank, she would call me to go with her even though it was only a block away. After my detention, she took care of the children, confronted the entire public, and handled all the media. God gave her the strength. I never knew that she could do all that work or that the children could be so strong. They handled the entire situation very well. Once they understood that our only fault was being Muslims after 9/11, they were able to face everyone.

The first time I met Uzma in the jail, I felt confident and satisfied also. I was surprised at my own change. Before my imprisonment, I used to call home 20 times a day. If my children went anywhere, I used to keep tabs on them. Now here I was in jail, and I didn't even know how they were getting food or clothes. At that time, the Koran really gave me the support and explained to me that as a human being I don't have the power to give anything. Only Allah has the power to provide. I am only the facilitator.

The jail allowed me to become a strong Muslim. The long months in solitary confinement allowed me to reflect on my life and myself. Before my imprisonment, I was not a very good Muslim and I did not pray five times a day. Reading the Koran and saying my prayers made me strong. I am glad for this change. By the time I met Uzma, I had become such a strong person that I did not hesitate to meet her in cuffs or shackles. When she saw me all chained up, she started to cry.

(Uzma) We made a huge scene at the jail, and we were finally allowed to go and see Anser, who was still in solitary confinement. Adem came with me. At first, they refused to let me in. Then I showed them my marriage certificate. Adem told them, "This woman has not seen her husband for three months." Finally the guards allowed me to see him, but they told me that I couldn't take my child with me to the ninth floor. Adem took care of him for a couple hours downstairs.

The meeting area was small, and they locked me up also. Anser wore an orange jumpsuit and was shackled. It was strange and we both cried. At first, I could not talk to him for a while. I knew that he was worried about the children and me.

(Anser) Uzma told me that everything was okay and that she had taken care of all the basic needs. I was thankful to Allah.

(Uzma) The time he spent in jail brought us closer. I often knew what he was thinking, and then later when we talked on the phone, he would confirm it. In his letters, he wrote about things that had been on my mind. I still keep some of Anser's letters.

The following is an excerpt from one of Anser's letters that Uzma read in a PBS program on March 15, 2002:

I am missing you a lot, which you cannot imagine. They put me in a very, very small cell where I have to wait until FBI completes its investigation. Since I am innocent, I don't have any problem with this investigation, only when I think about you and kids, trust me, I start crying.[31]

(Anser) Our life got a bit easier in the jail after Uzma started speaking publicly. Before that, the guards would not allow us to sleep. They would bang on the walls, make loud noises in the middle of the night, and keep the lights on. Because Uzma spoke, the lights started to go down and people began sleeping and getting food. Most importantly, the guards learned that we didn't have any connections with terrorism. They realized that the prisoners were there for minor crimes, such as credit card fraud.

Ahmar, Uzma's brother, also acknowledged that the weekly protests organized by various community and legal organizations outside the MDC jail helped them to gain some basic rights, like getting the lights shut off at night.[32]

(Uzma) I stayed in the U.S. for five months after my husband was detained. Then I told Adem from ICNA to arrange a ticket to Pakistan for me because it was very hard for me to go on living like this. The other kids were giving my children a hard time by calling them "children of terrorists," and they were getting into fights. I started getting complaints from the schools about them on a daily basis. The school administration did not realize that the children were in a bad circumstance. They were Americans, and they saw my children as troublemakers. They felt that Anser must have been arrested for a legitimate reason.

(Umair) I did not have anger before my dad's arrest, but now I get angry. One day, when I came home and heard that mom had gone to see our dad, I became angry because she had not taken me with her. I was very close to my dad and missed him. I smacked the table and it broke into pieces. Then I broke a window, and blood started to gush out of my arm. I was angry that he was being blamed for 9/11. I got angry with the children who bugged me.

(Children) The day we left, about 20 boys and girls came to our house to watch us leave. They were primarily white kids, and some of them were older than us, and some were the same age. Some were sad, but the others sat in front of the steps and taunted us, "Take off the American clothes. Leave the American things, take only the Pakistani things. You are terrorists. It is good that you are leaving." There were a lot of racist people there that day. They were laughing at us, and we called the police and reported them. The police came. We were not scared, but we felt very angry.

(Uzma) I returned to Pakistan on February 29, 2002, and Anser returned in May. By that time, he had been moved to the general population unit at the MDC, and Martin had promised that he would be released soon. Martin was a strong lawyer, and I trusted him. After Anser moved to the general population unit, my kids visited him on a weekly basis.

I wanted to return to Pakistan and settle in the house with the children so that by the time Anser returned, he would have a place to live. If he had been deported while I was still in the U.S., it would have been really difficult for him. I wanted to provide him with a relaxing environment after he returned home. I struggled a lot in Pakistan. First, I put the children in school, and then I fixed up the house to make it livable. By the time he came back, we were pretty much established. I went to the airport to receive him and noticed that he had gotten very weak. He was not wearing handcuffs or prison clothes.

Moving to the General Population Unit and Getting Deported

(Anser) On February 4, they moved me to the general population unit at the MDC and said that they would deport me to Pakistan shortly. Martin asked the court why they were still detaining me and requested my deportation. On March 29, the guards took me to Manhattan and charged me for working under my nonauthorized social security number. I had told the immigration agents about that on the first day of my interview.

My second judge was Barbara Jones. The prosecutor argued that he needed another month to get additional reports, but the judge said, "I don't need any more reports for this person. How can we make sure that he does not have to waste more time in a jail?"

"Your honor, it is under your discretion," Martin said.

"I will make the decision tomorrow," said the judge.

"Have you ever seen a case like this before?" asked Martin.

"No, I have not. That is the reason that I am making this decision tomorrow. I can't keep him in the jail any longer." The next day, she decided that I had served my time and could finally be deported.

By early February, Anser was moved to the general population unit of the MDC, which meant that the FBI had cleared him of all terrorist charges. However, on March 15, 2002, the then FBI counterterrorism chief Bob Blitzer implied on the PBS program NOW *that Anser still might have terrorist connections. It is important to note the inflammatory and insinuating metaphor of "smoke," which tries to link Anser with the September 11 hijackers:*

> *We have a foreign national here out of status. He has multiple passports. He has been licensed to drive large vehicles, there's always concerns he also has a hazardous materials license. I think all of those things drawn together would make an investigator say, "What have we got here. . . . I think there's a lot of smoke concerning this fellow. But whether there's any—whether there's any fire, I mean, I don't know. Time*

will tell....I don't think law enforcement is going after every illegal person in this country... but they're certainly concerned about the same kind of people that we saw on September 11th. Arresting them before they might commit a crime is—is really the prudent thing to do.[33]

Martin Stolar, Anser's attorney, provided the following explanation on the same program:

What's suspicious? He's a Muslim and he has a hazardous materials license. Well, of course he has a hazardous materials license—that's his business. Most truck drivers have hazardous material licenses. He had two passports—both in his own name, both legitimate Pakistani passports. There's something suspicious about that. The problem was that he lost the first passport, so he went and got a second one, and then he found the one he'd lost. This guy who's a law-abiding—except for the fact that he overstayed a visa. He paid his taxes. He supports his family. He's totally unconnected with September 11th.[34]

Soon after Judge Jones's decision, I moved to Passaic County Jail, and on May 10, I was deported to Pakistan. Initially, deportation officers handcuffed me, but my children had informed the U.S. media about my case. The deporting officer noticed the media at the John F. Kennedy airport and decided at first to cover up my handcuffs with a jacket, but then he changed his mind and unlocked them. In Pakistan, they did not ask me any questions, and the Pakistani immigration officers were very courteous. They offered me tea and took care of me. My brother-in-law was waiting for me.

Life After Deportation:

Uzma came back to Pakistan in February 2002 and settled in a house owned by Anser's father. Although she found a bit of solace among family members and the community, she started to confront new issues. The children's adjustment to the new environment and financial hardship were the hardest issues to face, though they were among many others. Uzma and Anser lost everything in their 40s and had to start all over again.

(Anser) Currently I am unemployed, and I don't have any money because they froze my account. They took my house, my computer, my trucks, and my business. What can I do now? I had a van. It must still be standing there. In the U.S., I used to make $8,000 to $10,000 a month. Suddenly everything is gone. It is a big shock to absorb, but I am not sorry for the loss. I trust my God. The prison has brought me closer to Islam and Allah. This is America's gift to me. Maybe if I had stayed in the U.S., I might have strayed away from my religion. I had started missing my prayers, but now I pray five times a day. This is good for me. This deportation may feel like a loss now, but I am confident that something good will come out of it.

I still have property and business in the U.S., and if I get an opportunity, I will go back there. That country has given me a lot. John Ashcroft's policies or George Bush's decisions will not change the values of the entire nation. I don't have any complaint towards that country, only towards the justice system. Today, there is no sense of justice; they threw me out because my name is Mehmood.

(Uzma) My husband worked so hard over the last ten years to build his life, business, and property. He had even taken money from Pakistan to establish his business in the U.S. from scratch. Ten years we spent there and lost everything, including the savings that we brought from Pakistan. The U.S. government made him leave empty-handed, and they did not even think about all that he had struggled for. What kind of justice system is that?

We understand that the 9/11 attacks were a big deal and that they had the right to investigate us. But after the investigation, when they did not find any terrorist links, they should have given us some time to collect our assets so that we would have something to survive on after we returned to our home country. In Pakistan, there are not enough jobs for the people who already live here. What did the U.S. government expect us to do when we returned home with nothing? How are we going to find employment and settle down? His time in jail has become part of his record. Wherever he goes, people will say that he has been in jail. The American government doesn't have any understanding of this problem. They don't realize the mistake they have made. They are calling innocent people terrorists, and they don't even realize what impact that has afterwards.

This practice is not good for America. Some people told me that the U.S. government interned the Japanese during World War II and that they were doing the same thing again to the Muslims. The government is making detentions a habit. When I was leaving the U.S., a Japanese American organization invited me to a Memorial Day event. They said, "It has happened to us and now it is happening to you. Tomorrow it could happen to someone else." I realized that it was true. Some African Americans told me about what the white people had done to them, and I saw that the American government was behaving the same way towards us. The American government lumps everyone together into a group instead of seeing people as individuals. With this kind of attitude, no one is going feel safe over there. America was once a dreamland for immigrants and everyone wanted to go there. That dreamland is vanishing now because minorities are afraid of discrimination. The American government should change its strategies.

Worries About the Future

(Uzma) My kids are not settled in, and I am extremely worried about it. In the U.S., their father had a job and he used to provide the very best for them, but he can't do that anymore. My children opened their eyes there and grew up there. They were constantly having fun, eating and doing whatever they wanted to do.

They used to go out and have fun every weekend. Not everyone does that, but my husband liked to take them out. They would stay in a motel for the weekend and go swimming. They liked going to the gym and were about to get their black belts. The kids are used to that lifestyle. Their needs have stayed the same, but we can't provide them with everything we did before.

Now, they don't know that their parents can't afford it. My husband still does not have a job, and he is not mentally ready to work. His temperament has changed, and now he loses his temper over everything. He used to be so humble and he never used to get angry with us, but now he gets angry so fast. His eyes get red as if he is going to kill someone. The anger he holds inside is very difficult to describe. We can't relieve him of the mental torture that he experienced in the jail. He was treated like a terrorist without any evidence. I am afraid to talk to him and don't share everything with him like I used to. He is still in shock, and I am afraid that if I say anything, it could be detrimental to him and his health. His eyesight has gotten so weak because of the high-powered lights that were on 24 hours a day in the small cell.

Whoever the hijackers were, the government should have investigated them in secrecy. My sons told me that according to the law, they need to investigate you first and then charge you with something. It is not fair to just pick up people and throw them out of the country. They did not just destroy the life of one person; they destroyed the life of the entire family. My children's lives are always going to be impacted by it. Who is responsible? With God's help, they will make money and recover financially, but how will they recover from the mental torture and pain of that experience?

The hardest thing is that my children are not settled. They blame me for coming back to Pakistan. But this is not how I wanted to come to Pakistan [crying]. They miss their school, their friends, and their life in the U.S. If they are not happy, how can I be happy? They constantly ask me, "Why did you bring me here?" They are not adjusting to life here because they are at a difficult age. My youngest child will adapt. Anser and I grew up here, so we will be fine. What will happen to my three other children? They are not doing well in school, and they are not making friends because they are not comfortable in this environment.

They have had to face a huge change at such a young age, and it has been really difficult for them to handle it. Neither they nor Anser and I can justify what happened to us. They constantly ask strange questions and make weird comments. We try to explain to them that they have to live here now, so they should study and do well in school. They say, "No. We don't want to. Our dad worked so hard all his life and what did he get? Why should we work hard? Why did it happen to us? There are millions of illegals living in the U.S. Why did it happen to us only?"

My children's thinking has changed. Now, whenever they see any kind of fighting, they become very interested. They ask, "Why is this person fighting with that person? Why is this person beating up that person?" We can't answer all these questions. Today's kids know more about terrorism than we do; they know what it is and what it is not. The things that we want to protect our kids from, they want to know more about.

My children are teenagers. At this time, they need a certain education and a lifestyle. What impact has the U.S. government had on them? What will they be like tomorrow? I don't know. I am trying my best to keep them oriented towards peace. However, the mantra of "your dad is a terrorist, your dad is a terrorist" is stuck in their head. What are they supposed to think? Before this, they never knew about terrorism.

In the U.S., my children were under the impression that the situation was going to change or that they would be able to return to the U.S. They didn't grow up in Pakistan, and they are not familiar with the educational system here. In Pakistan, the schools and teachers are different, especially when it comes to discipline. When the teachers say something, my children talk back to them. I get complaints every day from the administration about their behavior, and they even threatened to kick my child out of school.

One day, I got really angry with the teacher. I asked, "Is this all you can talk about? You don't understand from which circumstances the child has come. You are constantly threatening to kick the children out of the school. If you throw them out, what is going to happen to them? Where are we going to take them? What is their future?" How many children really want to study at their age? Very few! Parents can only provide guidance and encourage them to study. The American justice system destroyed all of their ambitions. The children tell us that they don't want to study and that they don't like the teachers. They are stuck between two cultures and don't fit anywhere.

But it's not their fault. It is like giving a toy to a child and then suddenly snatching it back from him. The American administration doesn't understand the impact on the children because they don't realize how much children idealize their parents at that age. My children idealized their father, and the American administration converted him into a terrorist. Other people are constantly reinforcing that by repeatedly saying, "Your dad is a terrorist." How do they explain to others that he is not a terrorist? How do they explain that the American administration made him appear to be a terrorist even though he wasn't? It is going to take time. It is my wish that they adjust to Pakistan, that my husband gets a job, and that we become financially strong. Then we won't have to go to other countries.

My children want to go back to the U.S. They believe that with a new administration the circumstances will change and they will be able to go back. They say that the American people are good because their friends and a lot of the people who helped us were Americans.

(Children) We used to watch Pakistani dramas. I never knew what Pakistan was like, and initially, I was very excited about coming here. Mom asked us if we wanted to go to Pakistan or Canada and we said Canada. But our dad was in jail, people were beating us up, the conditions were bad, and we had to sell our furniture. For a while, we slept on the floor. Our dad wrote us a letter advising that we go back to Pakistan, but we regret coming back now. We spent years over there and got used to it.

We don't know if we will be able to go back to the U.S. I was thinking that it was going to be short term. We did not know about the immigration laws and deportation. Now we are stuck here. My mom was saying that we would go back in March, but now we don't know if that's going to happen.

We don't talk like this in front of our dad because he gets angry. We just talk to our mom because we are not afraid of her. Our dad suffered a lot of mental torture. The guards hit him and broke his hand, so he is very angry.

We also have major problems in school. Last term, I failed in every subject, except for English. This term, I may pass in a few subjects. We have been having major problems in math. In the U.S., they teach Algebra in 11th grade, and here they teach it in ninth grade. The teachers tell us to learn Urdu, but it is very difficult to learn a new alphabet. Everyone in school talks in Urdu. I don't want to learn Urdu because I feel that it does not have any use and that the teachers just teach it to us for fun. Here in school, they don't teach you anything, but we still have to study. The teachers are useless, and we can't understand their English. Just like computers get viruses, we feel that we got some kind of virus also.

Teachers here are only interested in money, not in education. You ask them a question and they get angry. The teacher talks and no one understands. I sleep in class because I don't have any desire to learn. I put my books in front of me and think about my life in the U.S. After school, we used to go out and play, instead of studying. The schools in the U.S. are more focused on activities and sports than Pakistani schools. There are no sports over here. We don't understand the rules of cricket, and people push you a lot. We were close to getting our black belts in the U.S., but towards the end we did not have the money to pay for classes. We tell mom that we want to go back to our house in the U.S.

(Umair) My teacher says that I misbehave. I never wear the uniform correctly because I am not used to wearing one and I don't like belts or dress shoes. Sometimes, I forget to wear the belt, and then the teachers complain.

(Harris) One day, another student's book ended up in my bag by mistake. I don't know how it got into my bag, but I did not steal it. I don't even like that book, so why would I steal it? Maybe it was sitting on my desk and I put it in my bag by mistake. Later I pulled it out of my bag. Another student saw it and asked, "How come this book was in your bag? I am going to tell the teacher." I got angry and slapped him. They checked my bag and found the book. The teacher asked me why the book was in my bag, and I said that I didn't know and pushed my desk in anger. The teacher continued to harass me.

Two to three weeks ago, someone stole 3,200 rupees from a student. The teacher took me aside and asked me, "Did you steal 3,200 rupees? Do you have any idea who did it?"

"How much is 3,200 rupees?" I asked, surprised.[35] "No, I don't have any idea." Then some other student got in trouble for stealing the money. I told my dad about it, and he became angry and asked why the teachers would suspect me.

Over here, there is racial discrimination. Some people tell us that we are Americans, not Pakistanis. They call us "American cocks." I think that we should go back. All of them tell us that if we don't go back to the U.S., we will destroy our lives.

They think that there is crime in the U.S. They also have misconceptions about us. They ask us questions like, "Did you ever smoke? Did you drink? Do you have a girlfriend? Did you do anything with your girlfriend?" Strange questions. My dad thinks that kids in Pakistan are not capable of asking these kinds of questions. America is much better than Pakistan; even its worst parts are better. Here people don't know how to behave. We think that we can go back, but we don't know how.

I asked them if their schoolmates might bother them again in the United States.

We don't think that they will beat us up anymore. I think that the children will understand us now. Right after 9/11, they were angry, but by now they must have figured out that we did not do anything. People of every race and ethnicity have been through bad times. The Christians, Hindus, and Jews have all suffered in other places and times.[36]

Things were improving at the end of our stay. In our last month, we were hanging out with white kids again and the Jewish people were saying hello. They let us come back to the library. It was getting back to normal. Now, if we go back, we can take all the newspapers with us and show them all the articles. The entire nation knows that whatever happened to us was wrong. We think that America will recover.

One problem is that detainees don't speak out. We will speak and tell them the story. We asked our dad why he did not say anything and told him that if he had told his story the Americans would've felt sympathetic and let him go. They let murderers go over there.

(Uzair) I wanted to join the NFL. If I had stayed there, I could have joined it during college. Now I don't know how I am going to do it.

(Umair) I wanted to become a doctor. I used to read those big books. I know that I will go back to America for sure. How? I don't know. If they take me to court, I will tell them that I came here to make my life, like my dad. They will recognize that and then leave me alone.

(Harris) There was a factory close to my house and it was my dream to own a big factory. I still have the same goal. I want to go back and own that factory. What is the way to go back?

In the United States, these children were driven to become useful members of their community. Now, they are confused, lost, and unmotivated. Instead of dreaming of becoming doctors, football players, or factory owners, they dream of changes in the United States' political situation so that they can return to the United States. In many ways, they are avoiding establishing themselves in Pakistan because they want to reestablish their lives in New Jersey. They are angry and hurt, and the sudden deportation has created nostalgia about the United States.

This narrative reveals that what happened to Anser at the MDC was not limited to him. His family also deeply suffered the torture and pain of his detention. Umair, Uzair, and Harris felt alienated in the United States after their dad was detained. They were hoping to find a sense of community and belonging in Pakistan, but they experienced a different kind of alienation and cultural shock in Pakistan. Unable to speak Urdu (Pakistan's official language) and unfamiliar with the cultural nuances, they became misfits in their home country. They constantly think about moving back to the United States. The detention and subsequent deportation of their father shattered the lives of these young children, and they are caught between two worlds.

This narrative exemplifies the impact of detentions on detainees' families and illustrates the devastating aftermath of their collective deportation. Along with financial loss, discrimination, and name-calling, the effects of deportation and the stigma of detention are exacerbated by the fact that the children are so young. A close look at the lives of detainees' families reveals some of those emotional traumas. Specifically, this narrative illustrates what it really means to live with the stigma of a "terrorist father" or a "terrorist husband." It also explores how pain and fear of the unknown changes individuals.

Anser and his family are not alone. Over 1,000[37] individuals detained after 9/11 have families who experienced major financial and psychological problems as a result of the detentions of their loved ones. Anser's father summarized the long-term impacts of these detentions:

> *One hundred and three people arrived today in Pakistan.[38] We feel that the U.S. is targeting Pakistan. The reaction of these deportees is not going to be good for the U.S. The 103 people have 103 families, which are also impacted. The U.S.'s actions are magnifying the anti-American feelings that already exist.*

Life Today: In fall 2008, I met Anser and his family in Islamabad and completed a video interview with them. Anser has established his own business and has been slowly rebuilding his life. Uzma is busy helping her children with their education and her husband with his business.

Figure 4   Nabil Ayesh, Jerusalem, August 2010. Photograph by Irum Shiekh.

Loss of Civil Liberties for Muslims after 9/11: The National Security System's Guinea Pig

Nabil Ayesh

Nabil Ayesh, his wife, and their two children came from Israel to the United States in December 1997 on a visiting visa. Nabil's wife had Israeli citizenship, whereas Nabil was a Palestinian citizen.[1] After arriving in the United States, Nabil and his wife had two more children, and they started to establish themselves slowly. In 1999, on one of their trips to Seattle, law enforcement officials arrested the family.[2] Nabil's wife and children accepted the deportation orders to Israel; Nabil decided to stay in the United States and fight his deportation. He spent 52 days in a jail and was released on a bond with a pending deportation appeal. An immigration lawyer was working on his case.

On September 11, 2001, Nabil was arrested for allegedly running a red light.[3] Within days of his arrest, he was classified as a "High Interest" case and was moved to the MDC in New York, where he stayed for over a year. On September 27, 2002, Nabil was released in New York without any explanation. Apparently, immigration authorities could not get permission from either Jordan or Israel to send him to Jerusalem to join his wife.

Immediately after his release, Nabil got a job with a construction company in New York and started to work with various lawyers to legalize his status and to get his wife and children back to the United States. In March 2003, Nabil was arrested again. Apparently, immigration authorities had managed to obtain permission from Israel and planned to implement the order of removal. A month later, he was deported to Palestine.[4]

Meeting Nabil

I met Nabil in an office building in downtown Syracuse, New York, in January 2003 after getting his contact information from Adem Carroll of the Islamic Circle of North America. Nabil was in his late 30s or early 40s and wore his work clothes—a T-shirt, jeans, baseball hat, and heavy construction shoes full of dust—to the interview. He was forthcoming about his detention experience, and we talked for hours. It was pretty late at night by the time I finished the interview. The snow had blocked the roads, and I spent the night in a local motel. The next morning, I went back to the same building and talked to Nabil for a few more hours. In the fall of 2008, I went to Palestine to meet with him again. Nabil reviewed his story and gave me some additional comments. The following narrative is based on those two audio-recorded interviews, telephone conversations held with him after he was deported to Palestine[5], his review of the narrative, conversations with his lawyer, newspaper articles,[6] a review of his legal files, and a documentary featuring his case.[7]

Moving to the United States

Nabil, a successful developer in Palestine, explained his reasons for coming to the United States:

I moved from Palestine because of the killing of Palestinians and Israelis and not because I wanted to make more money. Back home in Bethlehem, I used to make much more, and I had two new cars and a big house. My business was building houses and developing land for different companies, and 27 contractors worked for me. In spite of my success, I came to the U.S. because I wanted to raise my kids in a peaceful country. I wanted to live in a place where people never asked me for ID or stopped and searched me in the streets. I didn't want to live in a place where I saw blood and heard things like, "The Jewish people took the Palestinians' country. The Jewish people live in my country." These are not my sentiments. The Jewish people are there to stay, and we have to live with that.

Given my financial situation, I could've moved to any country in the world, but I thought about the United States. Within five minutes of showing the consulate my papers, I got my visa. First, I came for a 20-day visit. I figured out that the country is good, that I could do something here, so I went back and told my wife that we should move to the U.S.

"Are you crazy?" she said. "We cannot go to that country. We don't speak their language. We don't know anybody there."

"We are going," I said. "I am not staying here. If you want to come with me, you can come. If you don't want to come with me, then just tell me."

"No, I go with you wherever you go."

When we went to the interview, she was nine months pregnant. We got the visa, and four days after we arrived in Philadelphia, the baby was born. I came with $17,000, so I was able to stay home for the first four months. It took me a while to get to know the city. I used to be afraid of getting lost and never finding my way home when I would go to the supermarket.

Within the first few months, I met an American guy who told me that I was the stupidest person he'd ever met in his life because I'd brought my family here without knowing anything, not even English. He helped me, though, by giving me a job. I am a contractor, but I worked for him as a handyman so that I could learn English and see how people in the U.S. work. Sometimes he paid me $20 for three or four days, sometimes $60, but I didn't care.

When I learned a little English, I told the American guy, "Introduce me to a Jewish guy, any Jewish guy." One time I was doing a small job for the American guy when he heard someone speaking Hebrew on a construction site. He told me to go and talk to him, so I went over and said "Hi" in Hebrew.

"Where are you from?" he asked.

"Jerusalem," I replied. We talked in Hebrew.

"How can I help you?"

"I used to work as a contractor for big hotels in Israel," I said and gave him some names of companies that I had done work for. He told me to stay put while he called his partner, who asked me to come to the office on Market Street right away. I didn't know where anything was, so the Jewish guy drove me over. At the office, the partner asked me some questions and offered me my first job for $4,000. I finished it in a day and half.

My main job was working on houses and commercial buildings for the Jewish guy. He gave me a nice big house to live in. It was a better neighborhood than my old one, and it had good schools. When I got arrested in Seattle, he also helped my family and paid my bond.

Nabil's Jewish friend had a business dispute with his partner and ended up leaving the country broke. On September 11, Nabil's friend was out of the country, and so Nabil could not ask him for help. After his release in September 2002 in New York, Nabil found out that his Jewish friend was back in the United States. He contacted him and got a job with his company in Syracuse. I met Nabil in January 2003 in New York, and he explained how he got arrested on September 11.

September 11, 2001

On September 11, 2001, I was driving on Sixty-ninth Street in Philadelphia around 5:30 p.m. I'd just finished work, and I was going home when I noticed flashing lights in my rearview mirror. I pulled over, and a cop walked over and asked, "Where are you from?" The question surprised me because the police had never asked me that before.

"Why are you asking where I am from?"

"I am just asking. I want to know. Give me your license."

He took my license, and five minutes later he came back and asked, "Do you know why I stopped you?"

"No."

"You ran the red light."

"The light wasn't red because I saw you behind me two blocks away and I saw a cop in front of me. I wouldn't be stupid enough to cross a red light in front of two cops."

"Where are you from?"

"I am from Israel."

"Arab or Jewish?"

"What's the difference?"

"Big difference," he replied.

"Okay, I am Arab."

"Give me the keys of your van and stand by my car." Ten minutes later, more cops came.

There was a sticker on the back of Nabil's car, which said, "God is Great," in Arabic. Nabil thinks that the sticker made the cop suspicious. He believes his looks don't necessarily connect him to the Middle East.

One of them said, "Put your hands up. You are under arrest."

"For what?"

"You are wanted by the INS."

"I am not wanted by INS."

"You have a green card?"

"I don't have a green card, but I have a pending case with immigration and I am just waiting for the appeal. I was in jail before, and they released me."

Nabil Is Referring to His 1999 Immigration Arrest and Appeal.

"You are under arrest. We're going to the station to see what's wrong."

"Okay, fine. I'll drive behind."

"No, you come with us and someone else will drive your van." They drove me to the police station and took my fingerprints. After that they took my wallet and license and put me in a cell.

Fifteen minutes later, the officer came and said, "Look, I am sorry. The INS doesn't want you. Just sign this ticket and you can go."

"What ticket?"

"You ran the red light."

"Look you know it was not a red light."

"If you go to court for this ticket, we won't come." He gave me all my stuff and I walked out. I had barely gone down four steps when four officers came after me.

"We need you again," one of them said.

The one that was wearing a suit asked, "Where are you from?"

"Sir, he is Arabic," another officer replied.

The guy in the suit ordered, "Arrest him. I want to check him out." They took me back inside and took my stuff again. This time I knew I was going to jail.

"Hey what's going on?" I asked.

"Just shut up. You know. The INS wants you and they are coming to pick you up."

Around 9:00 p.m., two agents came and introduced themselves as INS agents. I didn't believe them because I realized quickly from their questions that they did not know anything about the INS.

"Hey guys, are you FBI agents?" I asked.

"What do you think? We are the FBI?"

"I know the INS doesn't want me. If the FBI wants me, that's fine. I have nothing to hide."

"No, we are not INS. We are FBI and we are taking you to a holding place because there is no INS right now."

"You just said that you were INS."

"Yeah, but we are special." They took me to a holding cell and put a red sticker on my hand. At the time, I thought everybody got a red sticker.

Later, when I asked for a phone call, the guards said, "Oh, you got a red sticker. You are not allowed to make a phone call." After the shift changed, I saw prisoners who were in jail for committing a crime and they got phone calls right away. I asked for a phone call at the end of every shift, but they always refused.

The next morning, two men came, and I could tell they were INS from their clothes. They gave me breakfast, handcuffed me, and took me to another building. I thought it was a mistake and that it would clear up very soon because I knew that the INS didn't want me. I thought they knew everything about me, but one of the agents started to ask me questions.

"When did you come to the United States?"

"Hey guys, how come I am wanted and you don't know anything about me? I have a pending immigration case with you guys."

"What is the case?"

"You don't know about my case?"

"No, I don't want to search in the computer."

"But you must've searched it already if you know that I am wanted by the INS."

"I don't know. Just tell me about your case. If you want me to search in the computer, then give me your number."

"The case will prove that I am not wanted by the INS." I gave him all the information.

Afterwards, he said, "Okay, fine. You know what we need from you?"

"No, I don't."

"The FBI is going to talk to you, do you mind?"

"No, I have nothing to hide."

A very nice lady from the FBI came afterwards. She asked me general questions about my family and about my INS case. At the end she said, "You are clear. I will try to get you out tonight. Let me talk to them. Do you mind if I call you at home tonight?"

"No," I replied.

"I'll make sure that you go home tonight. You are a good guy."

She left, and after a few minutes, the INS agent came back with a paper and told me that they were revoking the $10,000 bond that I'd paid to get out of jail in Seattle and that I was under arrest.

I got frustrated with him, so I said, "I was under arrest yesterday but not today. I am not signing any papers. I want to talk to my lawyer."

"We are going to give you a phone call but not now."

"I want to call my lawyer right away because of what you are doing. The FBI agent told me that she'll make sure that I'm home tonight. But now you are putting me in jail."

"Yeah, yeah. We can't give you a phone call right now." The agent put me back in the cell again. There was a phone inside, but it didn't work. They took me out after an hour to ask me a couple of questions and take my fingerprints again. There was a switch near the door, and because I do construction, I realized that it turned on the phone. When they told me to wait outside, I turned the switch on and returned to the waiting area. Later, when they put me in the cell, the phone was working. Immediately, I called my friend and told him, "Look, I am in the INS building."

"We told your lawyer already and he is on his way."

The agent saw me talking on the phone and started screaming, "Who turned the phone on? Who gave you a call?"

"Look, the phone was on and I called. That's it."

"Who did you call?"

"I called my lawyer, who is coming right now." I don't know if the lawyer came or not. Around 5:00, they took me back to a holding cell, and the guards put the red sticker on me again.

The next morning, the exact same thing happened again. The INS brought me breakfast and took me to another building. "I am not talking," I said. "I want to call my lawyer."

They didn't let me call. They brought an Indonesian guy into the holding area, and when he asked for a phone call, they said they would turn the switch on. I grabbed the phone so that when the guards turned the switch on, I had the receiver in my hand. "I am calling first," I told him. The Indonesian guy protested, but I didn't care and called my friend. He told me that the lawyer came yesterday, but the guards told him that I wasn't there.

This is a very typical response that many lawyers got when they tried to find their clients.

When the guard saw me making a phone call, he started screaming. "Who are you calling?"

"My lawyer is inside this building. I want to see him." Immediately, they took me to a van in the parking lot and drove me to the York County Prison, about three hours from Philadelphia. A Pakistani guy and two Indonesian guys were also in the van. In York, they put me in a cell with a pay phone, and I called my lawyer to tell him where I was.

"What the hell are they doing? I am in the building. Why did they take you to York?"

"I don't know."

"Okay, I am going to talk to the judge and we are coming to get you."

"Look, they are going to put me in a different cell, so I won't be able to call again."

"I know where you are. Don't worry."

They put me in a different cell and said, "You are going to stay here for three or four days until we move you to the INS general population section. Right now, we don't have a place for you."

In the cell, my cellmate advised, "Tell them that you want to talk to your counselor."

"I don't want to talk to my counselor," I said because I thought he was talking about the embassy.

"No, no, there is a counselor for the inmates. If you ask him for a phone call, he gives you one." So I asked to see the counselor, who let me call my lawyer. The lawyer told me to stay calm and that he had talked to the judge and was going to get me out.

The counselor asked me if I had any questions. I asked him why I was there and he told me it was because of the INS. I didn't understand. "I have my immigration case in Philadelphia and I have not done any fraud. The INS doesn't want me. Why did they arrest me?"

"You are the guy arrested for September 11?" he asked. I nodded.

"Look the administration wouldn't like it if they found out I gave you a phone call, so don't tell anyone." I went back to my cell, and around 2:30 a.m., some guards came to my cell, handcuffed me, and put me in a car. There were three other cars behind us. They took me around the building, to a place with an eye scanner. After the eye scan, they started clapping and saying, "That's him, that's him, that's him."

"What you are talking about, 'that's him, that's him'?"

"Shut up, you terrorist."

A few minutes later, they asked the eye scanner lady to do the scan again. She redid the scan and repeated, "That's him."

"Who's 'him'? Man. Just tell me who's 'him'?"

One of the officers spoke. "Put your hands up."

"Come on, I am handcuffed. How can I put my hands up? What are you doing?"

The guards pushed me to the wall and told me not to look up. I didn't know what was happening. They took me back to the holding cell, and I noticed that they had guns. I felt something was wrong here. Either they had made a mistake or they were looking for someone who looked like me. They gave me the clothes I was wearing when I got arrested and took me back out to the car. Then they changed their minds and decided to put me in a van. At the last minute, they changed their minds again and put me back in the car. During this switching around, I got a chance to look around, and I saw about 20 people pointing shotguns at me.

By this time, I knew something was wrong and that I'd been arrested for the attack on September 11. Half an hour before I went to work on September 11, I had watched the news and thought that it looked like a movie. I went to work, and when I got arrested, I had no clue how many people had died, who did it, or why. Nobody knew anything yet, but I knew that bin Laden hadn't done it. I couldn't imagine that Arabs had done this.[8]

The guards then brought in a Pakistani guy. I don't know if he had also had his eyes scanned, but he had come to the U.S. only a month ago and could not speak English. He told us he was British, so I was surprised that he couldn't speak English. They put us in separate cars, and six or seven cars followed behind. The air conditioner was on, and I was freezing, so I said, "Guys, can you put the heater on? I am freezing."

"That's what we want."

"Why do you want that?"

"We don't want you to move."

"I am not moving. Where are we going?"

"You are going to get fucked up."

"Fucked up! For what? I didn't do nothing."

"Yeah? You didn't do nothing?"

"No."

"You know how many people died in New York?"

"No."

"He doesn't know that he killed 5,000 people there."

"Okay, so I am going to New York now?"

"No, we are going somewhere else." On the way, the two agents were joking around, which made me really angry.

"Look, I don't see you people feeling sad for the deaths of 5,000 people. You are talking about getting overtime and the big check you're going to get because you are driving somebody to New York. I am the only sad one here."

"Wait until you get there."

"I am telling you right now, I have nothing." On the way, they stopped three times to check my handcuffs. They got out of the car with handguns. I started laughing.

"Keep on laughing. You don't know what's waiting for you."

"Okay, let's see what's waiting for me." Anyway, I figured out they were taking me to New York when they took the exit.

Moving to the MDC

They drove up to a building, and I saw about 30 officers waiting for me. They put me in a cell with glass walls and a glass ceiling. I was extremely tired, so I went to sleep. An officer said, "We brought you to this building and you are sleeping?"

"Don't talk to me."

"Wake up. We want to take your fingerprints."

Twenty minutes later, they brought in the Pakistani guy. One officer said, "He falls in the same category as you, so translate for him."

"No, he is from Pakistan and I don't know any Pakistani."

"You all talk Pakistani. You all talk Afghani, okay? Big Islam translator."

"I am not going to translate. I don't know Pakistani." They took my fingerprints and then took me to another room. It was so packed with guards that I couldn't even tell what color the walls were. An officer started reading something to me.

"Mr. Ayesh, you are a WTC suspect. You eat when we tell you to eat. You drink when we tell you to drink. You dress when we tell you to dress. You strip when we tell you to strip. If you complain about anything, we will take you down and hurt you. You listening?"

I said yes, and they told me to strip, but I refused.

"We're going to strip you then."

"Go ahead, I am not gonna strip. You could force me but I am not gonna do it."

"Ah, he is religious. He is embarrassed."

"You say whatever you want. I am not gonna strip." So they jumped me and stripped me. After that, they gave me a pair of pants and a shirt and put me in a cell.

"You are gonna stay here for a while."

"For a while? For what?"

"You are gonna stay here for the rest of your life."

"Okay, thank you, bye," I said. It was 5:00 a.m. and I decided to sleep. I thought once those guys realized that I had nothing to do with the attacks, they would release me.

Life on the Ninth Floor

Each cell in the Special Housing Unit can hold two guys and has a bunk bed. When criminals in the general population unit have problems, prison guards bring them here for punishment for several weeks or sometimes even several months. The cell is nine or ten feet long and has a sink, a toilet, and a shower. The idea is that they don't have to take you out for any reason.

There was a large light right in front of me, and I couldn't sleep for the first three days because it was on all the time. After that, I didn't care and fell asleep anyway. There was also a window looking on to the ocean, which they painted later so that I could not look outside.

The prison guards would put food on the floor, and you couldn't take it until they said so. By the time they said okay, they would be far away from the cell door. I remember the very first time they left the plates and said, "We are gonna come and take all the empty things. You are not allowed to keep anything in your room."

I like to use toothpicks after eating, so I took some from the plate. When they saw that the toothpicks were gone, they asked me why I had taken them. I told them that I didn't know that I wasn't allowed to take them. It was not a big deal, but they handcuffed and shackled me and put me in the hallway. They searched the cell for 15 minutes and moved me to a different cell. They were upset.

One guard said, "He's trying to make something in here, big guy."

Whenever I asked them why I was there, I got the same answer: "You don't know, but we know. You are gonna stay here for the rest of your life. You are not getting out." I thought that nobody from higher up had told the officers to be hard on us, so it didn't really matter what they said. Let them say whatever they wanted. To them it was just a job.

Each day, we had recreation time for an hour. Prison guards would come at 5:00 a.m. and order us to go outside in a jumpsuit. I would refuse to go outside because it was freezing, but they would make me.

In the beginning, there were no cameras on the ninth floor. Later, they installed video cameras inside the cell and in the lobby area. They would record everything with a handheld camera when they took you out. From the small window in my cell door, I could see what the camera was recording. When they twisted somebody's hands or fingers, or whenever someone screamed, the camera would stop recording.

The jail administration installed video cameras in the cell and the lobby, and guards were required to use handheld cameras when they moved detainees around. The Office of the Inspector General's report about the MDC explains why video cameras became mandatory:

> *Around October 5, 2001, as a result of an incident involving a detainee who alleged that he was injured by MDC staff members, the MDC instituted a policy requiring officers to videotape detainees with handheld video cameras whenever they were outside their assigned cells, including when they first arrived at the MDC. As described below, however, we found that staff members did not always adhere to this policy.*[9]

Prison guards would strip people in their cells, or they would take them elsewhere and strip them. Out in the hallway, I would hear prison guards talking about who they were going to strip: "We are going to strip this man, or we are going to strip that man." They never came to strip me after that first time. They used to say, "This is not a country club."

I used to reply, "It's not a strip club either."

The OIG report on the MDC confirms that detainees were subjected to excessive strip searches and that sometimes these strip searches were used solely to inflict punishment.[10]

Even though there was a shower, you could not take one whenever you wanted and had to wait for them to tell you that it was okay. I took a shower whenever I wanted, even if they were screaming. I know the guards were just making up the rules so I didn't listen. The water was never hot, just warm.

In the beginning, there were only a few of us there. Then they started to bring other people. Hallways separated the cells, and no one talked at first. I remember the first people that I talked to were four Jewish guys.[11] We talked in Hebrew, and I told them that they had nothing to worry about because they were INS cases. However, at the time I thought that the Jews were responsible for the September 11 attacks, and as a Palestinian, I was proud not to have anything to do with that.[12]

The Arabs did not talk to each other right away. For the first three days, they were sad and some cried. Then they started to talk and exchange names and birthplaces—Egypt, Palestine, etc. I could only hear their voices. Till today,

I don't know what they look like, except for the people who came to the general population area after me. Everyone had their own stories—some had a fake passport or ID, some had crossed over from Canada. Small violations.

Then they brought in an Indian guy who had lived with four of the hijackers. Everybody got nervous, "Why is this guy with us? It means we are all the same." His name was Mukkaram Ali,[13] and I think he is in Virginia now. It looked like they'd broken his hand. Mukkaram started talking and told us that he was applying for asylum.

> "Shut up," I said, "You shouldn't be here with us. I don't know why they put you with us."
> "I'll ask them to put me in your cell," he said.
> "Look, you don't know me. If they put you in my cell, you might not come out alive. So don't talk to me at all. Because of you guys, innocent people are now in jail." I stopped talking to him. One time they took me out to search me, and I saw that there was a magnet on the door that had the words "WTC suspect," which was used for the World Trade Center suspects.
> "Hey, I am not a suspect," I said to the prison guard.
> "Shut up! You were a suspect from the first day."
> "Are all these guys suspects?"
> "Yes." I felt that they were jailing all the Muslims so that they could say to the American public that they'd captured the terrorists. I told them that I wanted to see the FBI directly. I wanted to know why I was here because I'd never taken flying courses. I'd never even faked documents like the people around me. I was convinced that I was going to get released one day.

A lot of people cried in the jail. An Iraqi guy tried to kill himself. "Why are you trying to kill yourself?" I asked. "That's stupid. Look, at your age talking about suicide is unacceptable. Don't talk to me about it anymore, because you are not a man."

> "Why are they doing this with me? Why? Why? Why?" he asked.
> "Why did you come to this country?"
> "To look for freedom."
> "Okay, to look for freedom. You ran from your own people, you ran from Iraq to look for freedom. So wait until the Americans know that it's okay for you to be on the streets. If you are ready to kill yourself, then that means someday you'll be ready to kill other people, too."
> "Okay. You are right, you are right, you are right."

Later, an Egyptian guy told me that the Iraqi guy tried to hang himself, but the guards found him at the last minute.

I said to the Egyptian guy, "If I was the guard, I would've let him die. That's it. Leave him. He came to live a life. I know the beginning is hard, but to kill yourself. . . . No, it's not right to even think about it."

Meeting the FBI

Ten days after they moved me to the MDC, the guards came and told me to put on my clothes. I could not see anything outside the cell. When I came out, a lot of officers were standing in the hallway, and three guards followed me with a digital camera. "Hey, where are you taking me?"

"You are going somewhere, man."
"For what? Tell me for what?" I think we went down to the first floor where there was a man standing behind a glass door.
"Who is this?" he asked.
"He is Mr. Ayesh."
"He's not who we want." They took me back and forth between my cell and the first floor three times. Each time they took me down, he'd say, "This is not him, this is not him." I began to wonder where I was. I knew that they do things like this in Egypt or Libya, but I didn't know that they could also do them in the United States.

After spending 30 days in the MDC, I met with the FBI for the first time and talked to them for an hour. One of the officers told me that I wasn't a WTC suspect and that they were just asking questions. They asked me questions about everyone in my family and a couple of general questions about Arabs and Muslims, but no questions that would imply that I was a suspect. I was surprised at the questions.

I figured out that these officers were just playing games, even though they had put the WTC magnet on my cell door. At the end, one of them said, "I promise that within the next two weeks you are going to the immigration court." Another officer told me that he was from the INS and that I could ask him anything.

"I am not arrested for an INS problem, so why do I need to go to the INS? I have not done anything, I am clear. Tell me why."
"I don't think you'll have a problem in front of the judge. They are going to release you and retain your bond. Then you'll wait till the appeal," the INS officer told me.
Three weeks later, he came back with another FBI officer and the same thing happened all over again. This time, he said, "I want the story about Seattle, fast!"
"Okay. In 1999 I went to Seattle at 8:00 p.m. I got arrested at 10:00 p.m. I stayed in jail for 52 days, and then I got out with a $10,000 bond."

"No, no, no, not that short."

"You asked me to make it short. You can ask me specific questions."

"You seem to have heavy stuff on your shoulders." On hearing that, I got angry.

"I don't have heavy stuff on my shoulders. If you think that, then you should charge me with something. I work 16 hours a day, that's the heavy stuff. I have a wife and four kids who got deported. That's what I am worried about. More heavy stuff? The FBI and INS have offices in Philadelphia, but I am in New York? I want to know, why am I here? I want to talk to my lawyer and that's it. I have nothing to do with what happened in New York. You have to tell me that I am not clean for me to stay here."

"Oh, no, no, dude, you are angry."

"No, I am not angry. I am so happy that it feels like I am on vacation in my cell 24 hours a day."

"Whatever is happening here is legal."

"If I was in an Arabic country where they jail 70 percent of the people, I would understand. But we are in the United States, not in Libya or Egypt. If you have anything against me, just charge me and that's it. At this point, I can't even call my lawyer because I don't have a case."

"I'll tell you why you are here. Do you have a green card?"

"No."

"You are legal here?"

"No."

"That's why you are here."

"I don't think I am sitting with the FBI because I am overstaying my visa. I am talking to you so that I can get some help. If it is going to make it worse, I don't want to talk to you then. I got arrested in Philadelphia and my case is pending in Seattle, so either send me back to Philadelphia or send me to Seattle."

"Okay, I'll tell you that I know a lot of stuff about you. There were four guys talking about you."

"What did they say about me?"

"I can't tell you that."

"What are you going to do with what they said? Tell me that much."

"They said bad things about you."

"No, this is not true because there are no bad things to talk about. The only bad thing I have done is that I have a girlfriend and I have a wife. That's the only bad thing about me."

"You know bin Laden is Sunni?"

"So, there are billions of Sunnis, and according to you, they are against the United States. There are Shias in Iran, and they are also against the United States. I could be either Sunni or Shia. What does it mean? About bin Laden, this guy was looking to become famous and you made it happen for him by putting him on television."

"What do you know about him?"

"I don't know nothing about him. I know only that he is a Muslim."

"He is talking about jihad."

"His jihad is something totally different."

"No, he is saying jihad."

"He is not a prophet. People don't listen to him or care about what he says."

"Where do we find those people who are doing bad things?"

"Simple answer—if they are Muslims you find them in the mosques, if they are Christians you find them in the churches, and if they are Jewish you find them in the synagogues. That's how you find these people. They found me in the street."

"Are you going to tell me that you don't go to the mosque?"

"It's bad that I don't go to the mosque, but I would not be afraid to tell you if I did."

"Why don't you go the mosque?"

"I can't have a girlfriend and go to the mosque. It's a lie to God."

"So you never drink?"

"No."

"You go to Atlantic City."

"Yeah."

"Do you play games?"

"Yeah."

"That's gambling."

"Look what do you want to prove? That I'm good or bad? If you want to prove that I am a good guy, I can appear good. If you want to prove I am a bad guy, I can appear bad."

"Those hijackers used to drink and go with girls..."

"I got arrested on September 11 and I have been here since then. There are no newspapers here, and I don't know who did it. I don't know anything."

"Bin Laden did it."

"Even if he did it, what has it got to do with me?"

"You are from that miserable country."

"Whatever you want from me, just tell me right now. You know, this is like Egypt. All the charges you want to put on me, just write those down and I will sign it. That's all."

"Take him to his cell." I could not understand these FBI officers. If I were really a WTC suspect, would they send in an inexperienced 20-year-old FBI officer? If I were a real suspect, they would come and sit with me every day. They would keep up with the news and know what was going on. They wouldn't ignore me for 40 days and then come to ask for my mother's birth date or my father's birth date. My father doesn't even know his own birth date. I am not say-ing that I am smart or that I was playing games with them or even that I needed more powerful people to investigate me. Those FBI officers made me feel like they were there to learn. It was like school for them . . . real-life school. It is similar to how medical students get a real dead body to cut up and learn from. In the same way, they gave the FBI officers real bodies to learn with.

You may think it is crazy, but this is how it looked and felt to me. In the jail, people were saying that the government needed an excuse to keep people inside so that they could tell the American public that they were talking to terrorists in prison. Everyone was waiting for the FBI clearance.[14] Whenever they called their lawyers, they asked them to get their FBI clearance. I said to them, "Guys, look, lawyers can't make that happen. The FBI can give a lawyer the clearance if they want to, but he can't push for it. We are here because the FBI is keeping us for some reason. We are in the United States and the FBI is not stupid. We could get clearance in two days if they wanted to give it to us because they know everything. FBI knows more about you than you know about yourself. I think we are here for the FBI training. They want to know how much we can handle. For example, if you put an American guy in a cell, the first thing he would do is kill himself. So they want to know about Muslims. They want to figure out things like whether we are against suicide and how we handle jail."

Immigration Court Hearing

One day after I had been there for 52 days, the jail administrators allowed me to call my lawyer. It wasn't time for a phone call, but they gave me one because I had my court date the next day. They just wanted to be able to say, "We gave him a phone call."

We went to the court, but it wasn't really a court because it was behind closed doors. I was not eligible for any bond, and the prosecutor told me that I was going to get deported within 45 days. My lawyer got angry with the prosecutor and told him that he was going to appeal, but he didn't do it. The entire court session lasted 15 minutes, and no one was allowed to speak. The lawyer told the judge, "Look, if you don't want to hear about his employment history, about his company, about his tourist visa, and his bond, then that's fine."

"No, I don't care if he has 25 million workers in the United States. He is not eligible to stay."
I told my lawyer, "The decision was made before we came." The judge was my enemy. A judge is supposed to keep the balance between the scales, but this judge was tipping the scale, away from me.
The judge told me that I was going to get deported, and my lawyer said that I could appeal it, if I could deal with staying in jail a bit longer.

"How long is it gonna take?"

"Not more than a month because you are already in jail."

"Appeal then. I don't wanna get deported like this because I didn't need to get arrested to get deported. I could have left myself."

That was the first and the last time that I visited court. My lawyer had also asked the judge to transfer the case to Philadelphia, but the judge said, "I am not going to send him back to Philadelphia, so that you can get him out with a $300 bond. He is in New York, he is going to stay in New York and he is going to get deported from New York." The judge was laughing with the INS prosecutors. There were also two FBI officers there—a man and a woman.

"He is not eligible, he got the final order of deportation from the fourth judge," said the FBI officers. They never said that I broke the law or that I was wanted. Because I'm an Arab, the judge saw me as a bad person, even before I showed up in court.

Passing Time in the Cell

In the cell, I liked talking about my kids and hearing about other people's kids. If people were not talking about family stuff, then I wasn't interested. I wanted to hear about their marriages, their kids, how they had come to the U.S. If they started talking about something else, like the jail, the government, the cell, or when we'd get out, I wouldn't give them 100 percent of my attention.

I really enjoyed talking to Ali Yaghi[15] about his three kids. They brought him from another jail, where he had stayed for 52 or 53 days. When he came, he said, "I am Arabic from Palestine." He was the first Palestinian person I met. As you know, people from the same countries like to talk to each other—Pakistanis like to talk to other Pakistanis, Egyptians to other Egyptians, etc. So when he said that he was from Palestine, I asked him his name.

"Ali Yaghi," he replied, and then he told me wanted to sleep. In other words, he did not want to talk, and the next day I didn't say anything to him. Other people asked him how he was doing.

"Where is the Palestinian guy?" he asked.

"Yeah, how are you?" I replied.

"Fine. I know you felt bad yesterday because I said I wanted to sleep."

"No, it's fine with me."

"I was thinking about my family. I am sorry."

"It's fine man."

"Actually, I am from Jordan. I am Palestinian but I live in Jordan. I have been here for 16 years, but I don't have papers. I was the first in my family to come here. I brought them all from Jordan and all of them got papers except for me. I am the donkey." Ali Yaghi is a fine guy. He is 45 years old and married with three kids. After I had been living in the general population unit for three months, they brought him down and I saw his face for the first time.

"Where are your wife and kids?" I asked.

"My wife is from Afghanistan."

"From Afghanistan? That's why you are here." [*Laughs*]

You miss your kids when they are not there. I used to sit and think about them for hours. I would remember things like my kids asking me to read them a story. I'd look at the story and even though it was only three pages long, it felt like too much at the time, and I would send them to their mother. When I was in jail, I felt terrible about not reading the story to them. Or I would remember the times when I came home and couldn't find parking so I'd go to another block. They would jump up and down and would want to follow me, but I would drive away. It is not a big deal—all parents do things like that.

In jail, though, you start remembering things you don't usually think about, things that happened five or six years ago. Small things, like the time when I smacked my son. I remembered it in jail, and it seemed like a big deal.

Nabil talks about the time when his wife and children were getting deported to Israel from Seattle after getting arrested for an expired visa.

I feel really bad about the way I treated my son in Seattle. They had released my wife and kids. My younger son was only six months old, and he was on the floor. While I was talking to my wife, he was holding my leg and he wanted me to carry him. I didn't carry him because I was occupied with talking with my wife, and the deportation officer was rushing us, saying, "Let's go, let's go, let's go!" I could have picked him up, but I didn't. You know it was not a big thing, and it happened two years ago. But when I thought about it in the cell, I cried.

Overall, I am happy that I gave them everything I could. I used to take them out three or four times a week and spend $100 to $150 at a time. I could have done more but I didn't because I was busy, busy, busy. Sometimes, my wife used to tell me that I liked my work more than my family. That's not true. I just wanted my kids to live in a peaceful environment.

One time, I remembered the time they wanted me to take them to Six Flags after they saw an ad for it on television. They were only kids, and there were things that they wanted to see.

"I am taking you next week," I told them.

"Don't promise the kids. What if you can't take them?" my wife said.

"No, I am taking them next week."

"Don't tell them, just take them. If you tell them, they are going to wait, wait, wait, until Saturday. If you don't take them, then they'll cry." I reassured my wife that I was taking them, but when Friday came and they started talking about Six Flags, I told them that I'd take them next week.

"Why next week?" my wife asked.

"Take the kids to the market and buy them some toys."

"You think you can lie and then make them feel better by buying them toys?"

"I am busy, I can't take them now." The next week came, but I was still too busy to take them. The day before they left for Israel, I said, "I want to take you to Six Flags."

"No, you are not taking them anywhere, we are going back home," my wife said. I never took them to Six Flags, and I should have. I promised them 20 times that I'd take them, but I didn't.

At the airport, I told my wife, "Change your mind, don't go. I swear, I don't care about the plane tickets. Don't go."

"I am going to lose my citizenship if I don't go back to Israel. Finish what you need to and come to Israel in two or three months," she said.

I told her I'd come, but I wasn't able to go back so soon. One day, I was driving and I saw a sign for Six Flags. I swear, I cried for 12 days when I saw that sign. I am not a bad father. I am telling you that I love my kids and my wife. Sometimes you think you're doing the right thing, but you're not. I bought them a lot of toys because growing up, I never had a single toy. You don't want your kids to miss out on the things that you missed out on. But kids need more than toys. They saw me for an hour, sometimes only 30 minutes a day. Most people work eight hours a day, but I worked 12 to 15 hours. After working all day, I had to drive workers to their homes and look for other workers. I'd come home at midnight when they were already sleeping and then I would leave early in the morning again. I saw my son only when I took him to school, and I hardly saw the other three.

In the cell, I spent my time writing and telling my stories. I wrote a lot of letters to my friends. I knew that I could not send them, but I wrote them anyway to pass the time. I did what I could. I was hoping that after I had written a lot of letters, the guards would say, "Okay, because you wrote 20 letters, you can mail them." Later, I was finally able to get some free stamps, but I didn't have enough to send a letter to Israel. I sent the letters to my friends with one stamp and asked them to send them to my family. I don't know if they threw the letters away or just kept them, but later they claimed that they never received those letters. I know they are lying.

Sometimes I wrote letters to myself, and other times I addressed them to my wife and kids. After writing the letters, I would read them over two or three times. To tell you the truth, I did not want to read them and get reminded of why I was in the MDC. I wanted to forget about it. Today, my time at the MDC is a memory that I carry with me all the time.

The MDC Guards

The guards used to strip this guy, Mohammed [a pseudonym], whenever they wanted. It was inhumane, and there was no reason for doing it. Usually, guards strip inmates when they come back from visiting their lawyers or families to look for drugs. But Mohammed hadn't left the cell, so there was no reason to strip him. They just did it because they were bad and did whatever they wanted, not necessarily what the government told them to do. I don't think the government ordered the guards to tell me every morning that I was going to die in my cell either.

The FBI knows that I was innocent, but the guards wanted to show that they love their country more than anything else. How do they prove their love? By mistakenly telling themselves that they must outdo each other in their tough talk. For me, telling inmates things like, "you are going to die here," or "I am going to feed you for the rest of your life in this cell," does not prove that you love your country. They could help their country by working 12 hours without overtime, but they would never do that. They were always talking about how much overtime they got last week or how much double pay they were going to get in their next paycheck.

Sometimes they said things like, "If these Arabs go back home one day, where are we going to work? We will have to go back to our eight-hour shifts." The guards worked 12 hours and got paid overtime for four of those hours.

One day, the guards were in the hallway, and I think by that time there were only 42 of us left on the ninth floor. Every week, one or two guys left. I heard a guard say, "Look, half of them are gone."

"They will bring more people."
"No, in these two weeks, they didn't bring anybody. I think they've stopped. I am used to getting that fat check every week."
"Aren't you guys embarrassed to talk about these things?" I said. "You are talking about people's lives and all you care about is getting paid."

"Shut up! You can't listen to us. Stand away from the door." I looked down on these guards. I didn't care about what they thought or said because all they cared about was their fat checks and not the people who got killed in the World Trade Center. All they cared about was what would happen when we got released and they would have to go back to their old shifts. They were worried about what they would tell their wives, who had also gotten used to the big checks.

Jail guards take it on themselves to harm people. They are not told to say anything, but they do. They did not beat me, but I heard the other prisoners say that they took them downstairs and punished then. I didn't see it. Do I believe these inmates? Fifty-fifty. Some guards didn't hate the prisoners, but there were others who cursed at us, gave us the finger and did random strip searches. This was normal behavior for them.

Moving to the General Population Unit

One of the lieutenants was really nice. Whenever we asked him any questions, he answered us nicely. One day, I was sitting on the bed with a Yemeni man. He came and said to him, "Tell you what?"

"What?"
"He is going downstairs today, you are not."
"Look man, don't joke with me." I said.
"You are going downstairs. You are innocent. Get ready; we are coming to take you in five minutes, I am counting."

When they take you to the general population area, it means that you are done. If you are innocent, you are going to get out or if you are not, you get deported. So I shook hands with the Yemeni guy, told him that he was next, and said, "*Inshallah* [God willing] we'll meet again."

They took me to the hallway, and all the officers started laughing, "You are innocent man! We can't believe that."

"You were a suspect at one time, now you are innocent. We are glad to hear that, we are happy for you, but there are people waiting to fight you downstairs. They are angry because they know that you are a WTC suspect," said one officer.

"Don't worry. I can take care of myself." Everybody looked at me when they took me downstairs. I had a bushy long beard because they hadn't give us razors on the ninth floor.

The day before I went to the court, I asked for a razor because I didn't want to appear in front of the judge with a big beard.

"No, you're dreaming! We are not going to give you a razor," the guards said.
"I swear to God, if you are not going to give me a razor, I'll never ever shave in the jail, trust me."
"We are not gonna give you a razor."
"Okay, I am not going to shave. Even if you give me all the razors in the world, I won't shave."
So they brought the razors after that and said, "Now shave. Take that."
"I am not shaving. You don't know me yet."
To protest, I didn't shave for months, and my beard grew long. Anyway, when I went downstairs, one Pakistani guy came up to me and said, "Where did they bring you from?"
"I am from the ninth floor."
"Oh my God, are you special baggage? They call people from the ninth floor 'special baggage.' If you are, then don't come to my cell."
"Why?"

"Man, these people will kill us."

"Look man, they don't know me. They won't kill me."

He went to his cell and brought me cigarettes. "You smoke?"

"I haven't smoked for a hundred days, man."

We went to the red gate and smoked a cigarette. I said, "Look Mohammad, I don't want you to come near me if you think they'll hurt you because of me."

"No, I don't care, but you know you'll have to defend yourself."

"Don't worry about me. All these people will be my friends in one week."

"You'll be surprised. Over here, they throw the Koran on the floor and step on it."

We sat on the table. The first guy who came and talked to me was called Santagnino. He was a big mafia guy in the '70s and '80s, and there are a lot of books written about him. He asked me if I was Muslim.

"They brought me from the ninth floor, and I see all these people looking at me," I said.

"Don't worry about them," he said, and we started talking. I told him that a lot of people on the ninth floor are innocent but that they just tell lies about us on the TV. I told him about an Indian guy who was caught with $5,000 on the train, and they had brought him to the ninth floor. Later I saw his pictures on TV and I knew he was not connected to terrorism.[16]

"I know these guys. I don't know what they look like but I know their voices. These people are innocent. They are in there because of fake passports or some fraud," I told him. A lot of people don't understand that things are different from what the news says.

Within a few days, everyone started coming and talking to me. You only need to speak a few words me to before I'll make you laugh. Soon, everyone was my friend.

People came and went, but my situation was bad because I didn't know what they were going to do with me. Was I going to get deported or not? How long was I going to stay? Santagnino, who was in his 70s, was hoping that he would go home and settle with both of his wives. My INS case could not be as bad as those of the people around me. Everyone who heard my story said, "We don't believe this guy's case. He is here without a court hearing, without a lawyer, without phone calls, without a counselor, without anything."

So it was hard for me to wait. The only thing that I thought about and wanted to find out was when I was going home. I wanted to know the exact time, if it was a year or two years or whatever. In jail, I met people with a ten-year sentence. Each day they would count down "ten years less one day" and "ten years less two days." I couldn't even count because I didn't have a sentence. They could call me anytime, and that is exactly how it happened, but waiting for that moment felt like forever.

"The Saga of the Beard"

There were four other Muslims besides me in the general population unit. Three of them were Pakistanis and one was Somali, and we used to pray together. One day, they said, "It's a heavy time for us as Muslims so you should cut your beard."

"No. I swore I wouldn't cut my beard."

Then they brought in a Jordanian guy and a Moroccan guy. After living there for months, we became close friends. They also told me that everything would be fine if I would only cut my beard, but I refused. One day, the Jordanian and the Moroccan came to my cell; one held me down and the other cut my beard with a blade. Everything—from the way the guards talked to me to the counselor's reaction—changed after that.

Before that, the counselor wouldn't give me a phone call because of the beard. He talked to everyone except me, and whenever I tried to talk to him, he would cut me off before I could even say a word. "You piss me off. I don't want to see you," he would say.

After the shave, the counselor said, "Come if you want to talk to your embassy, come call. Make a phone call. You look nice, you look better now."

"You don't know why I had the beard. I am not religious."

"Why did you have it?" I told him the story.

"So you shaved for the change?"

"No, my friends held me down in the cell and cut it, because it's awful."

"This is better, man."

There were two sheriffs who looked after the jail and the inmates. They also changed their attitudes and started treating me nicer after I cut my beard. I think they thought that I was a September 11 suspect because I got arrested on that day. I told them to look at my picture, which showed that I was clean-shaven when I was arrested. Officers think that if you don't have a beard, then you don't care about being Muslim. There were some Spanish and Jewish guys with beards, but the guards didn't even look at them. I grew the beard to prove a point, not because I was religious, but because I was Muslim, it made me appear guilty.

Getting Released

One day, an officer came to my room and said, "Pack up, you are going." I had already spent a year and 17 days there, but I didn't believe them because the guards had tricked me three times before. In the past I gave all of my stuff to my fellow prisoners, hugged everyone, and walked all the way up to the exit door, only to find out that they were playing a prank. This time, the one who told me to pack up was the nice Chinese officer who everyone praises.

"Look man, I can't handle any more jokes," I told him.

"I am not joking with you. They called me from downstairs and told me to tell Nabil Ayesh to pack up. You are going."

"Can you go and call them again?" I asked and went back to sleep because I was sure it was a joke. A Moroccan guy came to my cell and said, "I saw this guy coming with a trash bag. I have a feeling that he is coming to our cell."

"They are joking with me."

"Let me see." The Moroccan guy went to the counselor and asked, "Mr. Kaffi, do you know if Nabil is going to get released today?"

"Tell him, this is a good time to sleep. He is not going nowhere."

"Are you sure?"

"I am the counselor. I know everything before everybody."

So the Moroccan guy went to the unit manager, who also told him that I wasn't going anywhere. He then went back to the Chinese officer and said, "So, you asked Ayesh to pack up?"

"My boss asked me to tell him to pack up. He is leaving the building. I don't know where he is going."

"Call them again because the unit manager said he wasn't going."

"They don't know anything."

"They say that you don't know."

"I don't know about the unit manager, but they called me from downstairs and told me to tell Mr. Ayesh to pack up. I called them three times, and they told me the same thing each time."

"I can't believe it. He is not going nowhere," said the unit manager.

"I'll be back, man," I told the Moroccan guy and started to pack. It was early in the morning, and most of the guys were usually asleep at that time. This was the first time in the nine months that I had been there that the entire unit was awake. They were saying, "Nabil is going out, he is going out. Maybe he is going in the street, maybe he's going to get deported." I saw that people were happy for me, more than I was for myself. I kept thinking that I was going to the airport and that this was not going to be a happy moment for me. Everyone around me was laughing. They made a big noise as if it was a party. Every day, people get released and nobody cares. But when I got released, there was a big noise. It took me two hours to shake everyone's hand and give them hugs. I went with the officers and they gave me green clothes.

"Guys, just tell me where am I going?"

"The lawyer is coming to take you."

"I am going to the airport, you know." I had seen them take people to the airport, so I thought I was going there, too.

"Sign here," they said.

"Where am I going?"

"You from Jordan, right?" said an agent.

"Yeah, I am a citizen of Jordan from Palestine."

"Then where else should you be going?"

"I am not going nowhere. Send me back to the jail."

"No, you are going to Eleventh Street."

"Look, you are scaring me. Tell me the truth. Where am I going? I don't think you are taking me to the airport."

They put me in a room and took my picture. "Excuse me sir, where am I going?"

"To the airport, where do you think you are going?"

The other officer then fought with them and said, "Hey, why you fucking lie to this guy. Hey, you are going to the street."

"What?"

"You are going to the street. I will take you to the sidewalk downstairs." It felt like a big rock rolled off my heart.

"Hurry up guys, I want to go."

"Your lawyer called, and he sent you a Greyhound ticket and directions."

"Just put me in the street, man. I don't want directions. I don't want anything."

I still couldn't believe it. They took my pictures and fingerprints and took me to a door.

When the guy opened the door, he said, "Your papers are gonna be sent to your lawyer, you are going man."

I said, "I am going?"

"Yeah. I am taking you to the sidewalk. You are a lucky man, you got released."

"Thank you."

"What you are gonna do?"

"I'm going to buy coffee and cigarettes, and I am not gonna look back. I wanna run man." So I ran. I bought the coffee, I bought the cigarettes, and I took a taxi to the Greyhound and came to Philadelphia. It was September 26, 2002.

I am working right now. Life is alright, but it is important for me to have my wife and kids here and I am talking to lawyers about it. If they come here, I will never think about going back. My house in Bethlehem is worth half a million dollars. I will sell everything.

Even though my wife is an Israeli citizen, she can't leave the house. There are no schools for the kids, so they stay at home. She wants to come back and I am trying, but it's a big deal to get them a visa. I don't care if the U.S. gives me papers or not. I just want to live here. What happened to me was because of September 11. I was here for four years, and they never bothered me before that. There are millions of people who live here like this. I just want to live here in peace.

Throughout the interview, Nabil was in an upbeat mood because he had been released within the United States. He was optimistic that he would be able to bring his wife and children back to the United States. I also noticed a sense of anxiety of the unknown. He was at the mercy of the U.S. immigration officers, and he did not know what may happen to him in the upcoming months. Despite this anxiety, after his release, Nabil had been giving interviews with several media organizations and had participated in a documentary entitled Persons of Interest.[17] *ABC* Nightline *aired his interview in the beginning of January 2003 in a special segment about 9/11 detainees.[18] At one point during his interview, Nabil expressed a sense of concern about his media publicity and wanted to take precautions.*

During February and March 2003, I met several MDC detainees who had been deported to Pakistan, India, and Egypt. Whenever I told them that Nabil had been released within the United States, they were completely surprised. They could not believe that the U.S. government would release an MDC detainee within the country. It was a huge liability for the government.

In March 2003, Nabil was arrested again by the local traffic police in Syracuse, New York, and was handed over to the immigration authorities. Within a month, Nabil was deported to Israel. Authorities claim that Israel accepted his travel documents in April 2003, even though before that both Jordan and Israel had been reluctant to accept him.[19]

I talked to Nabil on the phone about his deportation. He said that initially the U.S. government wanted to send him to Jordan, but he insisted on Palestine and that's why he ended up there. At first the U.S. government told him that he wasn't allowed to come back for 30 years, but Nabil refused to sign the papers. Later, they reduced it to ten years. A July 2003 article in Reuters *provides basic details about his deportation:*

> [Nabil] said he was handcuffed on a plane with about 25 detainees to Amman, Jordan. Ayesh and five others were driven by bus on May 16 to the Israeli checkpoint and admitted to the West Bank nine hours later.
>
> "They refused to let us go. I said there is a deal between the Americans, the Jordanians and Israelis. They said nobody told us about you guys. After hours and hours they let us go."[20]

Law enforcement officials are not forthcoming, and it is difficult to know what really triggered his deportation a few months after his release. During a telephone conversation in November 2007, Nabil stated that he was deported because he had been talking with the mainstream media and the U.S. government wanted him to stop. "They could not kill me in the U.S. and they could not stop me from talking. It is hard for me to believe that Israel could not accept me for a year and then later on they accepted me after 19 days."

The OIG's April 2003 report, which exposed patterns of systemic abuse on the ninth floor of the MDC, might also have contributed to his third arrest and subsequent deportation. The OIG completed a thorough investigation on the physical, psychological, and emotional abuses that occurred when the government put individuals in solitary confinement on the ninth floor of the MDC. The official report was released to the public in June 2003, but it had started to circulate for internal Department of Justice review in February 2003 and was fully released to the DOJ in April 2003. Nabil might have been deported because he was confirming the findings by talking openly about his own experience.

Another contributing factor might have been the Turkmen v. Ashcroft *lawsuit[21] filed by the Center for Constitutional Rights in April 2002, which challenged the government's decision to incarcerate immigration detainees in the Special Housing Unit of the ninth floor of the MDC. Everyone placed on the ninth floor had been deported to their home countries by early 2003 except for Nabil and another anonymous individual, who also left the country in 2008.[22] Nabil's presence in the United States could have been a liability for the U.S. government because he was living evidence for the case. His interviews and testimony were a threat to the U.S. justice system. Today, Nabil is forgotten. The law enforcement officials have effectively safeguarded themselves by getting rid of him.*

At the micro level, Nabil's string of arrests and detentions and his final deportation point to the incompetent efforts of a government bureaucracy to ensure national security. However, at the macro level, Nabil's case fits into a larger pattern of detentions and deportations of Muslim males and reveals that the civil liberties of Muslims in the United States are at stake.

Life Today: Nabil and his wife and children live in an undisclosed city in Palestine/Israel. In the fall of 2008, I met them and conducted a video interview. Nabil's health has deteriorated, and he has lost a lot of weight. In the last two years, Nabil has suffered a stroke and has been hospitalized for a heart condition. When I asked him about his health, he joked as usual and said, "My heart was not feeling good and that's why it failed." He is the primary breadwinner for his family, and I found him constantly smoking and living with anxiety—it was the same anxiety I observed when I met him in January 2003 in New York.

Figure 5   Mohamed E******, close to New York City, date unknown. Courtesy of Mohamed E******.

CHAPTER 5

Propagating and Maintaining the Global War on Terror

Mohamed E******

Mohamed E****** entered the United States from Egypt in May 1999 while working on a ship. A few months later, an inexperienced lawyer filed an asylum application for him in which he tried to legalize Mohamed's immigration status by establishing a false relationship with Al-Jihad, a political group that claimed responsibility for Egyptian president Anwar Sadat's assassination in the 1970s. After marrying a U.S. citizen, Mohamed withdrew his asylum application.

On October 25, 2001, Mohamed was leaving a New Jersey courthouse after attending a hearing for his immigration case when two law enforcement agents arrested him and placed him in the Passaic County Jail. After 11 months, Mohamed was deported to Egypt in custody with two deportation officers and a file that falsely established his connection with Al-Jihad. Upon arrival in Egypt, Mohamed was arrested and placed in a high-security jail, where he was tortured for about three weeks. After his release from the Egyptian jail in March 2003, he remained under Egyptian surveillance.

Meeting Mohamed

It was a late, warm afternoon in April when I arrived at the Zimalk Sporting Club in Cairo. I got out of the taxi and looked around for Mohamed. I did not know what to expect. I had only talked with him once on a public phone and had hinted at my Pakistani looks. Mohamed had assured me that he would recognize me. I stood for a few minutes orienting myself to the area. I had already spent three weeks in Cairo and was becoming familiar with the surroundings.

The street was busy with traffic, and a lot of people were entering and exiting the many large gates surrounding Zimalk. From a distance, I saw a man standing who looked to be in his 30s. I smiled at him and he walked toward me. "Irum?" he asked. I nodded my head. "Good to meet you," he said. "Can you follow me?" Again, I nodded my head in response. He entered the gate and started to walk briskly a few feet ahead of me, and I followed him. He continued to walk ahead of me and exited the gate. I did not know how to respond, so I just followed him. Then he entered another gate, walked for another five minutes, and exited through a side door. Finally, he entered a garden area in the club and looked for a seat. Both of us sat down on green plastic chairs around a round table.

"I am sorry for all this walking around," he said. "The Egyptian FBI is watching over me, and I just wanted to make sure that no one was following us." I nodded my head again, took a deep breath, and started to introduce myself. We talked for the next few hours, and I audio-recorded his interview. That night, when I returned back to my hotel room, a cold chill went through my body. I was scared that local authorities might jail both of us for doing the interview.

I met up with Mohamed several other times during my stay in Cairo. He introduced me to some of his friends and relatives. These meetings, however, were always in crowded public spaces. Mohamed suggested that for security purposes I should mail the interview tapes via DHL to the United States instead of carrying them with me. I followed his directions, but right after sending the audiotapes, I felt very empty—I had suddenly lost control over the materials that I had collected laboriously over the last four months. I was nervous going through the customs clearance at the Egyptian airport, but nothing happened. I called Mohamed after the clearance and confirmed our safety. A few weeks later, I received my DHL packet intact in California.

The following narrative is based on an audio-recorded interview with Mohamed; conversations with Steven Watt, a lawyer at the ACLU who is familiar with his case; conversations with Sin Yen Ling, a lawyer at Asian Law Caucus who is also familiar with his case; a review of FBI documents that Mohamed provided me; legal files from the New Jersey Immigration Court;[1] an ACLU report featuring Mohamed's case;[2] e-mails from Adem Carroll, a community organizer;[3] and a few newspaper articles.[4]

Entering the United States

I entered the United States on May 5, 1999, through Portland, Oregon, while I was working on a ship. I used to dream of coming to the U.S. and building a life here. People had told me many stories about how America was a country of immigrants, a nation where everyone found jobs and a better life. I wanted to be a part of this country.[5]

After I arrived in Portland, I tried to find a job, but I realized quickly that my English was not very good and that people couldn't understand me. However, there were a few people who were helpful. Someone told me that I should try to find work in New York. I took that advice and went to New York with $200, which was all I had at the time.

I rented a room in Manhattan on 116th and Broadway for $70 a week. I shared that room with some Spanish[6] people, and since I was living with them, I started to learn Spanish and got a job in the same neighborhood. This job paid me $200 per week, which was very low, but you know that Spanish people don't pay a lot. Very soon, I realized that I needed more money to live in the United States, and I started looking for other jobs. However, wherever I went, people told me that they couldn't give me a good salary because I didn't speak English well. After hearing this over and over, I decided to attend English classes in uptown Manhattan and work on my language skills.

As soon as I started learning basic English phrases, like "good morning" and "how are you," I began looking for a better job. I got a job in a pizza store in downtown Manhattan for $250 per week. Two months later, when I learned more English, I looked for a better job again and got a job that paid $300 per week with Poly Cleaners, a Korean-owned dry cleaning store on Park and 75th Avenue.

This was very good income for me at the time. I delivered clothes to the customers, and even though it was winter and freezing in New York, I liked the work and it was good pay. Slowly, I started to speak English more fluently, and I began practicing with my customers. I was very happy with my job. Some of my customers were big movie stars like Dustin Hoffman, whom I had only seen in blockbuster movies. I started to have conversations with my customers, and they gave me tips, which would add up to another $100 per week. Soon I had enough money to buy a car, so I bought one, but I did not have a driver's license.

Trying to Gain Legal Status

Mohamed was interested in obtaining legal status in the United States because it meant higher pay, stability, and security. Many immigrants who are unfamiliar with the maze of immigration laws and regulations become victims of incompetent and greedy lawyers who take advantage of their vulnerability. Mohamed remembered his encounter with one of these lawyers.

When I was still working in the Spanish neighborhood, a customer came and asked me, "Do you speak English?"

"No, I can't," I replied.
"Where are you from?"

"I am from Egypt."

"You speak Arabic?"

"Yes. Where are you from?" I asked him.

"Palestine," he said. We started to speak in Arabic, and he told me that he had been living in the U.S. a long time and that he was an immigration lawyer. During our conversation, I told him that I wanted to meet more people to improve my English. He asked me how much money I made, and I told him $200 per week.

"Two hundred is not good. If you have the right papers, it does not matter whether you speak good English or not. You will make more money," he said.

"How do you make papers?" I asked.

"I can make a green card for you for $3,000."

I told him that I was interested in getting papers, and he asked him to tell him everything about myself and my family and how I entered the country. He told me that he would make a good story for me and after one or two years I would get a green card. I was happy about the possibility of getting a green card, so I agreed and gave him $500 to start the process.

Five hundred dollars was a lot of money for me at that time. I was only making $200 per week, and out of that I had to pay $70 per week for my room. I was living pretty cheap; I paid a dollar a day for food at the store and slept the rest of the day. I worked at night, and I was not a smoker or a drinker, so my expenses were low.

Every week, I saved some money to give to my lawyer. He put together an asylum case for me by making up a story about how I used to belong to a Muslim organization called Al-Jihad. He wrote that I jumped ship because I was scared of living in Egypt, and then asked me to sign an application. I gave him another $500 and showed the application to my friend since my English was still very weak at that time. My friend explained what the lawyer had written. Shortly after that, I started receiving letters from the immigration office and I tried to find the lawyer, but he had disappeared. Every time I called, I got his answering machine. By that time, I had paid him approximately $1,400 or $1,500, and I could not give him the rest of the $3,000 because I never found him again.

I went to the immigration office because one of the letters warned that if I did not come in, I would be deported. At the office, I tried to explain to the woman there that I didn't have any relationship with Al-Jihad. She told me that my case was very complicated but that if I decided to change my statement, I would have to go to the immigration judge. I decided to make a change. While I was waiting for a date with the immigration judge, I found a lawyer who spoke Arabic. I explained the situation to him, but when he saw the paperwork, he told me this was not a good case and that he could not do anything. I pleaded him to do something, and he said that he would try. He talked to the judge and told him that he needed time to prepare for the case because he had just met me. The judge agreed and gave us another date. At the next appointment, he told the judge that I did not speak English and that he needed a translator, so the judge gave us another date.

Between these hearings, Mohamed met a naturalized U.S. citizen from Puerto Rico who lived close to his house. They got married, and afterward, Mohamed filed an application to change his immigration status based on his marriage to a U.S. citizen. He paid $1,500 for an illegal entry ticket, and on September 6, 2001, he received his social security card and work permit, which was valid until September 5, 2002. Based on his lawyer's advice, he also made a request to withdraw his asylum application. The lawyer told him that he had an appointment with the immigration judge in October for his case. Mohamed finally started feeling a bit more secure and settled.[7]

Racial Profiling and Harassment

Many Muslim- and Arab-looking individuals became victims of racial profiling after September 11. Mohamed recollects his first investigation, which occurred right after September 11.

After September 11, I lost my job at the Korean dry cleaner and I got another job as a delivery person for a phone card company in Bridgeport, Connecticut. On September 14, I was driving on the highway between New York and Stamford and stopped at the card company store to pick up money. When I came out of the store, I saw that two cars were blocking my car. Two officers told me to freeze and to put everything on the floor, including the bags I was holding. Then they handcuffed me. A Jordanian man named Mohamed, who also worked for the company, was with me. They pointed guns at us and took both of us to separate cars and started questioning us. I am not sure how they found us, but I think they saw my face when we were driving and noticed that I was a Muslim. They probably checked the license plate number, realized that the car belonged to an Arab, and decided to follow us. At that time, I had my work permit and my marriage license with me.

They searched everything in the car and checked my driver's license.

I was very scared, and I asked them why they were investigating me. They checked my wallet, my cellular phone, and all the telephone numbers in my phone. Then they started questioning my friend and I about Muslims and September 11 and asked questions like what do you think about September 11? Who did the September 11 attacks? What have Muslim people been saying after September 11? Do you pray? How many times do you pray? What kind of Muslim are you? Are you Sunni or Shia? They also asked me about my friend. They asked me his name, his family name, how long he had worked with me, and a lot of other questions, like did he visit Jordan before? Does he pray? Does he go to mosque? Is he married? Is his wife married? Is she an American citizen? Is she Muslim or Christian or Jewish? I don't remember all of the questions. After five or six hours, they came back and told us that they had good news from their supervisor. They took our name, address, and other information and released us. I was very happy that they let us go.

On October 25, 2001, I appeared in the court with my paperwork. The lawyer told the judge that I wanted to withdraw the asylum case because I was married to an American citizen. The lawyer showed the immigration judge all the papers and confirmed that they were valid and that I was in the country legally. He argued in front of the judge that someone took money from me and made up a false asylum case for me. He said that I did not speak English, was unfamiliar with the system, did not belong to the Islamic organization Al-Jihad, and was not a terrorist. He said, "If my client was a terrorist, he would not have appeared in front of a court after 9/11." The judge accepted the request to withdraw the asylum application and to use my marriage status instead. He gave me an appointment for January 17, 2002, and said that I had to appear in front of the judge with my wife. My lawyer also requested a change in location from New York to Bridgeport, Connecticut. The judge agreed and told me, "Have a nice day. Come back early in three months with your wife." That was October 25, 2001.

Getting Arrested

When I left the immigration court, I saw the same two officers who had arrested me on September 14 waiting for me. I said to one of them, "Hello Officer, I hope you did not come to arrest me this time."

He replied, "Your problem is not with the FBI but with the INS. We are here because immigration authorities want to investigate you."

The other officer said, "Can you do me a favor? Just come with us to the immigration court since we have been asking about you for a while." I did not want to go with them.

I replied, "I just came from the immigration court where I appeared in front of the judge." At that time, my lawyer was with me. He told the officers that I was married to a U.S. citizen, that I had a social security number and a work permit, and that I did not have any criminal record. He also told them that I had paid the illegal entry fine and taxes. They insisted that they needed another investigation. My lawyer had to go to another court hearing and told me he was leaving.

I begged my lawyer, "Please don't leave me with INS alone. I don't know what is going on. I hear a lot of stories about the INS, that it has been arresting too many Muslim people."

"Don't worry. You are legal in this country. They can't arrest you. I have another court hearing right now. I will contact you on your cell phone after I am finished with the other client," he said. I was at 26 Federal Plaza at the time, and I had just completed a hearing date on the 13th floor of the building in front of the immigration judge. After my lawyer left, the officers took me to the sixth or seventh floor in the same building. All the immigration offices are in the same building, and all the immigration papers are kept and prepared there.

These officers told me that they wanted to talk in front of an immigration judge. I agreed to go downstairs with them, and we started walking. On the way, one of the officers opened a door and the other officer pushed me inside. Once inside, I realized that it was a bathroom.

"What is going on?" I asked.
"Your face towards the wall, hands up. Open your legs!" they shouted together. One of them said, "We need to check that you are safe. Do you have a knife or anything?" I took everything out of my pockets: my passport, wallet, keys, and everything else. They patted my body up and down and afterwards looked through my passport.
"What is this written in your passport?" they asked.
"It is my name written in English and Arabic."
"We don't understand Arabic. What is this?"
"This is my address in Arabic."
"If you lie, we have translators who can reconfirm the information."
"This is an official document for immigration purposes," I replied, feeling more and more scared.
"Enough of this. Put your stuff in your bag and put your jacket on." We were going to be passing by the immigration court, and the officers did not want the immigration judge to see that they had handcuffed me. I did not realize that at the time, but I understand it now. They told me to be quiet.
"We are going to take you to the immigration court downstairs. After they check you out, we will release you." I was under the impression that I would be released. They put my jacket over my hands so that nobody could see the handcuffs and took me to an elevator and told me that we were going downstairs. I did not know which floor they were taking me to because they were pushing the buttons of the elevators. After we got off the elevator, they took me to a room, unlocked the handcuffs, and told me to sit down in a chair. One of the officers told me that he was going to go and check all of my records, and the other one started asking me the same kinds of questions about Muslims and September 11 that he had before. I was really surprised.

"Why are you asking these questions? Are these questions for the INS or the FBI?"

The officer put his feet on the table and said, "Mohamed, read the news. Now there is no difference between the FBI and the INS. Both the INS and the FBI are working together. You have to answer all of my questions."

I felt that what he was telling me was illegal. However, I did not argue with him because I did not want to offend him and go to jail. I thought that maybe the government had created temporary new laws because of the 9/11 emergency. I thought that if I resisted and fought with him, he would put me in jail, but that if I answered all his questions and satisfied him, I would be able to leave. I answered all his questions. Afterwards, the other officer came back. Initially, one of them had said that my situation was very good and that I would be able to leave. Now, they talked with each other in the back of the room. After talking, they told me that I was under arrest. I was very surprised and asked, "Why am I under arrest?"

"Your situation was very good before September 11 but your situation is very bad after September 11," one of them said.

"What is my relationship to September 11? I don't have any relationship to September 11."

"No, you have a good relationship with September 11."

"What is the relationship between me and September 11?"

"You are a fucking Muslim. That is the relationship between you and September 11."

"Do you mean that you are arresting me because of my religion not because I am legal or illegal?"

"We are going to send you to the immigration judge, and he will decide about your immigration status. Don't bother us right now."

"I was with the judge about an hour ago and he gave me an appointment for January 17, 2002. Why don't you accept what this judge says?"

"We have another judge in New Jersey, and you need to meet with her. Right now, you have to come with us."

"How long will I have to stay in jail before I see the other judge?"

"If you have a good lawyer, maybe one week or two weeks at the maximum. You have a good situation."

"If my situation is good, don't arrest me."

"Things have changed after September 11. Before September 11, we were not arresting anyone. Now we have an emergency law. The situation is bad for Muslim people. When you go to jail, you will find a lot of Muslim people."

Afterwards, the officers left and some other officers told me that they were sending me to another floor in the same building and that later they would move me to a jail. I wanted to call my lawyer's cell phone from my cell phone, but they didn't allow me to.

Mohamed can't continue with the story, and he needs to take a break. I watch him quietly. After he drinks a bit of water, he becomes calm again. He tells me he is ready and then continues.

Before they transported me to the jail, they handcuffed my hands in the back so tightly that they turned blue. They checked everything in my pockets. I had over one thousand dollars in my wallet that I had just withdrawn from Chase Manhattan Bank to pay my lawyer for the October 25th hearing. They took the money, and I asked them what they were going to do with it. They replied that they would put it in my account in the jail. Then they sent me to the INS building, where they wrote a receipt, which I signed.

I was very confused and did not know what was going on. I was arrested for an immigration violation, but I had all the correct immigration papers and a pending case. If I were illegal, why would they process immigration papers for me? I just couldn't make sense of the situation. My lawyer called and reassured me. He told me, "Don't worry. You are legal in this country."

Passaic County Jail

Mohamed was taken to Passaic County Jail in New Jersey. It remains unclear why certain individuals were taken to the ninth floor of the MDC while others were sent to Passaic County Jail. The OIG report states that both of these jails were used to hold immigrants who were suspected of any links to terrorism. However, Passaic County Jail generally held individuals whose connections to terrorism appeared weaker.[8]

I did not have any money with me when I entered the Passaic County Jail. There were about five or six Muslim people there. I tried to call my lawyer, but he did not accept collect calls. Then I tried sending him a letter, but he did not answer. I wrote to so many people. Some people tried to make a three-way phone call to my lawyer for me, but he still did not answer. My lawyer told one of my friends that he would visit, but he never did. I did not know what was going on.[9]

I kept asking about my money because I wanted to buy some stuff from the jail. They only give you one pair of pants, one pair of shoes, and one shirt. Nothing else. They don't even give you a toothbrush, toothpaste, pajamas, T-shirt, or underwear. If you want anything you have to buy it, slippers and everything. One shirt and one pant for sleeping, eating, and living.

I also wanted to contact my wife and my friends, but I couldn't get in touch with anyone. Finally, I got a hold of my wife. She told me that after I got arrested, she could not pay the rent and had moved back in with her family. I did not have her family's phone number, but a friend of mine in Bridgeport knew her family. He managed to talk to her, and she told him that someone from the FBI visited her and told her that I was a terrorist. If she tried to help me, she could be charged with helping a terrorist. I called her and told her that I was being charged with an immigration violation, not terrorism. I told her to come to jail and check out everything for herself. She was scared, though, and she did not come.

When she did not respond to my letter, visit, or try to help, I realized that I had to forget my wife. Even though she was scared, she should have come to see me, her husband. I thought that I married her for life, not only for love. I don't want to marry for love only, which can be a short-lived experience. I want to marry for life, which means living together through thick and thin. Now that I think about it, I realize that she was young. She thought that by staying with me, she would have a hard time. I stopped contacting her.

I tried calling other people instead to complain that the immigration authorities stole my money and that I needed some. Someone from Washington, D.C., came to talk to me and wrote a report about what happened. He said that he would send the report to Washington, D.C., and that they would investigate about the money. No one got back to me, and I stayed in jail for the next three months without knowing what was going on. Meanwhile, other prisoners around me entered the jail, got court hearings, and left. I was just stuck there.

In the middle of January 2002, I finally got a call from my lawyer. He told me that he was trying to find out why I got arrested. The INS had told him that I had to appear in front of another judge because I was in a New Jersey jail. He told me that doing all that research took time and that was why it took him so long to get back to me. I knew that he was lying, but he told me that I had a court date on January 18, in an immigration court in New Jersey. He told me that I should make a request to withdraw the asylum case at the next hearing and that I should inform the judge that I was married to a U.S. citizen. He promised that I would get to stay here in the U.S. and that he would file a complaint about the INS stealing my money. He also said that I had a clearance from the FBI and that I was okay.

On January 18, 2002, I appeared in front of the immigration judge at 9:00 in the morning. She was a strong woman. The court officials told me to swear, and I swore. They started by asking me my name. My lawyer told them that I wanted to withdraw the asylum case and restart the case. The judge asked if I wanted to withdraw the case, and I told the judge that I did but that I didn't want to go home to Egypt and that I was married to an American citizen. The judge agreed to start a new case and told me that I had until February 2002 to reapply. My lawyer did not reapply, and that was the last time I saw him.

On February 19, I was waiting in the court and trying to contact my lawyer, but I could not find him. Finally, through a three-way call, I contacted him.

"What is going on?" I asked.

"You have deportation orders."

"Why do I have deportation orders?"

"The INS doesn't want you to stay here."

"Why?"

"Because of the earlier asylum case, the INS says that you are a terrorist. You can't stay here. Whether you are legal or illegal, you just can't stay here."

"Did you apply for the other case?"

"No. The INS did not accept the case." I was surprised.

"I haven't lived in the country very long, but I know that the INS can't stop someone from filing a case. The FBI can refuse, but not the INS. If I am a danger to the community, they have to charge me. I don't want to be deported."

"I can't do anything for you. You may want to try a different lawyer."

After that, I contacted the ACLU and talked to a lawyer who was from Sri Lanka. He was a good guy and told me that he would find a lawyer for me. He found a bad lawyer who was originally from Pakistan. She came to visit me one time in the jail and wrote down everything we talked about, but she did not have any experience. I think she had just finished college and that this was her first job and that I was her first client. I tried to contact another lawyer and asked him to make a motion to reopen the case and stop the deportation order. The entire time, I was waiting to hear back from the immigration court.

Finally, I received a letter from the INS saying that I had a redetermination hearing at the immigration court. There was a 1-800 number in the letter that I could call for additional information. By this time, I had heard about a lawyer from an Asian American legal organization that was helping people like me. I contacted her, and she said that she had heard about my case. She was a great lawyer, and she did not want anything for her help. When I talked to her, she said that she would be there in court. She told me not to worry and that she would contact my lawyer because she needed to talk to him before she could review my file. Since she was leaving for England, she asked the judge to postpone the hearing, and he gave me a new date for September 20. By this time, I had been in jail for almost a year. This was my last appointment in the immigration court.

My Pakistani lawyer came to the court on September 20, 2002, and this was the second time I saw her. She approached the judge, and they both talked together in very low voices. I could not understand what they said, but my lawyer told me that she had gotten a letter from someone that I had worked with in the past and that I had a clearance from the FBI. She also told me that I didn't have a criminal record and that she would ask for bail. I was sent back to the jail.

I could not understand what was going on. I tried to contact my lawyer again after that, but her telephone system would not accept collect calls. I called ACLU again, and they told me that they would contact my lawyer for me on Monday. It was Friday, September 20, 2002. They were closed on Saturday and Sunday.[10]

Getting Deported

On Monday, September 23, guards told me to pick up my stuff. "You are released," they said. Again, I was surprised.

"Am I being released in the United States?"

"Yes, you may be released in the U.S. We don't know what is going on in the court, but we will release you from this jail, and the INS will come and pick you up."

"But you said that I am being released?"

"Yes, released from here, but not from the INS. They will come and pick you up."

I just waited for the INS, and after they came, they collected my badge, my bag, and my other belongings and asked me, "Is this your shit?"

"Yes, this is my shit," I replied and asked them, "What is going on? Someone from the jail told me that I will be released."

"Yes, you are released and we are sending you to the airport."

"I have a pending case. I had a court date last Friday, two days ago. How could you make the travel documents, the ticket, the reservations so fast over the weekend?"

"We don't know. We are just told to do so."

"I am not going anywhere."

"No, we have to deport you today. You have a flight at 11:00." They took my check. Some people and organizations had sent me money to help me in the jail because I had a special case and had been there for 11 months. During that time, I tried to work as a leader for the Muslim people in the jail. I led the hunger strike, so a lot of people wanted to talk to me...

Mohamed breaks down and can't continue with the interview. We take another break. Mohamed drinks a little bit of water from the glass while I watch him and wait. A few minutes later, he is ready to talk.

The civil rights lawyer Steven Watt told me that Mohamed had signed the deportation papers at his last court hearing. It is unclear if Mohamed understood the significance of his signature or whether he was aware that he was signing his deportation papers. Perhaps he got tired of waiting in the jail and was thinking about another way to approach his case with the help of another lawyer. Perhaps he was not expecting such a fast turnaround for the preparation of his travel documents.

After the deportation officers left the jail, they did not want to cash the check because I had refused to sign the deportation orders. They told me that if I signed the deportation papers, they would cash my check, and they wanted to give me a hard time for not signing the papers. I refused to eat food all day from seven or eight in the morning till the flight at 11:00 at night. Finally I admitted that I was hungry.

"We will stop at the McDonald's on the way to the airport."

"I am hungry, I need some french fries."

"We'll buy you a hamburger."

"No, I can't eat that food. Please buy a fish sandwich or some french fries for me."

"We already bought the food. This is the only food that we have, and we don't buy french fries."

"Okay, give me some soda."

"You will get some food on the flight." There were two INS officers with me, one on the right and one on the left. I told them that I had a last request and wanted to contact my lawyer from the airport. They allowed me to make a phone call from the public booth, but I got her voice mail and left a message for her. "Please help me, I am at the airport. We have one hour before the flight. Please help me. When you hear this voice, please help me." I had tried to contact her many times before I left. I didn't have anyone's number except for hers. All the offices were closed, and there was no one else to call.

After I hung up, I just couldn't stand anymore. I felt that I didn't have any energy left inside me. The two INS officers or maybe they were the FBI had files with them. I didn't know what was in those files, but I recognized them as the old ones. I was scared because I know the Egyptian government. I was scared—really, really scared. I knew that whatever was in those files wouldn't be good for me. I felt that my heart was going to slow down or maybe stop, and I just couldn't stand up anymore. My legs felt as if they were going to collapse, and then I think I fainted.

After I regained consciousness, I found ten people standing around me. They told me to stand up, but when I tried, I fell on the floor again. Since I couldn't walk, they held me up and put me on the flight. The officers told the flight people that I was a bit tired and that I couldn't talk or walk at this time. I said I don't want to go home, and after that I didn't feel anything. I didn't have any voice left. I lost my concentration and my consciousness.

I was on a direct flight from New York to Cairo. There were no stops in transit, and if there were, I would've asked for asylum at the stop. In Egypt, we are under emergency law, which means that the government can put anyone in jail without reason. We are not a free country. There are a lot of things happening in the U.S., but it is still a free country, unlike Egypt. There are supposed to be no emergency laws in the U.S. In Egypt, you can be arrested just for staying at home. Under the emergency laws, you don't need to be charged with anything. They don't take you to a judge; they don't make any decisions. People just stay in the jail. On the flight home, I was scared that the Egyptian government would lock me up.

After I boarded the plane, I ate and slept, and after that I felt okay. I could feel my legs again. I could not do anything at the time, so I tried to sleep some more. On the plane, the deportation officers kept a close watch on me and followed me the whole time. Even when I went to the bathroom, they would stand outside the door and wait for me, one on each side.[11]

Arriving in Egypt

When the plane landed in the airport, both of the deportation officers came out with me and asked for the local police. When someone from the local police came, the deportation officers asked, "Do you speak English?"

They said, "Someone does." After the English-speaking person came, the deportation officers went with the Egyptian officials, handed them the old asylum files, and talked to them for a while. I was watching them from a distance. My heart was beating, and I was scared about what was going to happen to me.

The transferred files included a report titled "Significant Incident Report." This report established Mohamed's connection to Al-Jihad, an Egyptian organization convicted for the assassination of the Egyptian president Anwar Sadat in 1981. Mohamed had fabricated that connection to obtain a U.S. visa and withdrew the asylum application after his marriage to a U.S. citizen. Mohamed believes that law enforcement officers knew this but deliberately highlighted his false connection to Al-Jihad. The travel document reads:

> *Subject Mohamed E****** (A . . .) an Egyptian National is a crewmen that jumped ship. On 1/18/02 he withdrew his asylum & withholding claim before (Judge) I. J. Cabrera. A review of the file indicated that on his asylum application he admitted to being a member of the terrorist organization Al-Jihad (courier & recruiter) between 1996 and 1998.*[12]

The U.S. procedures for Asylum and Withholding of Removal establish the following confidentiality regulations in regard to disclosure to third parties:

Information contained in or pertaining to any asylum application, records pertaining to any credible fear determination conducted pursuant to §208.30, and records pertaining to any reasonable fear determination conducted pursuant to §208.31, shall not be disclosed without the written consent of the applicant, except as permitted by this section or at the discretion of the Attorney General.[13]

I assume that the U.S. government made an exception to its regulations for what they characterized as national security reasons.

Someone at the airport had a cell phone, and I borrowed it to call my brother. I told him that I was at the airport and tried to explain the situation to him.

"I'll be there, I'll give you a ride," he said.

"I feel bad. I feel I am not going to see the outside."

"Don't worry. You have not done anything wrong. You don't have any criminal records here or in the U.S. The worst thing is that you were illegal in the U.S., and you got deported for that. You did not do anything, and there is nothing wrong with that." We hung up after that, but I never got to see him.

Investigation and Detention

The Egyptian officials started to ask me about the reasons for my deportation. They told me that the Americans had told them that I was from Al-Jihad and that I had asked for political asylum. I told them that that was a lie. I tried to explain how my lawyer had made up the whole thing to get a visa for me, but they didn't believe me. After I talked to them for five or six hours at the airport, they sent me to another building in Nasar City.

This building is like a cemetery. They covered my eyes, handcuffed my hands in the back, and put me in a small room. I couldn't see anything, not even light. I don't know if this room had been darkened or if it just didn't have any windows or light. I was alone there and the door was locked. I couldn't hear anything either. The toilet was a small hole in the room.

My eyes remained covered, and hands were tied in the back. I couldn't see or feel anything. I didn't know how to see. When I sat, I wanted to sleep, except I didn't know how to sleep. I kept waiting. When I asked them anything, they cursed at me and hit me on my face and legs. I stopped asking. I started to cry because I didn't know what was going on or how long I would have to stay there. I'm not sure how long I stayed in that situation. Maybe three days.

During those three days, I didn't eat anything. Sometimes, they brought me some food, but it smelled bad and I didn't want to eat it. The bread was hard and old. They told me to eat it but I told them that I didn't want to. They cursed at me and I was scared, so I just took the food and put it on the floor. When they opened the door three days later, they found a lot of food on the floor.

"You did not eat for three days?" they asked.

"No."

"Why?"

"I don't want to eat."

"It is not your choice. You have to eat." Then they started to hit me.

"I can't eat this food. I am a vegetarian."

"You have to eat this food." Then they started to hit me again, and I don't know what happened after that because I lost consciousness. They sent me to the hospital, and that was the first time that I saw light. I saw the doctor and noticed a policeman standing with a gun next to my bed. I asked him what day it was, and he said Saturday. I started to calculate the days in my head. I came from the U.S. on Tuesday or Wednesday, so I'd spent three days in the jail. The doctor came and asked me, "Why you don't want to eat? Your blood is not circulating properly because you are not eating."

"I have a hard time eating this food. I am a vegetarian. I can't eat everything."

"You have to eat," he said as he put blood in my body. "You have lived outside the country for a long time, so you don't know what the Egyptian police do to people if they refuse to eat."

"Okay, but I can't eat just anything. My stomach does not allow it. I have been a vegetarian for a long time."

"I will talk to the police," he said. Then they started to give me special vegetarian food, like cucumber, beans, etc. The Egyptians felt that I might die, and that was the only reason they sent me to the hospital. After I recovered, they sent me back to the same building with the Egyptian police.

As soon as I got to the front gate, they blindfolded me so that I couldn't see anyone and handcuffed my hands in the back. I don't remember how long I stayed in that condition. I couldn't figure out how long I slept because I was constantly blindfolded. There was no way for me to find out what was going on around me. It was completely dark, and I couldn't see anything. I couldn't feel anything either. Half of the time I slept, and then I would wake up. From a distance, I heard people cry. Sometimes, I heard faint voices and water dripping. I realized that I was in a basement, somewhere underground. I began to question if I was dead or alive. I didn't know because I couldn't feel anything. I felt as if I was already dead. My hands, legs, eyes, and everything felt the same. Nobody talked to me.

After I stayed in that dead condition for a long time, the police started to talk to me. They removed the handcuffs and put chains on my hands, feet, neck, my entire body. They asked me my name, where I'd been, my family relationships, my marital status, everything about my life. I didn't know how many people were asking me questions because I was still blindfolded. Only one person talked to me at a time. Then they told me to take a break. I don't know how long the break was. I was exhausted because every part of my body was chained up, and I fell asleep. Then they called my name again and I woke up. They asked me how long I had stayed in jail in the U.S. and the reason for my deportation. Then they started questioning me about Al-Jihad and my relationship to it. I told them that I had no relationship with them. They asked me about my asylum application. I explained that I put it on the application to get a U.S. visa.

Then the torture began. They started with electric shocks to my hands, legs, and my private parts. They put something on my head, which made the electric shock go directly to my head. It was so strong that I couldn't take it and I fell down. When they were giving me the electric shocks, I felt as if the angel of death was going to come and ask me what I'd done in my life. I did not feel alive. Then they sent me to a hospital again, and after I came back, they stopped giving me electric shocks. Instead, they hit me on my head and on my legs. They hit me with an electric thing on my leg and deliberately pushed my leg so that the joint broke. After that, they sent me to the hospital again, but this hospital was inside the jail. Last time, when I was in the outside hospital, I tried to complain to the doctor about the police.

Eventually they stopped the electric shocks with me because they began to notice that I could withstand them. I think I could take the electric shocks over seven, eight, or ten times. They continued for hours and hours. Every time they brought me in for questioning and torture, I wished that I was dead. With electric shocks, you can't feel anything in your body. I was hand-cuffed and my legs were tied. They would come to my cell and call my name. I wished that they were calling for someone else. I was so scared every time and hoped that my heart would stop before I go. I tried to make it stop in any way possible. I didn't eat anything because I just wanted to die. I wanted to kill myself, but I could not. They would return me to my cell and tie my hands in the back and also tie my legs. I could not do anything. Then they would bring me back and start all over again. They would give me shocks, take a rest, and then start all over again. I don't know how long this lasted, but it was extremely long. I told them over and over that I had not done anything, that I was just a normal person, that I wasn't interested in politics, and that I didn't know anyone.

One day, they told me that I would go to the jail and that really scared me. Because this place was already so bad, I wondered how much worse the jail would be. I asked them what the jail was like. The jail had strong security, which means that it is so secure that you can't see the sun. They don't torture you there, but you just stay in an underground cell.

When I went to the second jail, I asked the people what the date was. They told me, and I figured out that I had spent 20 days in the first investigation jail. It felt more like 20 years. I never knew the time in jail, and every day felt like a year. I reconfirmed the date with the warden. He told me that he knew my situation and that some people stay in that emergency situation for 8, 15, or even 20 years. I felt lucky that I was out so soon.

The jail was better. The food was still bad, but it was better than the emergency jail. Anything was better than the electric shocks. No more hard time, no more questions, just being held in a jail.

My family tried to help me a lot. There are people who have suffered more torture in the jails than I have. They take off nails from fingers and toes and cut off private parts. They can do anything and everything. They were telling me that they would take my nails off, too, but I think they were only trying to scare me. I think they stopped torturing me because they believed what I said or maybe because my health was not good and I lost a lot of weight. I think the doctor might've told them that I could die because I had not been eating for the last 20 days. I did not eat anything except for cauliflower. Only when they let me rest a lot did I eat. I would eat something vegetarian like cucumber or fruit. When I was alone, I wouldn't eat anything.

The last time that I was in the hospital, I complained to the doctor that I'd lost a lot of weight because of the electric shocks. When I came from the U.S., I was about 230 pounds and was overweight. But in the Egyptian prison, I lost a lot of weight because of the torture and because I could not eat anything. The 20 days I spent in the Egyptian jail were worse than the entire 14 months I spent in the U.S. jail.

In the U.S. jail, the INS officers would sometimes put the handcuffs on too tight, which would cut off the circulation in my hands. Two or three fingers of my hand still don't work, and my hand still feels numb because the blood doesn't circulate so well. When I go to the hospital now, I do some exercises for my hand. Sometimes, my hand shakes and I can't hold anything, not even a cup. I am still on medications and have to go to doctors and hospitals on a regular basis. There are too many doctors and too many medical therapies. I try to stay around the people who can understand me.

Here is an e-mail from Mohamed's mother, Swsan Mohamed, which Adem Carroll forwarded to me. She expressed her pain and her determination to find her son.

*We know that Mohamed E****** is detained in Tora jail after long time of investigations (3 weeks) and mistreatment from Egyptian authorities. I have contact with the head of the Egyptian human right organization Mr/Hafaz AbouSeda and he promised me to help Mohamed. I gave him your E-mail.... Please try to mail Mr. Hafaz to encourage him to work hard with Mohamed case and I think also as much* *liberties and human right organizations can mail him to encourage him and support him if he needed.*[14]

When I was inside the Egyptian jail, I tried to ask the people around me to contact my family. They got my brother's phone number and contacted him. My brother is a major in the Egyptian military and has a lot of friends in high positions. It was because of him that they put me in a better jail. Even though I could not go outside or have visitors, this was a better jail than the emergency jail. Later I found out that I was moved very quickly from the emergency jail to the better jail because I had family and they called everyone they could to help me. I've heard about cases where people stay in the emergency jail for over ten years. It depends on who you know. If my brother was a big politician, I wouldn't even have been tortured.[15]

The Final Release

My brother contacted tons of people, found out where I was, and used his influence to get me transferred to a better jail. Even though he knew where I was, he wasn't allowed to see me. He contacted human rights groups in Egypt, like Amnesty International, and they contacted human rights groups in the U.S. and other people in high positions. Because of this publicity, a lot of people in the media were writing about me. My brother tried to gather all my immigration papers and contacted lawyers in the U.S. who could explain to the Egyptian government that I had been deported because of immigration violations, not because of my connection to Al-Jihad. Even after all this effort, I had to stay in the jail till February or I don't remember, maybe it was January.

I don't remember a lot of things. I have lost my concentration. Maybe they did transfer me from the torture jail to the other jail in January. After they realized that I don't have any relationship to Al-Jihad, they let me go. During my imprisonment, they wanted to make sure that I don't have any connection with anyone. I had visited many countries so they had to check with the U.S. and Egyptian governments.

Now I am too scared to even go and pray in the mosque here in Egypt. If I have to pray, I just pray at home because I'm afraid they might arrest me if they see me at the mosque. After they released me, I had a medical examination. The doctor told me that everything would be all right. I hope that everything will be all right, but the doctor said, "You can't marry anymore because you've taken some electric shocks in your private places." He added that sometimes things get better and that it is not necessarily permanent. He told me that if I rested for a long time, I might be able to go back to living a normal life, but he is not sure. The doctor told me that if I get married, I should tell him.

I am okay now. I can walk and do things for myself. Before this, my family had to help me with everything. I could not even drink a cup of water. Now, I can go to the bathroom alone. Before, someone had to hold me while I used the bathroom. Now I walk a little. I am talking to you. I am almost normal. I am hoping that after I finish my therapy and take a rest, I will be normal like everyone else. I hope to have a family someday. I hope to find another wife and to have kids. But I don't know. Maybe this is a test from God and I have to just pass it. Sometimes, I wonder why I had such a hard time migrating. There are so many people who leave the country, and they don't have problems.

Sometimes, I forget my name. I lose my concentration, and I can't remember my name. I don't even know what language I speak. Is it English, French, Spanish, or just Arabic? You may not believe what I am saying, but sometimes I feel that I don't live in this land or this world. I can't explain it to you. Sometimes, I feel that I am dying, as if I am in a cemetery. I remember something else. I remember a life when things were different. Now I don't remember anything. I forgot all of my friends, my family. I always think about myself. Where am I? Where am I living? Am I alive or dead? Maybe I am dying now? Maybe I am still alive? I really don't know. Believe me, I don't know if I am dead or alive. Let me finish the story now. I will tell you another story later.

Life Today: In July 2003, Mohamed escaped to Switzerland, where he currently lives as a political asylee. He is happily married to a Muslim Swiss citizen with a two-year-old son, Tarique, and a newborn daughter, Nura. He is still undergoing medical treatment and can't hold a steady job because of back problems. His health has improved over the years, and now he can sleep without medications. He hopes to recover and establish his life in Switzerland.

Mohamed has talked about his case at several conferences and is interested in publishing his story in detail; however, he fears persecution from the American and Egyptian governments—especially since he heard that in February 2003 CIA agents arrested Hassan Mustafa Osama Nasr, an Egyptian who had sought asylum in Italy. The CIA agents arrested Hassan in daylight in Milan, flew him to Germany, and eventually handed him over to Egyptian authorities. Hassan was kept in an Egyptian prison for years and allegedly tortured. In November 2009, an Italian judge convicted 22 CIA agents, one U.S. Air Force colonel, and two Italian secret agents for the 2003 kidnapping of Hassan.[16]

Hassan's and Mohamed's cases are not exceptions. Since 9/11, there have been several other well-documented cases in which the U.S. government extradited individuals of Muslim origin without substantial evidence and transferred them to countries notorious for torture.[17] *The Human Rights Watch report titled "List of 'Ghost Prisoners' Possibly in CIA Custody" provides a list of 26 individuals arrested worldwide and kept in undisclosed locations and prisons.*[18] *For additional discussion about the larger global and transnational impacts of 9/11 detentions, see the conclusion.*

Mohamed's experience attests to the fact that both the Egyptian and American governments collaborated and shared erroneous intelligence, which had far-reaching and negative impacts on Mohamed's life. Through Mohamed's narrative, I want to reveal the human cost of sharing erroneous intelligence between two states and more specifically the impact of torture.

Figure 6 Yasser Ebrahim, Egypt, 2008. Photograph by Irum Shiekh.

CHAPTER 6

Reclaiming Our Civil Rights and Liberties

Yasser Ebrahim

Yasser Ebrahim and his younger brother, Hany Ibrahim,[1] *two young men from Egypt, were living in a two-bedroom apartment in Brooklyn, New York, on September 11. They shared the apartment with two Egyptian friends, Ahmed Khalif and Walid,*[2] *who were also from Alexandria. Shortly after September 11, a young man from Morocco who had a valid green card also moved in with them. Their lives were good and resembled their lives in Egypt in some ways. They cooked Egyptian rice, grilled kabobs, and ate together. Jokes and laughter continued late into the night, and this carefree lifestyle inspired Yasser to stay. Yasser's visiting visa had expired, and initially his undocumented status had bothered him. However, after noticing that New York was swarming with undocumented immigrants, Yasser slowly forgot about it. During his stay, Yasser never experienced any problems with immigration officials until after 9/11.*

A week after September 11, Yasser's mother called to inquire if he was doing okay. She had heard on the news that people were getting arrested and wanted to know whether Yasser and his friends had been affected by the sweeps. Yasser told his mother, "Nothing is happening and nothing will happen to us. Mother, this is America, and in this country they just don't arrest people without a crime, without a charge. I will be fine."

A few weeks later, on September 30, 2001, all the men in the apartment except for the young Moroccan man were arrested and taken to the Metropolitan Detention Center in New York, where they were kept in solitary confinement for several months. Months later, all were deported to Egypt on minor immigration charges.

Meeting Yasser

In April 2003, I met Yasser in Alexandria, Egypt, in a crowded coffee shop. Ramy Ahmed,[3] another former 9/11 detainee and Yasser's MDC cellmate, accompanied him. Hany, Yasser's brother, briefly stopped by during the interview.

This coffee shop, a popular spot among the locals, is located in the center of Alexandria. While listening to the recorded interview, I was struck by the sounds of the bustling crowd in the background. Initially, I recorded Yasser and Ramy together. However, after an hour, when I noticed that Yasser was more comfortable talking to me, I expressed my interest in doing solo interviews with Yasser. At that time, Ramy left the coffee shop after agreeing to meet me the next day for his interview. I continued my interview with Yasser that evening, and his interview proved to be deeper and more reflective after Ramy left.

The central location of the coffee shop, Ramy's presence, and Hany's appearance during the interview were all meant to ensure Yasser's safety. Yasser did not know me personally, and he wanted to make sure that I did not work for the FBI or any other intelligence organization. He confessed this fear during the interview. He had been called in by the local Egyptian intelligence organization just a few months before for investigation, and he believed that the American government had asked Egyptian intelligence to do so. Despite this ongoing questioning, Yasser had come to see me and talked with me at length. After I returned to the United States, he sent me a written account of his arrest and detention. The following narrative is based on that recorded interview, his written account,[4] a review of his legal file,[5] conversations with his attorney (Rachel Meeropol at the Center for Constitutional Rights), and newspaper articles.[6] Yasser and Rachel reviewed the final story before its publication. Both of them had minor comments, which I incorporated into the narrative.

I also interviewed Yasser's roommates Ahmed and Walid separately, and they corroborated Yasser's story.[7] Ramy,[8] Yasser's cellmate, also confirmed his story in a separate interview. I decided to concentrate on Yasser's narrative because he was an identified plaintiff in Turkmen v. Ashcroft,[9] which is a class-action civil rights lawsuit filed by the Center for Constitutional Rights on behalf of Muslim, South Asian, and Arab immigrants who faced lengthy and abusive detentions after 9/11. Yasser decided to join the lawsuit against the then attorney general John Ashcroft, the FBI director Robert Mueller, the former INS commissioner James Ziglar, and employees of the MDC, where he was at the mercy of those same officials.[10] This narrative attests to the courage of Yasser and many other individuals like him who were kept on the ninth floor of the MDC. It highlights their spirit of resistance. The powerful government machine could not convince them even in the most difficult circumstances that they were "illegal" and therefore should forget about their legal, constitutional, and human rights.

The Arrest

It was late morning on September 30, 2001. Yasser was contemplating his plans for the day and was still in the house with his housemates when about 20 FBI agents entered the apartment.

They were heavily armed, carrying shotguns, and wearing bulletproof vests and helmets. From their appearance, it seemed like they were going to war instead of picking up a few guys with immigration violations. The FBI agents treated us harshly. They demanded to see our passports and searched our apartment, even though they did not have a search warrant. They went through our drawers, papers, and passports. They did not even read us our rights or allow us to make a phone call.

The FBI officers arrested Yasser, Hany, Ahmed, and Walid. The young man from Morocco with a green card was not arrested. From a national security perspective, immigration status should not preclude someone from being associated with terrorism.

When the FBI/immigration officials were arresting us in our apartment, I told them that there was no need to handcuff us because we only had immigration violations. We were not criminals, and I did not want my neighbors to see us in handcuffs because I could not predict their reactions after September 11. The FBI insisted on handcuffing us.

"We can cover your faces if you want," they said.

"That would be worse," I replied.

When we went down to the street, half of the building's residents were standing outside, watching us get arrested by the FBI. It seemed like the officers were making a scene and terrorizing us on purpose. Maybe they were taking revenge on us for some reason.[11]

From the apartment, the FBI agents took them to the Varick Street police station. They spent the night there, and some FBI agents interviewed them the next morning. This interview became the basis for their classification as "High Special Interest Cases" and for their detention on the ninth floor of the MDC. After the interview, all four of them were transported to the MDC.

Reception at the MDC

When Ahmed, Walid, my brother, and I entered the MDC, a reception squad met us. They dragged everyone by the handcuffs; the dragging was very painful and bruised our hands. They also smashed our bodies against the walls.

"Do not open your mouths. Do not do anything," they threatened. I witnessed how harshly they treated Ahmed and Walid. When it was my brother's turn to come out of the van, I had to shut my eyes because I did not want to see him being treated like that.

I was still very confused. I had nothing to do with the attacks at the World Trade Center, and I could not imagine that they would arrest innocent people in the U.S. because of religion, color, or ethnic background. I was very shocked at everything. Then they took us inside, and it got worse. They tried to slam us against every wall and metal door that we passed. I felt it was my turn to face my fate as a Muslim in the U.S.

After I entered the MDC, everything changed because I started to witness other things that I never imagined could happen in the United States. The MDC staff was very unprofessional. They should have treated the detainees better. I am not suggesting that they should have treated us like guests, but until the law enforcement officers determined our crime, the guards should have stayed neutral. Instead, their attitude reflected a desire to take revenge on us for the deaths of 3,000 Americans at the WTC. They thought it would be heroic to abuse us for our supposed involvement in the 9/11 attacks.

At the entrance, they did a medical examination. One doctor discovered that I had sharp eyesight and asked loudly in front of the prison guards, "Did you ever think about flying?"

For a few minutes, I could not open my mouth. The doctor was trying to be funny while my life was falling apart.

I thought, "Just because I have 20/20 vision, I'm responsible for 9/11?" Then they strip-searched us. While doing this, one of the officers asked, "What is your crime?"

"Nothing. I just overstayed my visa."

"Oh, I don't think so."

"I don't know what you mean."

"If you are here it means that someone somewhere thinks that you are connected to September 11th."

It was very weird for me to hear that because it was so off the mark. The guards treated us like dangerous terrorists. They didn't have any clue about our case and were scared of us. When we told them that our only crime was violating immigration laws, they didn't believe us. Every time the guards took someone out of a cell, four guards and one lieutenant had to be present. They were that terrified. There was a small slot located on the lower third part of the cell door. The guards wouldn't open it until the lieutenant was present. What if they opened it? What if they left it open? What could we possibly have done?

FBI Investigation

On October 15, FBI agents came to talk to me. This was the first and last time that I saw FBI agents at the MDC. Up until then, I had just been sitting there without a clue about what was going on. The FBI guys were very nice, and they promised me that I'd be sent back to Egypt very soon. The agent also told me to sign a paper, which said that I was willing to talk and to waive my rights to see a lawyer.

From our initial conversations, they gave me the impression that if I talked to them, I would be out very soon. On the other hand, if I waited for the lawyer, it meant waiting in the cell for two or three more weeks. I had already spent two weeks in the cell, which had been terrible because I didn't know what was going on. When they came to talk to me, it was the first time since my arrest that I had the chance to talk to someone, and I was desperate enough to do anything to get out of the cell. There was no opportunity in the near future to talk to anyone from the outside, such as a lawyer or someone from the Egyptian embassy. The guards in the jail had told me that I could not contact the outside world. I asked to talk to the embassy, and the jail administration refused. I asked to talk to a human rights activist, and they refused that too. I knew talking to a lawyer was unrealistic. At that point, I couldn't bear to wait indefinitely for the lawyer and decided to talk to the FBI. During the investigation, the FBI agents showed me photos of September 11 suspects.

> "Do you know them?" they asked.
> "No," I replied. "I've only seen them in the newspaper or on television."
> "Do you pray in any mosques?" At that time I didn't pray, so I replied no.
> "Do you know or have you heard anything suspicious in the Egyptian or Muslim communities in Brooklyn?" Again, I replied no.
> "Do you have any knowledge about flying? Have you transferred money back and forth from the U.S. to Egypt?" The questions went on and on, and I kept saying no.
> At the end, they said, "If you know anything, tell us. We will help you."

Yasser is implying that FBI agents offered him a "snitch visa." FBI agents made a similar offer to Ramy, one of Yasser's cellmates, to wear a wire, sit in a coffee shop, and talk to people. If he identified anyone suspicious, they promised to drop charges and help him stay in the United States. In the beginning, Ramy thought about doing it because he was ready to do anything to get out of the situation. But later, when his lawyer explained that it was not going to be as easy as wearing a wire and talking to people in coffee shops, he became afraid and refused. After he refused, FBI agents started treating him differently, as if he had become an enemy.[12]

During my investigation, one of the FBI agents told me, "You are smart, you express yourself well, you are highly educated, and you have a political perspective."

"What is wrong in having all these things?" I asked. I think he was telling me that these characteristics matched the profile of the hijackers. This was so funny to me. They were so sure about me that I started thinking that maybe I *do* know something. Maybe if I thought about it hard enough, I would remember.

Later, I realized they were asking me the same scripted questions that they asked everyone.

"What is going on?" I asked them. "I am here for an immigration violation. Why is the FBI investigating me? What is the reason? How and why did the FBI become suspicious of me?"

"We can't tell you anything. If you don't have anything as you say and if your only crime is violating immigration laws, then you will be going home soon."

This was October 15, 2001. I stayed on the ninth floor until June 2002. They were all telling lies.

From their investigation, I felt that these people didn't know what they were doing. I told the FBI agent that if everyone else on the ninth floor was like my roommates, my brother, and I, then their only crime was violating immigration laws and that the agents were completely on the wrong track. I did not have a flying license, but even if I had one it did not necessarily mean that I was a terrorist.

This was not a real investigation. It was racial profiling. The arrests of my roommates, my brother, and I meant that every adult Muslim male was considered suspicious and subject to arrest. I remember that one of the guys on the ninth floor was arrested because he had a flight simulator game.

"Why do you have a flight simulator game?" an FBI agent had asked him.

"Go and ask Microsoft," he responded.

The FBI investigation was so absurd. One day, I was in the recreation area and I met Azmath Mohammed. He told me that the FBI agents had made a fake pilot license for him as evidence. Whenever I heard stories like this, I wondered about the FBI's behavior. In other words, the FBI agents knew that this guy did not have anything to do with the attacks, so why did they make a fake license? Were they looking for suspects or scapegoats? Why was the FBI wasting its money and efforts on people that they knew were innocent? Why not spend the same money and time to find the people who were really responsible?

I felt that the FBI agents who interviewed me could have been more skilled in asking the right questions. Instead, they asked me some routine questions. Sometimes, I felt that our Egyptian intelligence was better than the FBI and that the Americans could use some training from the Egyptians. FBI officials should send their agents to live in Egypt for a year or two. One thing was clear: if the U.S. government really wanted to investigate and successfully identify the hijackers, then they needed FBI agents who were knowledgeable about Muslims and Arabs. The agents who investigated me didn't know anything, even though it was their job to know. They needed better training.

Immigration Hearing

I went back to the cell and just waited and waited until I saw an immigration judge on November 6.[13] I was arrested on September 30, and I stayed in jail for two months before I saw a judge. This is a direct violation of immigration law because I should have seen a judge three days after my arrest. Whenever I complained, the guards told me, "Forget about these laws. Everything has changed. Things are not the same anymore." When another guy asked to see someone from a human rights organization to document the human rights violations we were experiencing, the jail counselor replied, "Forget about human rights. Three thousand people died in the World Trade Center. There is no such thing as human rights."

"We feel sorry for the deaths of the 3,000 people," the guy said. "But what does it have to do with us? Why are you taking revenge on us?" They did not care.

The immigration court hearing was on the second floor of the MDC, and I noticed that the judge seemed to be scared of something. I was predicting that because this was my first immigration violation, I would probably get bail. Even though I was assigned a legal aide, it was the wrong time to have an immigration violation in the United States. The jail administration had told the judge that I was too dangerous to be out of jail. Appearing in front of him in chains and shackles and with four or five guards didn't help my image. In this situation, how could anyone convince the judge to let me out on bail?

The Office of the Inspector General's report reveals the unwritten governmental policy of "hold until cleared" that prohibited bonds for September 11 detainees:

> *Officials from the FBI and the INS told the OIG they clearly understood from the earliest days after the terrorist attacks that the Department wanted September 11 detainees held without bond until the FBI cleared them of any connections to terrorism. This "hold until cleared" policy was not memorialized in writing, and our review could not determine the exact origins of the policy. However, this policy*

was clearly communicated to INS and FBI officials in the field, who understood and applied the policy.... In addition, an attorney with the FBI's Office of General Counsel who worked on the SIOC [...][Strategic Information and Operations Center] Working Group told the OIG that it was understood that the INS was holding September 11 detainees because the Deputy Attorney General's Office and the Criminal Division wanted them held. She said the Deputy Attorney General's Office took a "very aggressive stand" on this matter, and the Department's policy was clear even though it was not written.[14]

At the end of the November 6 hearing, Yasser tried to inform the judge about the abuse, but the judge stopped him by saying that he was not responsible for the detention center. The immigration trial transcripts include the following conversation between the judge and Yasser:

> **Ebrahim:** *Sir, one of the guards was bringing me here... he was pushing me to the walls. And he was saying "if it wasn't for the camera I would have smashed your face. You bla bla bla" and bad words.*
>
> **Judge:** *Okay, stop and let me explain. I don't run this detention center and there is not much I can do about that. So you have an attorney, if you think there is a complaint that you should make, Ms. Yeng can make the complaint for you. I don't work here, I work in Manhattan and I don't run this building or supervise these officers. You understand? Telling me this isn't adding anything to your case... —*
>
> *There was some muddled speaking between Ms. Yeng and the Judge.*
>
> **Judge:** *Excuse me Ms. Yeng, I disagree. I think there is a misunderstanding. The purpose of this record is for me to make decisions about things I have authority to make decisions about. If you have something to complain about I would encourage you to make the complaint to someone who has the authority to deal with it. As I have explained to your client, I don't. It doesn't actually belong in this record. Okay?*[15]

In the courtroom, a woman was talking with the prosecutor and the judge before the hearing. When they started taping the hearing, she became quiet. Whenever I spoke during the hearing, she would write notes on a piece of paper and would pass them to the immigration prosecutor and the judge. Who was that lady and what was she writing? I don't know.

I told the judge that I knew I'd violated immigration laws but that I had been locked up in solitary confinement for over two months in a maximum-security jail. I should've been in an immigration jail. I pleaded for him to move me to another jail or to let me out because if there were anything suspicious about me, the FBI would've found out by now. I told him to charge me with something or to deport me back to Egypt. The judge looked really uncomfortable during the hearing as if someone was watching over him. He wouldn't even look at me, not even when he was asking me questions. He occupied himself with writing down things instead. I could have explained my situation, but he was not listening, and I could tell his mind was already made up.

"We are waiting for a document. We need to show it to you," the prosecutor said.

"What is this document?" the judge asked.

"It is the FBI clearance, but the guy who is responsible for preparing this document is out of the office on a funeral leave." The judge postponed the hearing for another two weeks to wait for the document. I went back to my cell knowing that I was going to stay there for another two weeks. I felt like I'd rather be shot dead than wait in the cell.

Everyone on the ninth floor was waiting for this FBI clearance. We heard about it but we never knew what it was. It was ridiculous. How long was it going to take to get clearance for a guy like me? What would've happened if they had arrested Osama bin Ladin? How long would it take to investigate him?

In the next hearing two weeks later, the judge denied my bail due to a disappearance risk. Meanwhile, they had assigned me a new lawyer. My first lawyer, Ms. Yeng, was from a legal aid organization. She was very good and cooperative and felt really sorry for my brother and me. She had tried to talk to the judge, but he wouldn't listen. In the second hearing, my new lawyer advised me to ask for deportation because the situation was so bad. "Nobody is going to be released from the MDC in the U.S. Deportation is the fastest way to get out of this mess," he said. I took his advice.

> "If I accept the deportation order, how long it will take for me to go home?" I
> asked the judge.
> "Two weeks to 45 days."
> "So the maximum amount of time I'm going to stay is 45 days?"

He said yes, and I accepted the deportation order on November 20. However, I stayed on the ninth floor for eight more months, which is over five times longer than the maximum amount of time that I was supposed to stay. I don't know why. Some guards told me that I needed to be kept in maximum security because I didn't have the FBI clearance, regardless of the volunteer deportation. The strange thing is that they moved my brother to the general population unit in January 2002 after he got his clearance, but he stayed there for an additional four months until April. If he was cleared, then why did they keep him downstairs for an additional four months? They should've deported him. Someone mentioned that we were kept on the ninth floor for our safety . . . that's bullshit. If they were so concerned about safety, why did they send my brother downstairs and keep me on the ninth floor? It does not make any sense. Maybe they were more suspicious of me and wanted to pressure me into talking.[16]

Looking back, it seems like it was a very manipulative move. They were trying to pressure me into giving them any information that I had, into cooperating with them. But this is all speculation. I will never know the truth about why they did things the way that they did.

Incarceration on the Ninth Floor

I constantly asked myself why I was placed in the MDC. I am still asking this question. Was it a random decision? I don't know. Maybe the FBI agent who arrested me decided that I should be placed in the MDC. I don't know. Maybe I will never know.

In the beginning, they put my brother and me in different cells even though I begged them to put us in the same cell. Eventually, on November 3, they placed him in my cell.

Even though Yasser was primarily in solitary confinement, he had roommates during certain periods of his detention. Jail administration used the privilege of having roommates and company as another way to abuse detainees. For example, guards might bring in an inmate, allow the detainee to get accustomed to having company, and then suddenly move the roommate to another cell.

Up until then, I did not know where he was and what was going on with him. I was so worried about him.

On the ninth floor, we passed our time praying and reading the Koran like everyone else. Thank God that we had the Koran; we could have not survived this experience otherwise. I am a better person now. I started to pray and read Koran because of this experience, and I became closer to God. Later we got other books and spent our time reading and singing. We had to keep ourselves sane or we would've gone crazy and died. Everyone on the ninth floor was trying to stay lighthearted and to help others.

We went on a hunger strike over five times. We put on the first hunger strike to protest the fact that we didn't have any access to our lawyers. We coordinated it by talking through the doors. They didn't care. They said, "Listen, if you don't want to eat, don't eat. We don't care." The longest hunger strike I did was 72 hours, almost three days. I stopped because I was hungry. During the hunger strike, they told us, "Get off the strike and we will see what we can do." We listened to them many times and nothing happened, so we stopped trusting them.

Once, my cellmate was on a hunger strike, and I'd lost my appetite that day because they'd taken my brother downstairs and I was worried about him. I was still accepting food, so I gave my tray to Ramy. He ate, and I stood in front of the camera so that they couldn't see him eating.

Once the guards took away one of the detainees who was on a hunger strike. A few minutes later, we heard him screaming. We did not know what was going on and we thought that the guards were torturing him. When he came back, we asked him what happened through the doors. He said that the guards had forced a tube down his throat and then stuffed food into his stomach through the tube. It was painful. The guards warned, "This is what is going to happen to anyone who goes on a hunger strike."

An Iraqi guy, a refugee, was seeking asylum in the U.S. He tied a towel to the bed and tried to hang himself with it. He survived because the towel got loose from the bed and he fell down. Otherwise, he could've died. Later, they put him in a different cell.

This Iraqi man had come to the United States before September 11. After the attacks, immigration officials put him on the ninth floor. Many other individuals whom I interviewed told me about this attempted suicide case.

Everyone thought about suicide at least once. I told the psychiatrist about it, and she replied, "If you ever think about this thought, tell the guards to tell me." However, I never tried to commit suicide because it is against my religion. The guards were making extra money because of the overtime, and they openly admitted to us that they were happy to make this money. I remember asking one of the guards on Christmas, "Don't you feel bad about working on Christmas Day?"

"I don't give a damn," he replied. "I care about the money, and I am making good money." In the beginning, the jail administration divided the day into two 12-hour shifts. One group of guards watched over us from eight in the morning to eight at night and the second group worked from eight at night to eight in the morning. The 12-hour shifts allowed them to make lots of money.

Then, later when they went back to their normal eight-hour shifts, it seemed that they were feeling bad and wishing that something would happen again so that they could make tons of money with overtime. Not all the guards were selfish, however, and some of them felt sorry for us. Some even became a bit friendly and started talking to us. After working for eight months on the ninth floor, one of them said, "You know when the jail administration told me that I was going to be working on the ninth floor with the WTC suspects, I was very scared. But later, I found out that you were nothing. You were just in the wrong place at the wrong time." This guard was three times my size, and at that time I was skinnier than I am right now. He was scared of me because of the wrong information he had received about me. However, he only admitted that eight months after I met him. By that time, it was too late. I was about to leave.

Although the guards could be abusive, the person most at fault is the one who put us in the MDC instead of an immigration jail. These guards thought that we were responsible for the attacks on the World Trade Center. How else did the administration expect the guards to treat us? If the administration would have told the guards that we were immigration law violators and not terrorists, I believe that they would have behaved more professionally.

During those eight months of detention, the hardest thing to deal with was the anxiety and despair of not knowing when I was going to be released. Everyone around me was giving me the impression that I was never going to leave this place.

We were not allowed to contact anyone in the outside world. Even if we had been allowed, I could not have called anyone because I did not have any money in my account. When they arrested me, I had over $200 in my pocket. I kept asking them about my money, and they should have put that money in my account, but they never did.

Every week, guards came around with a sheet of paper, which listed items that we could buy from the commissary if we had money in our account. One night, my cellmate Ramy and I were very upset because they had moved my brother to the general population unit and I didn't know what was going to happen to him. Prison guards came around with the commissary sheet. I said to Ramy, "We don't have any money but let's order everything we can. What the hell?" We didn't have access to all the items listed on the sheet because we were on the ninth floor. The only items we could get were things like cookies and chocolate. For each item, we marked the maximum amount allowed.

The next day, we were sitting in the cell, and they started pushing the things we'd ordered through the slot in the bottom of the door. We got the maximum amount of everything we'd ordered. We were going crazy. We never thought that we'd actually get all those things. Later, I found out that Ramy's friend had put money in his account but that the guards neglected to tell him about it. They should have told him when it happened so that he could've bought some food. The guards did this on purpose. They took every opportunity to bring us down. They thought that if he knew about the money, he would buy some chocolate and find a little bit of happiness. They did not want to allow that. This was just another example of the violation of his rights.

Once, Mohammad Maddy[17] bought a small radio, and he was ecstatic. After a week or so, they took it away from him and told him that he would get it at the time of his deportation. They did not want him to know what was going on in the outside world.

Medical Problems

Ramy had a broken finger at the time of his arrest, and a guard purposely twisted his finger to torture him. I saw it happen through the cell door and complained to the jail authorities. They asked me to testify, and I wrote and signed a verification statement. Nothing came out of it. Ramy could not even make a fist. He needed physical therapy, but he didn't receive it because he was on the ninth floor.[18] No matter what kind of pain we were having, or how severe it was, all the jail doctors did was give us a Tylenol. I developed a kidney stone because we weren't allowed to have cups, not even plastic ones, and I had to sip water from the tap in the cell. I couldn't drink enough water this way, and living thirsty for eight months affected my kidneys.

I began having sharp pains in my stomach, and I told the doctor in March or April that I had never suffered anything like this before. The pain was so sharp that I was crying. I was told that I would be taken out for a urine test, but the doctor waited two weeks to do it. It could have been done in one second, but I was given a Tylenol instead and told to drink 12 cups of water a day.

"How can I drink 12 cups a day when I don't have a cup?" I asked.

"Why don't you have a cup?"

"The guards refused to give me a cup."

"Oh, I will talk to them." Then the doctor forgot about it. Two weeks after my complaint, I was taken out for the urine sample. I was wearing my chains and shackles, and four or five guards escorted me. Ten days after that, the doctor came back and told me that I'd been right about the kidney stone because there were traces of blood in my urine. Then the doctor took me downstairs and took x-rays and told me that I definitely had a kidney stone, but I was not given any treatment for it. I was furious. If I was going to die from kidney failure, let me at least die in my own country. Let me go to Egypt and get some treatment.

Harassment During Deportation

I landed in Cairo, which is about 240 kilometers away from my home, without a dollar in my pocket. I had to borrow money from the people in the airport to buy a ticket for Alexandria. I had $200 when I was arrested in September 2001, and at deportation time, when I asked the officers about it, they said that they didn't know anything about it. One said, "You should have asked the jail administration when you were being processed for deportation." It was my mistake that I did not ask.

My pant size is 32, but they gave me size-42 pants and no belt. They also gave me a T-shirt that was too small and sneakers without shoelaces. I had to hold my pants like this [*gestures with his pants in his hand*] all the way to Egypt. The trip was extra long because they sent me to Greece first. Everyone who gets deported usually flies directly to Egypt, but they sent me to Greece, where I had an 11-hour layover. The authorities did not speak English and did not know what to do with me, so they put me in jail until my flight left for Cairo. They did this because of the WTC label on my file. To make things more complicated for me, U.S. officials sent a note about my detention first to Greece and then to Egypt.

In Egypt, the authorities held me overnight at the airport in a small detention room and questioned me about what happened and why. They let me go the next day. I know a lot of other guys who also experienced a lot of difficulties after they arrived in Cairo. The Egyptian authorities sent them to other governmental buildings, and they underwent further investigation there. Some people spent two or three days in detention, while others spent weeks going from one place to another. I was released the next day from the airport.

During the investigation, the Egyptian authorities asked me what happened and wrote a short report. A few months later, they summoned me again for investigation. Their main question was why the U.S. had detained me for eight and a half months if they didn't have anything against me. I couldn't answer that question. They also asked me about my detention conditions and wanted to know what the FBI had asked me.

Reclaiming Rights

In May 2002, while I was still at the MDC, a guard told me that a lawyer wanted to see me. I always thought that they might pin false charge on me, so I was really scared when I went to see the lawyer. The lawyer introduced himself as Mr. Bill Goodman from the Center for Constitutional Rights. He was working on a legal case against high-ranking government officials with regards to what was happening to inmates at the MDC. He indicated that my brother and I had strong cases because we had only immigration violations, and he wanted us to participate in the case. I refused at first because I was so scared. I didn't know what would happen to me after suing all those people. That was in May.

"I can't do it because I am scared. My brother is by himself downstairs, and I don't know what would happen to us if we joined the lawsuit," I told Mr. Goodman.

"Just think about it, and I will come back to you," he replied. That was the first time I had heard about the CCR. On May 29, I found out that my brother had gotten deported. I was so excited and happy to hear that he was safely home that I didn't care anymore about taking precautions. I decided to go through with the case. Things couldn't get worse anyway.

The next time Mr. Goodman came, I told him, "I agree to join your lawsuit. My brother has been deported, and I am here by myself."

"Okay. I am going to leave now and come back on Thursday at 2:00 p.m. after preparing the paperwork for your signature," he said.

On Thursday I got deported. The guards came at noon to take me to the airport, two hours before Mr. Goodman came and six hours before my flight. I think they were listening to our conversation and knew that it would be a troublesome case. We got to the airport four hours early because the MDC is only a half-hour drive from the airport. The INS didn't know what to do with me, so they killed time by going to 7-Eleven, buying fried chicken, etc.

"Why did you take me away from the prison if the flight is at 6:00 p.m.?"

"We didn't know about the traffic and we didn't want you to miss your flight," they said. I think it was all crap. They just wanted to get rid of me so that I wouldn't be able to participate in the lawsuit.

After I arrived in Egypt, I called Mr. Goodman and told him that I had been deported on Thursday.

"I came for you but they told me that you were deported."

"Yes, they deported me before you showed up."

"Write down your story in full and send it to me," he said. I prepared a small file and wrote down everything that had happened to me. In the jail, I couldn't tell him about everything because I was scared that the guards might be listening to our conversation. Mr. Goodman completed the paperwork with the e-mail I sent him and sent it to me for the signatures. I signed the documents and sent them back. That's it.

I am very happy that I am participating in this lawsuit. I don't know what will happen, but I am going to go through with the legal process. This is the only way to make them compensate deportees for what they have done. What else can I do? There is nothing else to do. I am respecting the law and seeing if the legal process will work. If I hadn't joined the lawsuit, I would've always felt bad about not standing up for my rights. I just couldn't live pretending that nothing had happened. It would have always tortured me inside. Even if nothing comes out of this lawsuit, I will be happy and satisfied with myself. My participation in this case is enough.

I read the arguments that the CCR prepared, and it said that three or four constitutional rights were violated. What is more authoritative than the constitution?

Eight months after I came back to Egypt, an internal investigation officer summoned me. He was very nice when I went and spoke to him, and he said, "The U.S. government has sent us a memo and asked us to check on the two brothers again." He wanted to know why they had singled out my brother and me. I told him about the lawsuit and said that maybe the U.S. government was trying to harass us because we were participating in the lawsuit. I don't know if the U.S. government has sent similar memos to the home countries of the other five individuals involved in the lawsuit. Memos like this can lead to torture in other places. It only depends on the range of freedom and the relationship of the particular country to America. Foreign officials may want to make America happy and so they may tell the U.S. government that they'll do whatever it takes to get the guy off the case. Here in Egypt, the officials had integrity and did not torture us. They just asked us a few questions.

Sharing with Family, Friends, and Others

My family found out a month or two after the arrest that my brother and I had been detained. They had been trying to reach us by calling our apartment and cell phones. I don't know how my mother felt exactly during our detention, but you can imagine how awful a mother must feel when she has two sons in jail in another country and she can't find out anything about them. After my brother moved to the general population unit in the MDC, he was able to call her, but I never got an opportunity to call her. The whole time, she was asking my brother about me. She wondered why I wasn't calling and where I was. It was a horrible experience for us, for our family, for our friends, and for everybody who knew us.

I don't know what people outside of my family think of our detention. Even if they have negative thoughts, they won't tell us to our faces. They will talk behind our backs instead. I don't know if people believe my story or not. For some people, the whole situation seems strange, especially in the United States. Let's assume that I'd lived in the United States before 9/11 without any difficulties and had come back to Egypt after a few years. If somebody came from the U.S. and told me a story like this, I wouldn't believe it based on my past experiences in the United States. I would think that he was lying, that he did have some connection to the attacks but that he was denying it. Of course, I did not tell everybody about my arrest. Some people were suspicious about my brother and me because we disappeared and then suddenly showed up eight months later in Egypt. I told my close relatives and friends because they knew me and wouldn't be suspicious.

I got married after I came back to Egypt. I told my wife, who I knew before the arrest, everything because I have nothing to be ashamed of. She had heard about my detention and felt very bad for me. We were supposed to get married in July of 2002 and do our honeymoon in the United States, but we did not get that opportunity. When I came back in June 2002, it was too difficult to get married a month later. I felt like someone had knocked me out, and I had to get back on my feet again before I could even think about marriage. It took me six months before I felt ready to get married. I got married in January 2003, and it has been two and a half months since I have been married. It is a new life with new commitments, and it has given me the desire to let go of the past. I have to move on in spite of what happened and think about my future because I have a wife now, and maybe one day I will have a son or a daughter. I just can't sit and cry about what has happened. My marriage recharged my batteries.

When I first came back to Egypt, I was trying not to think about my detention. I was not denying it because it was too big to deny, but I was just trying to put it out of my mind. I didn't have any nightmares, perhaps because I was purposely trying not to dwell on it. In the first two months, I wouldn't even talk about it. I was talking about everything but the detention. I would go out, go places, but would not talk about it. After two months, I started talking about it. I told my mother, my family, my fiancée, and my best friends. Up till that point, they had only heard half of the story. They knew that we had been arrested, but they did not know about our time in detention. I told them what really happened.

Most of the time my mother doesn't want to hear about all the suffering that we endured because it makes her feel worse. She cries all the time. "Mother, listen," I say. "It will make me feel better if I talk about it. I want to share my suffering with you."

I want to talk about my experience. When my brother and I talk about our detention with my mother, we make light of it and laugh. When we notice that she is switching from laughter to grief, we change the subject. This is how I am trying to live with it. Sometimes, I feel proud of how I handled the whole experience. Maybe one day 50 years from now, I will sit down with my grandson and tell him, "You know 50 years ago, I was connected to September 11. Not because I did anything, but because I was at the wrong place at the wrong time." When I share my story, it will be a history lesson for him about September 11. I suffered because of what happened. Few people know about it now, and maybe even fewer will know about it in the future. That is why I like to talk about my experiences with researchers and newspapers. The truth has to come out.

I asked Yasser how often he met up or talked with his prison mates.

Since I came back, I've seen Ahmed only once. He was deported in early January. I saw Walid five or six times. This is the second time that I'm seeing Ramy. We talk on the phone from time to time, and we say that we want to meet up and talk about our detention, but when it comes down to it, talking about it is our last priority. Don't think that it is easy to sit down and talk about it. I talk about it because I want the truth to get out, but I'd prefer to talk about anything else. But this is the pain that I have to go through. I have to talk about it any chance I get.

Attitudes Toward the United States

Now, the way I see it, the U.S. has changed. I was a big believer in American democracy, freedom, and lifestyle. Before September 11, I always considered the U.S. a model of how humans can lead free lives in a democratic society. I used to believe that this kind of lifestyle was only possible in the U.S. and that this was the only place where people had freedom and respect for human beings. In any other country, things are unstable and can change in a minute.

I believed that the American people built this freedom and that they would fight to hold onto it for a very long time. But after what happened, my attitudes have totally changed. Now I see that what they used to tell us about human rights, democracy, and freedom is all crap. They were only waiting for an excuse to change the democracy to an autocracy... like any other dictatorship in a third-world country. They were just waiting for an excuse to undermine the respect for human rights. Maybe I would've accepted it if this change occurred among people who were indifferent to human rights or among those who hold stereotypes of Muslims and Arabs.

It is especially unacceptable when the shift away from human rights happens on the governmental level. It was a government policy that put us on the ninth floor. I remember that some guards felt sorry for us. They could not show it openly, but I could feel it by the way they talked to us and treated us. I think they felt that their government had committed a big mistake and they felt powerless to do anything about it. That is why I am more angry with the government and the administration than I am with Americans on the street.

I don't uphold the U.S. as a role model of how human beings should live anymore. I think if the government starts to discriminate against people because of their religion or color, then that government is like a third-world government or dictatorship. It is like Rwanda or Yugoslavia. The way I look at things has completely changed now.[19]

Losing Trust

I have a lot of good friends in the U.S. and a lot of good memories. I would love to walk down the streets of Manhattan, go to Times Square, or see my friends, but I am scared. Even if I get a chance to go to the U.S., I am scared. I don't feel secure in the United States. I am suspicious of everything now. I even had doubts about you before talking to you...

Now, it is hard for me to trust people. This is a new feeling for me. Before the arrest, I used to trust people and had faith in them. The fact that I was arrested really bothers me because it means that someone I know might've complained about me. Maybe someone called from my neighborhood, but that is difficult for me to believe because we had great relationships with our neighbors. We were very friendly to the entire building, which is small with two stories. There were only two apartments, and downstairs there were some shops. I don't know who made the phone call, but it shook my trust and still confuses me. Now, eight months after my deportation, the U.S. authorities have sent a memo asking for further investigation. This makes me feel that the fire is still burning.

Sometimes I feel afraid in Egypt. First, I believe that because of this arrest, my name has been blemished. Let's say that I want to get a job in any firm. I apply for a job, and when the company does a background check on me, they will find out that I have a security-related file and that I was suspected of a terrorist act. They would probably not hire me. This arrest and detention is going to affect me for the rest of my life. What if I want to teach? I used to teach at the American University in Alexandria. What if I want to go back and teach in the college? The university will not hire me now.

I don't know what the American government will tell the Egyptian officials about me. The American government can fabricate anything and send it over here. What are the Egyptian officials going to do with me? American officials have my fingerprints, and they update their files periodically. Eight months later, they are still trying to find out what I am doing. I don't know, but I don't feel safe anywhere.[20]

What if I want to go somewhere outside of Egypt for tourism or business? I am afraid. I will never go to England because the FBI and others have links to the security system with England and Israel and all the other allied nations. They share databases. What if my name comes up? The least they will do is detain me for 24 hours and send me back to Egypt. Why would I want to put myself through that? What if I am going with my wife? What if I want to go to France or wherever? I just want to live a normal life. I want to travel because I love traveling. My wife wanted to go abroad for our honeymoon because she has never left the country, but I felt scared and I told her, "No. I don't know what can happen to me. It is hard...."

In the United States, I was doing web design and computer graphics. I had a vision of establishing a company in the U.S. which specializes in web design and hosting at a global level. I incorporated a company in Newark, and I got the paperwork a few days before I got arrested. That company is gone now. Everything—the hardware, the software, the company—is gone.

I am more into business now. I don't know why, but something has changed in me. I used to teach, but it is difficult for me to teach now. I feel that to be a teacher, I have to have a certain point of view that I can convey to my students. After my detention, I feel that I have to reconsider all my beliefs, thoughts, ideas, and principles because everything I used to believe turned out to be a lie. There are a lot of things I encountered that I could not see before. So I am reevaluating everything—democracy, political views, and human rights—that I used to believe in.

I feel that my past beliefs are totally wrong. I was hoping to see Egypt have a democracy one day like the United States. Now I don't. I know now that it does not exist. Democracy is not just about winning elections or having elections every four years. Democracy is about what people want. It is about respecting human rights—that is the essential part of democracy. Human beings hold the highest value in life. For example, after two towers fall, you can build hundreds of new towers, but you can't bring back even one life.

Now if a government violates human rights, ignores the Constitution because of an emergency, and stops respecting human beings and human rights, then it is heading in the wrong direction. It means that it has forsaken democracy. What if the current administration says we have to postpone the elections in order to maintain national security? What are you going to do? What are you going to do as an American? What is America going to do? Nothing! Nothing! America is going to become a very powerful dictatorship. In other words, if you can justify something that is wrong once, you open the door to justifying anything, and people will accept it.

I fear the moment when I'm teaching in a university and my students ask me about human rights. What am I going to say? Before this experience, I used to say a lot of good things about America when I taught classes. I used to talk a lot about how people in the U.S. respect democracy and human rights. I used to tell my students that you can go there and even though you are not an American, people in the U.S. respect you. They treat everyone as equals. How can I talk about that now? A part of me is broken, and I am not fully the man that I used to be. A part of my life has twisted.

Now I think about business because I don't want to have assumptions about anything. Open-ended ideas, which require thinking, I don't want to deal with them. I just want to deal with facts now. I studied English literature and novels. I love reading literary books and learned a lot from them. However, someone said that real life is much worse than fiction. Now I am over fiction. Now I want to adapt to reality.

Yasser Today: In the fall of 2008, I met Yasser in Alexandria, Egypt, to do an interview for a documentary. He is married and has a young child. He is also working as a manager for an Internet company that sells books online. His Internet department is booming, and he is hoping to increase sales and personnel in the next few years.

In November 2009, Yasser and four of the Turkmen *plaintiffs accepted a settlement with the U.S. government for $1.26 million. In a statement from Egypt, he said,*

> *We were deprived of our rights and abused simply because of our religion and the color of our skin. After seven long years, I am relieved to be able to try to rebuild my life. I know that I and others are still affected by what happened and that communities in the U.S. continue to feel the fallout. I sincerely hope this will never happen again.*

Even though Yasser and four other individuals have accepted a settlement, the Turkmen *case is still ongoing. Currently, CCR is seeking permission from the district court to amend the complaint to add six new plaintiffs so that they can continue to hold high-level officials accountable for their actions.*[21] *Time will tell if a change in the political climate would bring a different outcome for the* Turkmen *lawsuit in the next decade.*

Despite the settlement, the government has not been held fully accountable for violating the legal and human rights of 9/11 detainees. On June 14, 2006, a federal district court judge in the Turkmen *lawsuit "dismissed the challenges to the racial profiling and prolonged detention of the Turkmen plaintiffs but allowed the conditions of confinement and religious discrimination challenges to proceed." Both the government and the plaintiffs appealed to the Second Circuit Court of Appeals.*[22] *On December 18, 2009, the Second Circuit affirmed the district court's dismissal of plaintiffs' claims about prolonged detention. The Second Circuit Court vacated the balance of the district court's decision, regarding abusive conditions of confinement, and remanded the case to the district court to consider the plaintiffs' motion to amend the complaint.*[23]

The June 2006 decision of the federal district court and the December 2009 decision of the Second Circuit Court are not surprising. History is full of examples when the American courts upheld the abrogation of civil liberties during wartime emergencies. For example, the U.S. Supreme Court upheld the internment of Japanese Americans in Korematsu v. United States, *an infamous lawsuit during World War II. It took 40 years for the government to recognize the unconstitutionality of its actions and to provide an apology and reparations for each surviving Japanese American internee. Just as the U.S. government apologized for its unjust actions 40 years after the internment of Japanese Americans, it will also eventually apologize to the immigrants targeted by its "security" operations after 9/11. Americans will look back at the post-9/11 era as a dark period in American history. I hope that the former detainees won't have to wait as long as the Japanese did.*

This apology may not stop the government from infringing upon the rights of vulnerable populations in the future, but it still carries significance, especially for the former detainees who were caught in the government's machinery. An apology would provide former detainees some psychological and emotional vindication and an opportunity to clarify their situations to their neighbors and community members who may not understand what it meant to live as a Muslim in America after 9/11.

Conclusion

The six narratives included in the book reflect the experiences of the 1,000-plus individuals who were initially arrested after 9/11 on suspicion of terrorism and quietly deported months later on minor immigration or criminal charges. The 9/11 detainees labeled as "High Interest" were incarcerated for prolonged periods on the ninth floor of the MDC and were subject to severe physical and psychological abuse, which involved sleep deprivation, sensory torture, communication blackout, and daily humiliation. Other 9/11 detainees who were not kept in very high-security jails—such as Mohamed E****** and Ansar Mahmood—experienced other hardships caused by suspicion of terrorism, such as inadequate legal access, coercive questioning, and sharing of erroneous intelligence. As a result of the detentions, Ansar lost his permanent residency and Mohamed suffered torture after his return to Egypt. If they had not been Muslims, they would not have been caught in the sweeps after the 9/11 attacks, and law enforcement officers would not have tried to find every possible means to keep them in custody.

Even though government officials continue to maintain today that they were following the law by deporting undocumented immigrants, these narratives challenge the government's argument and force us to question why undocumented immigrants were kept in high-security jails and deprived of their legal rights for immigration violations. If these undocumented immigrants suffered a loss of their legal and human rights only because of their religious or racial affiliation, then the government apology for the internment of Japanese Americans was lip service to the demands of Japanese Americans during the 1980s. Their detentions and deportations imply that the government can circumscribe the rights of Muslims today because they are perceived as enemies, just as the Japanese Americans were during World War II. It also means that in the future, with the change in the political climate, members of another ethnic or racial group might also be considered "enemy aliens" and their legal and human rights will be thrown out the window. This book not only challenges the detentions of the few thousand individuals who lost their rights in the chaotic uproar after 9/11, but it also serves as a warning that such losses could happen in the future to another group that the government chooses to manufacture into an enemy. Strong protective measures should be taken to protect the civil liberties of vulnerable populations, especially during wartime emergencies.

Scapegoats of 9/11

During my public talks, audience members have often asked me if the government knew that these immigration detainees did not have any connections with 9/11. Why did the government keep them in detention and in high-security jails without any evidence of terrorism? Was it deliberate? Did the Bush administration achieve any political gains? Was it just a byproduct of the post-9/11 chaos or the inefficiency of the intelligence community? Was the administration anti-Islamic and taking revenge on Muslims for 9/11? I explore some of these questions in the following section.

In the introduction of this book, I explain that despite repeated efforts government officials were unavailable or unwilling to answer these questions about 9/11 detainees. Some of the answers, however, can be found in two publications issued after 9/11, which include interviews with high-level administration officials.[1] A close reading of these publications reveals some insights into the post-9/11 climate in which these arrests occurred. In particular, the publications provide some explanation of why these individuals were kept in prolonged detention without any evidence of terrorism and imply that some government officials knew that the immigration detainees did not have any links to terrorism.

On September 12, 2001, President George Bush held a meeting with Attorney General John Ashcroft and the FBI director Robert Mueller and reminded them, "We need to focus on preventing the next attack more than worrying about who did this one."[2] The way this objective was achieved was not through smart intelligence but through roundups of Muslim males from predominately Muslim countries, especially those whose immigration papers were out of order. Ashcroft and Assistant Attorney General Michael Chertoff were in charge of these roundups, and they told FBI and INS agents that their goal "was to prevent more attacks, not prosecute anyone. And the best way to do that was to round up, question, and hold as many people as possible...round up anyone who fit the profile."[3] "To Ashcroft and his team, these immigration detainees were not defendants.... They were potential killers who had to be stopped."[4]

In other words, Ashcroft was employing a preventive strategy to stop additional terrorist attacks that was purely based on racial profiling. His strategy to round up undocumented Muslim males implied government officials believed that Muslim males were going to be involved in the next wave of terrorist attacks or that they knew about upcoming terrorist attacks. In September 2002, the Center for Constitutional Rights challenged the government's post-9/11 strategy in the class-action lawsuit *Turkmen v. Ashcroft*.[5] The CCR attorneys stated,

"Instead of being presumed innocent until proven guilty, they [the plaintiffs] and hundreds of other post-9/11 detainees were presumed guilty of terrorism until proven innocent to the satisfaction of law enforcement authorities."[6] In other words, imagine the outrage that would occur if after the 1999 Columbine High School shooting, the government had questioned all white male high school students in Colorado and detained those who had drinking problems or used antidepressant drugs. Anyone with any experience in the legal field would consider this strategy not only a waste of resources, but also impractical and illegal. The state can't simply punish thousands of white teens who have no connections to the shooting. Our deep familiarity with thousands of white teens with some drinking or drug problems who eventually become responsible individuals leads us to believe that only a very tiny fraction of them would arm themselves and shoot their classmates. Unfortunately, given the historical racial segregations within our society, we don't have the same familiarity with 2–7 million Muslims living in the United States. Many thousands of these Muslims have taken immigration risks to seek better economic opportunities within the United States, but a very small fraction of them have flown planes into tall buildings. To take the analogy a step further, the parents of many of the white teens arrested in the Columbine scenario would petition the senators and representatives within their communities, which would prevent the occurrence of such large-scale detentions. Unfortunately, most of the immigrant detainees were disenfranchised and did not have access to political power. They became the scapegoats for all social ills and were allowed to rot in detention centers for months and years.

Because the immigrant detainees were arrested through racial profiling, several government officials knew from the beginning that the immigration detainees in the MDC were not terrorists. The OIG report notes, "A current lieutenant at the MDC said that when the detainees arrived they were scared and visibly afraid. He said it became apparent to him that the detainees were not terrorists."[7] Within the DOJ, officials had also developed further classifications to focus their investigation. For example, in the OIG report, Deputy U.S. Attorney David Kelley makes a distinction between persons of "investigative interest" and the other "special interest cases" as follows:

> Several Department officials involved in the terrorism investigation also told the OIG that it soon became clear that many of the September 11 detainees had no immediately apparent nexus to terrorism. As a result, the terrorism investigation soon narrowed its focus to a few of the individuals who were detained, not the vast bulk of the aliens arrested in connection with PENTTBOM leads. For example, David Kelley, the Deputy U.S. Attorney for the Southern District of New York who immediately after the September 11 attacks came to Washington, D.C., to help supervise the investigation of the attacks, told the OIG that within one to three days of the attacks prosecutors were focusing on individuals of

198 / Detained without Cause

"genuine investigative interest," such as a person whose telephone number was linked to one of the hijackers or a person who lived in a building near a location of high interest to the terrorism investigation, as opposed to aliens identified by the FBI simply as "of interest." Other Department officials acknowledged to the OIG that they realized that many in the group of September 11 detainees were not connected to the attacks or terrorism in general.[8]

This research reveals that smart intelligence was at work when "within one to three days of the attack" the officials were already focusing on individuals of "genuine investigative interest." In other words, officials were able to realize quickly that immigration detainees were not connected to the attacks. The question, then, is why didn't the DOJ quickly clear those who were not of genuine investigative interest? Many of the detainees whom I interviewed during my research pointed out that they were waiting for this FBI clearance and were hoping that someone would come and talk to them so that they could be cleared. For some individuals who were kept on the ninth floor of MDC, such as Anser Mehmood, no one came to talk to them.[9] FBI officials talked to some, such as Yasser Ebrahim, once or twice and visited others, such as Nabil Ayesh and Azmath Mohammed, more frequently. In other words, FBI clearances were not issued systematically, in part because they were based on racial profiling and not on any genuine interest or suspicion.

Although the FBI knew that these detainees had no connection to terrorism, it established a policy of "hold until cleared," which required that immigration detainees had to be held without bond until the FBI cleared them of all connections to terrorism. According to the OIG report, this policy was not memorialized in writing, and its exact origin is not clear. However, this policy was clearly communicated to INS and FBI officials in the field, who understood and applied it.[10] The FBI clearance, which consisted of some background checks and interviews with detainees, was given haphazardly. In some situations, detainees received FBI clearances but remained in custody. For example, after Yasser's brother received his FBI clearance in January 2002, he was moved from the high-security floor to the general population unit of the MDC, where he stayed for an additional three months before he was deported to Egypt in April 2002.

Within the Department of Justice, discussions about the delays and legality of the "hold until cleared" policy began as early as the end of September 2001. An attorney from the Criminal Division of Terrorism and Violent Crime Section (TVCS) drafted an unsent memo[11] to his superiors that raised concerns about the FBI's lack of adequate resources to conduct detainee clearance in a timely manner. The TVCS attorney told the OIG,

After reviewing the files of these detainees it was "obvious" that the "overwhelming majority" *were simple immigration violators and had no connection to the terrorism investigation.* He said continuing to hold these detainees was a waste of resources and could damage the Government's credibility to oppose bond or release in more meritorious detainee cases. He acknowledged that the only way to know "for sure" if these detainees were linked to terrorism was to conduct clearance investigations, but he argued that the Government must provide the resources for such an effort.(emphasis added)[12]

This unsent memo reveals the legal frustrations of holding up individuals without any connection to terrorism and the difficulty of conducting an investigation with inadequate resources. The attorney's overriding concern is that these practices could undermine the government's credibility and diminish its power to prosecute individuals genuinely involved in terrorism. Assistant Attorney General Chertoff acknowledged that he was aware of the delays and addressed the issues with the FBI director, Robert Mueller, and Assistant Director Dale Watson. However, both Ashcroft and Mueller denied being aware of the problems with the FBI clearances. According to the OIG report, lack of adequate field office staff resources, poor coordination and monitoring of the detainee clearance process, and reassignment of FBI field officers to other tasks created tremendous delays in the issuance of clearances.[13]

This opposition to unnecessarily long detentions of undocumented immigrants did not only occur behind the doors of Ashcroft's office. Questions about the baseless connection of detainees to terrorism were also brought up during the "No Bond" hearing process set up after 9/11. The OIG report points out,

According to many INS officials we interviewed, implementing the Department's "no bond" position for every September 11 detainee quickly became very difficult.... On September 19, 2001, Cooper sent an e-mail to an INS Regional Counsel describing the problem and discussing his efforts to obtain more information from the FBI about September 11 detainees: "As for the information to support a no-bond determination, we are trying today to break through what has been an absence of information from the investigation to use in the immigration process." Other INS officials expressed similar concerns, even as late as the summer of 2002. In a June 27, 2002, memorandum, INS Deputy General Counsel Dea Carpenter stated, "*It was and continues to be a rare occasion when there is any evidence available for use in the immigration court to sustain a 'no bond' determination.*" An INS District Director brought to INS Headquarters to assist with the detainee cases told the OIG that in many instances the FBI would base its interest in a detainee on the sole fact that the alien was arrested in connection with a PENTTBOM lead. *Thus, even though from the INS's perspective it had no evidence to support a 'no bond' position, INS attorneys were required to argue that position in court.* (emphasis added)[14]

Despite these internal discussions about the legality of the holding policy, the FBI continued to delay the clearances. The OIG report states, "The FBI cleared only 2.6 percent of the 762 September 11 detainees within three weeks of their arrests. The average length of time from arrest of a September 11 detainee to clearance by FBI Headquarters was 80 days."[15] In some situations, individual FBI officers intervened for the release of the person that they had recently arrested. One such example is Purna Raj Bajracharya, a Nepalese Buddhist man. He was arrested on October 25, 2001, in downtown New York for videotaping buildings. Officers suspected that he might be a terrorist and imprisoned him on the ninth floor of the MDC in Brooklyn. Purna was deported to Nepal in January 2002 for an immigration violation after an FBI officer intervened.[16] In other cases, detainees with higher incomes were able to hire lawyers to get them out. Some detainees were also able to access legal organizations who secured a somewhat timely release.[17] The rest just remained stuck within high-security prisons, not because they had connections to terrorism but because they lacked adequate resources and connections and because they were Muslims.

Legally, immigrant detainees have to be deported back to their home countries within 90 days after a noncitizen has been served a deportation order.[18] Ashcroft and his allies did not want the immigration detainees to be deported until they were satisfied that they had gotten all the information they needed from them or the detainees had fulfilled all of their political purposes. "Chertoff had figured out that...there was nothing in the law[19] that said [the immigrant detainees] absolutely had to be deported immediately. They could be held still longer, until the FBI decided they were of no use."[20] What this meant was that detainees rotted in solitary confinement even after receiving their deportation orders from the court. For example, Yasser received his deportation order on November 20, 2001, but he stayed on the ninth floor of MDC until July 2002. Yasser, a plaintiff of the class-action lawsuit *Turkmen v. Ashcroft*, who with four other MDC detainees settled his claim with the U.S. government in November 2009 for $1.26 million, is not unique. Many other immigration detainees remained in custody despite the fact that the courts had issued their deportation orders.[21]

One can presume that in the chaos ensuing after September 11, government officials were trying hard to prevent future attacks and to avoid committing mistakes that might lead to another 9/11-style attack. Therefore, a thorough investigation of suspicious individuals linked with evidence to terrorism is justified. However, it is clear from the narratives included in the book and statements from some of the DOJ officials that the government did not have any evidence of their involvement other than the knowledge that these detainees were from predominately Muslim countries. This fact becomes more disturbing when we look at the way government officials characterized these arrests in the media for the general public.

Top government officials, including President Bush and Attorney General Ashcroft, highlighted these arrests and detentions as success stories in antiterrorism investigations at various public meetings, press conferences, and Senate hearings. In some cases, the administration said hypocritically that these "efforts have been *crafted carefully to avoid infringing on constitutional rights* while saving American lives" (emphasis added).[22] In November 2001, when hundreds of immigration detainees were kept *incommunicado*, Chertoff testified in a Senate hearing,

> Importantly, nobody is held *incommunicado*. We don't hold people in secret, you know, cut off from lawyers, cut off from the public, cut off from their family and friends. They have the right to communicate with the outside world. We don't stop them from doing it.[23] (emphasis added)

Later, Ashcroft claimed that in "a preventative campaign of arrest and detention of lawbreakers, America has grown stronger—and safer—in the face of terrorism.[24] In a similar tone, Assistant Attorney General Viet Dinh wrote, "These detentions may have incapacitated an Al Qaeda sleeper cell that was planning to strike a target in Washington, DC—perhaps the capitol building—soon after September 11."[25] In June 2002, when most of the detainees had been deported or released, President Bush praised the Department of Homeland Security by declaring that the homeland defense coalition "has hauled in about 2,400 of these terrorists, these killers—there's still a lot of them out there."[26]

Why did the administration characterize the arrests as a successful counterterrorism strategy when some officials within the agency knew that these individuals were just immigration detainees with no links to terrorism?

Coleen Rowley, an FBI whistle-blower and a *Time* magazine "Person of the Year" for 2002, characterized these arrests as a public relations strategy. In her letter to the FBI director, dated March 6, 2003, Ms. Rowley pointed out,

> The vast majority of the one thousand plus persons "detained" in the wake of 9-11 did not turn out to be terrorists. They were mostly illegal aliens. . . . [A]fter 9-11, Headquarters encouraged more and more detentions for what seem to be *essentially PR purposes* [emphasis added][27]

This "public relations strategy" allowed the government to appease the fears of the general public and gain their trust by claiming that they were responding to 9/11 efficiently and arresting those responsible.

Steven Brill writes, "The bureau, according to a well-placed FBI official, had few undercover informants in the Muslim community in September 2001."[28] One way to develop this pool of informants was to arrest and hold Muslim males until the FBI felt that they had learned something from their "lab animals." Therefore, it was not a surprise that "Ashcroft told Mueller that any male from eighteen to forty years old from Middle Eastern or North African countries whom the FBI simply learned about was to be questioned and questioned hard."[29] Nabil Ayesh in his narrative stated that he thought he was a "lab animal" for FBI rookie agents, who repeatedly asked him irrelevant questions about his parents and his background. He felt that these officers were using detainee interrogations to gather practical experience. In other words, through questioning and roundups, officials were establishing a pool of informants that they could use to better understand the Muslim community or to tap into terrorist networks. Ashcroft's Volunteer Interview Program, "which formalized what had been going on ad hoc since September 11,"[30] was established after these initial roundups. Its purpose was to gather information about the Muslim community by building a network of informants because the FBI did not have any of those networks before 9/11. FBI officials congratulated themselves because the volunteer interview program allowed the state to gather some information that led to the arrest of seven U.S. citizens from Buffalo who had attended training camps in Afghanistan in August 2001.[31] However, after their return from Afghanistan, they had not conspired to carry out any attacks. It seems these young men were attracted to Afghanistan because it offered possibilities for adventure and not because they were drawn to Islamist rhetoric about jihad.[32] Mr. Sahim Alwan, one of the young men who attended the camp, stated, "[T]he men had no plans, no hatred for America, and that when he walked away from Osama bin Laden, he left Al Qaeda behind. He explained his trip to Afghanistan as 'a lot of curiosity'."[33] While the national security adviser, Condoleezza Rice, characterized the arrest of young men from Buffalo as "victories in the war on terrorism," the *New York Times* stated, "Behind Washington's sweeping proclamations is a more measured victory over a profoundly ambiguous threat."[34]

Despite the intelligence failure to find "real terrorists," FBI has been using paid informants to infiltrate the American Muslim communities. The Lodi case—in which a Pakistani informant named Khan worked closely with the FBI to entrap a Pakistani Muslim family and received over $200,000—has revealed that informants will go as far as destroying the lives of others to get money from the government. In Lodi, the informant lured a young Muslim man, Hamid, into jihad and even fabricated stories to create a case against a Muslim family.[35] In taped conversations, Khan told Hamid that he should "be a man" and "do something." He also criticized Hamid for not having attended training camps in Pakistan.[36] Similar concerns of entrapment have been found in other terrorist convictions, such as the Fort Dix, the Newburg 4, and the Albany case of Yassin Aref and Mohammed Hossein.[37] Through these informants, the government has been able to create a sense of mistrust in Muslim communities and make people fearful of each other. More specifically, such entrapment operations suggest that the government continues to perceive the American Muslim community as a threat to national security.

The post-9/11 arrests were a result of ignorance about Islam and Muslim communities; even though there was no evidence to connect these individuals to terrorism, the top administration officials were unable to see these immigration detainees as anything but terrorists because they were racialized[38]—meaning that the government saw them as terrorists only because of their race and religion. Within the government, the majority of the decision makers are unfamiliar with the basics of Islam, even to the point of not knowing the differences between Shiites and Sunnis, the two major Islamic sects.[39] Sometimes, this ignorance results in extreme cases, such as that of a secret agent who wrote "Islam is evil, Christ is King" on a Muslim prayer calendar while searching the home of a Jordanian man in Detroit.[40] In general, because culturally and linguistically ignorant law enforcement officers[41] were eager to find a terrorist as soon as possible after September 11, they interpreted every book written in Arabic and Urdu as terrorist paraphernalia when they searched homes, often without legal search warrants. For example, Urdu spy novels became "terrorist paraphernalia" found in the home of one Pakistani American pilot.[42] Two ceremonial swords hanging in the home of a young man released on parole caused the probation officer to become so suspicious of the young man that he rearrested him.[43] Flight simulator games were the cause for suspicion in the case of another Pakistani American who had a green card.[44] A stun gun bought for a private investigation course caused a dramatic arrest for yet another Pakistani immigrant in the Bronx.[45] In other words, anything can become suspicious if a group of people is racialized; law enforcement officers could not see Muslims as anything but terrorists after 9/11. A young Arab man administrating the aviation section of Dubai International Airport, during his visit to the United States at an airport, would most probably be seen as a suspect for his aviation background and knowledge of a U.S. airport.

Other factors in the 9/11 detentions were the emotionally charged atmosphere right after September 11 and the political climate under which these immigration detainees were classified as "High Interest" detainees. These factors prevented the majority of field officers from thinking independently. The OIG supplemental report describes the emotional environment of the MDC immediately after 9/11:

> Many of the staff members we interviewed described the atmosphere at the MDC immediately after September 11 as emotionally charged. One of the lieutenants currently at the MDC said the staff "had a great deal of anger" after September 11 and that it was a chaotic time at the MDC. Another lieutenant, one of the lieutenants responsible for escorting detainees, stated that upon entering the institution the detainees were handed over to teams of five to seven officers who were "spiked with adrenaline." He said that there were some officers on the escort teams who were "getting ready for battle" and "talking crazy."

Another lieutenant responsible for escorting detainees similarly described the officers as "high on adrenaline."[46]

The OIG report mentions that many of the law enforcement agents were related in some way to people who died during the attacks,[47] and New York was the main site of the attacks. Passing "Ground Zero" every day and witnessing the demolition firsthand had a deep impact on New Yorkers. Consciously or unconsciously, the WTC suspects provided them an opportunity to vent their anger and frustration, and their desire for vengeance prevented law enforcement officers from thinking about the detainees' human and legal rights. Once classified as terrorists, they became subhumans who could be locked away for months in solitary confinement. While writing these narratives, I often visualized the ninth floor of the MDC and how it was reminiscent of the cages that held slaves centuries ago.[48] It is amazing to note that we as human beings are capable of such cruelty and punishment, especially when we convert the other into a subhuman being.

One can assume that detainees were converted into terrorists because of a combination of all of the factors mentioned earlier, such as a desire for vengeance, ignorance of Islam and Muslims, the need for a pool of informants, and attempts to appease the fears of the general public. More specifically, by constantly barraging the public with references to sleeper cells and detentions of Muslims, the state deliberately created a climate of fear in which Americans assumed that they were surrounded by terrorists who were plotting additional terrorist attacks against them. The more than 1,000 terrorists behind bars show the state's efficiency in stopping additional terrorist attacks and serve as a constant reminder that there are many more "sleeper cells" among us. As a result, the general public has to relinquish their civil and legal rights to stop additional terrorist attacks. I remember seeing photographs of Azmath Mohammed with a box cutter on television and fearing that additional attacks may be coming. If I—as someone who is aware of how the American government has historically manufactured enemy aliens during wartime—can feel this fear, I wonder how others felt. I can understand why members of the general public were willing to relinquish their civil liberties and trust the government to protect them from additional terrorist attacks. As a result of this fear, the U.S. PATRIOT Act was passed almost unanimously and attacks on Afghanistan and Iraq were approved with minimal opposition. In hindsight, it is clear that fear froze the independent thinking of decision makers.

Unfortunately, this fear is still present, along with the fear of Muslim-looking males and Al Qaeda, even though there are non-Muslim individuals and organizations involved in activities that could be considered terrorist. For example, a recent New York University study about terrorist convictions and trials reported that since September 11, the Revolutionary Armed Forces of Colombia (FARC) was the most commonly prosecuted terrorist organization in the U.S. courts. Al Qaeda ranked second.[49] However, given the constant references to Al Qaeda in the media, the general public continues to link it with terrorism regardless of its ability to carry out any terrorist acts.

Moreover, because government officials know that these detentions were illegal and that they could be held liable for racial profiling and prolonged detentions, they continue to justify the deportations by citing the undocumented status of 9/11 detainees and to assert, without any evidence, that these detainees had potential links to terrorism. For example, in December 2002, when most of the detainees had been deported, Jan Ting (a former INS official) linked deportees to terrorism without any evidence:

> We succeeded in removing hundreds, hundreds of individuals from the United States who should not have been here, who fit a profile that raised our concern about terrorism, many of whom we believed, our law enforcement believed, were involved in terrorism in some way. Again, we couldn't prove that. *But at least they've been removed from the United States and no longer represent a threat to us.* (emphasis added)[50]

The purpose of such statements was to keep the general public suspicious about 9/11 detainees. As a result, the common discourse around the 9/11 detainees has been that those individuals were potential terrorists. At the minimum, they were undocumented or had committed minor criminal acts and, therefore, whatever happened could be justified in the court of law. They have become the scapegoats of 9/11.

Transnational and Global Implications of 9/11 Detentions and the Manufacturing of Stateless Subjects

In Pakistan, Egypt, Palestine, and India, I met deportees who had been ambitious and hardworking in the United States. Whether they worked as high-tech engineers, entrepreneurs, taxi drivers, or gas station operators, America provided employment and advancement opportunities that their home countries could not. They took advantage of those opportunities and worked 10 to 16 hours per day. Their remittances strengthened the economies of their home countries and provided food, shelter, and amenities to immediate and extended families. However, their hard work not only benefited them but also contributed significantly to the U.S. economy. The National Immigration Forum states that immigrant workers are essential to the United States' expanding economy because they add about $10 billion each year to it.[51]

The 9/11 detentions not only caused individuals to lose their incomes, which were used to support families in other countries, but also had additional transnational implications. The sharing of erroneous intelligence created terrible situations for deportees in their home countries, as in the case of Mohamed E******, who was tortured after his deportation.

Even after his release from the torture cell, Mohamed remained under surveillance and had to report to the Egyptian authorities on a periodic basis. His freedom was so circumscribed that he fled the country by applying for political asylum in Switzerland. Although he is currently enjoying a happy married life in Switzerland, he is unable to return to Egypt, where all of his family and community live. Mohamed became deportable not only from the United States but also from his home country, where he grew up and lived for over 30 years of his life.

While E******'s case is extreme, the rest of the individuals included in the book and the other individuals I interviewed also fear the U.S. government and their home governments. The U.S. government has their personal information, like fingerprints and eye scans, which makes them traceable in any corner of the world, and they fear that serious repercussions could result if it decided to share that information with their home governments. For example, Yasser Ebrahim fears that the fact that he was once suspected of the 9/11 attacks could show up on an airport computer during international travels and that security guards might stop him. In the best-case scenario, he would experience questioning or humiliation. Why does he have to deal with this kind of questioning for a prior immigration violation? Why does he have to constantly explain that he did not have any connections to terrorism?

This fear of being a suspect is very real for Yasser and not just in his imagination. The Egyptian government investigated him after his return to Egypt, and he had to report to the authorities again when the American government sent an inquiry about him. Mohammed Azmath also fears repercussions from the Indian government because his name has been connected with terrorism. Both Ansar Mahmood and Anser Mehmood understand that anything can happen to them given that the Pakistani government has handed over several Pakistani citizens to the United States who were later placed in secret prisons.[52]

The fear that the United States will share intelligence is exacerbated by the fact that many nations working as client states for the United States have handed over their own citizens to the CIA and FBI for reasons of "national security." A Human Rights Watch report provides a list of 26 individuals arrested worldwide and kept in undisclosed locations and prisons.[53] Many of these prisoners may have connections with terrorism, but the report is critical of such "ghost prisoners" since "international treaties ratified by the United States prohibit incommunicado detention of persons in secret locations."[54] The report also mentions that some government officials speaking anonymously to journalists have suggested some detainees have been tortured.[55] Many other reputable newspapers and scholars have confirmed the presence of such secret prisons.[56] Although the Obama administration has signed an executive order to close all secret prisons and detention camps,[57] there is no way for us to confirm such information as they are operating under secrecy. However, on August 25, 2009, the Obama administration undermined the effect of the executive order by announcing its plans to continue the practice of sending suspected terrorists to other countries for interrogations. They claim that they will employ more oversight to avoid torture and inhumane treatment of prisoners.[58]

Nonetheless, under U.S. and international laws, all individuals—regardless of terrorist links—need access to their legal and human rights. In other words, they cannot be placed in secret prisons and tortured. These issues get compounded especially because several individuals have been handed over to the government based on false intelligence. One example is Maher Arar, a Syrian-born Canadian who was arrested in New York on September 26, 2002, after the Royal Canadian Mounted Police wrongly classified him as an Islamic fundamentalist and gave misleading and inaccurate information to U.S. authorities. This intelligence sharing very likely led to Arar's arrest and deportation to Syria, where he was tortured for ten months. After two years of inquiry, the Canadian prime minister Stephen Harper apologized and compensated him $8.9 million.[59] Another example is Osama Hassan Mustafa Nasr, an Egyptian man arrested by CIA agents in February 2003 in Italy and tortured in Egypt.[60] Another example of mistaken identity is Khalid El-Masri, a German national of Lebanese descent who was picked up by Macedonian agents on December 31, 2003.[61] He was sent to Afghanistan, where CIA personnel interrogated him in an unacknowledged detention center. Four months later, they discovered that he shared a name with an Al-Qaeda member and released him.[62] The Guantanamo Bay prison is another example of how the United States' global war on terror has falsely implicated hundreds of individuals as a result of incorrect information. Many of the Guantanamo Bay prisoners have been released without any connections to terrorism.[63]

The American government's practice of arresting individuals and keeping them in secret prisons regardless of a terrorist connection has created a new category of individuals that I call stateless subjects. In modern political systems, citizens and residents expect their governments and states to work toward protecting their rights. A German citizen should feel safe living within Germany's national borders or traveling for a vacation to Macedonia with a German passport because it is Germany's duty to protect his rights. Unfortunately, like Khaled El-Masri, there are several thousand examples of disappeared individuals who have become stateless—meaning that no state is willing to stand up to the United States for its giant size and power. This book concentrates on individuals primarily arrested on immigration or minor criminal violations. However, in the case of stateless subjects, one could be legally sitting in his/her home and sent to a secret prison. If we push this argument further, we can assume that a Muslim man, for example, cannot feel safe anywhere in the world, regardless of whether he is living in his native country of Pakistan, has sought political asylum in Germany and has

become a German national, or is living as an undocumented immigrant in the
United States. The United States' imperial discourse can convert any individual
into a threat and incarcerate him in a secret prison. This omnipotent prevalence
of the U.S. imperial discourse of national security, which means that the client
states weighs U.S. national security higher than their own national interests, is
very alarming and has major negative impacts for the security of client states. For
example, in 2007 Iftikhar Muhammad Chaudhry, the chief justice of Pakistan,
resigned over the disappearance of thousands of Pakistani civilians—many of
them have been reportedly handed over to U.S. intelligence.[64] Since 9/11, the
disappearance of thousands of civilians in Pakistan has brought additional tur-
bulence and antigovernment sentiment in the country.[65] I personally met several
relatives of these disappeared persons who expressed their anger at the Pakistani
government for its inability to protect their basic rights.

Demand for Reparations and an Apology

Through these detailed oral histories, I hope that readers allow themselves to see
detainees as human beings with ambitions and dreams. I would like the general
public to know what it feels like to be placed in solitary confinement for months,
cut off from the rest of the world without any ray of hope for the future. More
specifically, I hope the readers not only contemplate but feel at a visceral level
what it means to live with the stigma of being called a terrorist when one isn't.
Would they want to be compensated for each day of freedom that they lost?
What kind of compensation would they ask for? The compensation that readers
would want for themselves is what I am hoping the six individuals and the thousands who were in similar situations receive.

In April 2002, the Center for Constitutional Rights filed a class-action
lawsuit, *Turkmen v. Ashcroft*,[66] which challenged the Department of Justice for
arresting Arabs and South Asian individuals "on the pretext of minor immigration violations, and secretly detaining them for the weeks and months that the
FBI took to clear them of terrorism." The lawsuit also charged that some of
the 9/11 detainees were "improperly assigned to the Administrative Maximum
Special Housing Unit...[and] subjected to physical and verbal abuse...and
obstructed in their efforts to practice their religion." It claimed that the U.S. government violated the U.S. Constitution and international human rights law.[67]
In November 2009, five of the *Turkmen* plaintiffs accepted a settlement with the
U.S. government for $1.26 million. In June 2010, the CCR filed a motion to
seek permission from the district court to amend the complaint to add six new
plaintiffs. The case is still pending.

The Urban Justice Center also filed a lawsuit, which sued the government
for physically abusing detainees who were initially arrested for criminal charges

unrelated to terrorism and kept at the MDC in New York.[68] In February 2006, the government paid one of the plaintiffs, Ehab Elmaghraby, $300,000 during settlement but refused to accept any liability or fault.[69] The second plaintiff, Javaid Iqbal, did not accept the settlement and filed an appeal in which he argued that top administration officials, including the former U.S. attorney general John Ashcroft and the FBI director Robert S. Mueller III, were responsible for the abuse that he suffered during his detention at the MDC. On May 18, 2009, the U.S. Supreme Court rejected the lawsuit on the basis of insufficient evidence and ruled that Mr. Iqbal had not included enough facts in his complaint to show that the top administration had "adopted and implemented the detention policies at issue...for the purpose of discriminating on account of race, religion, or national origin" rather than "for a neutral, investigative reason."[70]

The wars in Afghanistan and Iraq and the constant threat of terrorism have created a pernicious climate of fear in which it has been difficult to hold the U.S. government fully accountable for violating the legal and human rights of detainees/deportees. The courts constantly excuse the illegal actions of the intelligence community and the administration and ask for additional evidence.[71] However, this fear and the Supreme Court's response are not new. During World War II, the U.S. Supreme Court justified the internment of Japanese Americans,[72] and it took the government over 40 years to accept its wrongdoing and to offer reparations.[73] I am certain that with time the same will happen for the 9/11 detainees. My hope is that the government will apologize to the immigrants who were unfairly targeted by its "security" operations and that Americans will look back to the post-9/11 era as a dark period in the nation's history.

Notes

Introduction

1. Click10.com, "FBI Investigates Mysterious United Airline Pilot: Anjum Pervaiz Shiekh Vanished Two Days Before Attack," September 17, 2001 (accessed July 2002). No longer available online; hard copy available from the author.

2. I use the general term *law enforcement officer* to refer to any government employee who is responsible for the prevention, investigation, apprehension, or detention of individuals suspected or convicted of offenses against criminal and immigration laws. In cases in which a detainee clearly refers to a specific type of law enforcement officer, such as an agent from the Federal Bureau of Investigation or Immigration and Nationalization Services, I use specific titles such as FBI agent or INS agent. Sometimes, detainees were not able to determine whether the individual(s) they were speaking with worked with the FBI, the INS, or some other government department. In these cases, I use the term *law enforcement officer*.

3. I define racial/religious profiling as a strategy in which race/religion is considered a criterion for the arrest of an individual instead of behavior or another cause. We can determine whether or not racial profiling is occurring if the arrest would not be made when "white woman" is substituted for "Muslim man." For additional information, see David Harris, *Profiles in Injustice: Why Racial Profiling Cannot Work* (New York: New Press, 2002).

4. Anjum Shiekh, interview with author, written notes, South Beach, FL, October 2002.

5. Reference to the historic period before the establishment of internment camps in the United States, when the governments and the general public started to discriminate against Japanese Americans because of their race and nationality. Before the mass internment, the government arrested 1,370 Japanese Americans classified as "dangerous enemy aliens." See Roger Daniels, Sandra Taylor, and Harry Kitano, eds., *Japanese Americans, From Relocation to Redress* (Salt Lake City, UT: University of Utah Press, 1986).

6. I use the term *Muslim-looking* to illustrate that some non-Muslim males, especially Sikhs and non-Muslim Arabs and South Asians, became targets of law enforcement policies.

7. Many government officials characterized these arrests as important steps in achieving national security. One example is from Attorney General John Ashcroft's prepared speeches. Department of Justice, *Attorney General John Ashcroft, Prepared*

Remarks for the US Mayors Conference of October 25 (2001), http://www.justice.
gov/archive/ag/speeches/2001/agcrisisremarks10_25.htm (accessed March 15,
2002). I provide additional examples in the rest of the book.

8. The following is a partial list of books that address the issues of civil liberties after
a wartime emergency:

Brown, Cynthia. *Lost Liberties: Ashcroft and the Assault on Personal Freedom.* New
York: New Press, 2003.

Cole, David. *Enemy Aliens: Double Standards and Constitutional Freedoms in the
War on Terrorism.* New York: New Press, 2003.

Daniels, Roger. *Concentration Camps USA: Japanese Americans and World War II.*
New York: Holt, Rinehart, and Winston, 1972.

Delgado, Richard. *Justice at War: Civil Liberties and Civil Rights During Times of
Crisis.* New York: New York University Press, 2003.

Dershowitz, Alan. *Shouting Fire: Civil Liberties in a Turbulent Age.* Boston: Little,
Brown, 2002.

Drinnon, Richard. *Keeper of Concentration Camps: Dillon S. Myer and American
Racism.* Berkeley: University of California Press, 1987.

Finan, Christopher. *From the Palmer Raids to the Patriot Act: A History of the Fight
for Free Speech in America.* Boston: Beacon Press, 2007.

Fox, Stephen. *American's Invisible Gulag: A Biography of German American
Internment & Exclusion in World War II: Memory and History.* New York: Peter
Lang, 2000.

———. *The Unknown Internment: An Oral History of the Relocation of Italian
Americans During World War II.* Boston: Twayne, 1990.

Fried, Albert. *McCarthyism: The Great American Red Scare : A Documentary History.*
New York: Oxford University Press, 1997.

Fried, Richard. *Nightmare in Red: The McCarthy Era in Perspective.* New York:
Oxford University Press, 1990.

Griffith, Robert. *The Politics of Fear: Joseph R. McCarthy and the Senate.* Amherst:
University of Massachusetts Press, 1970.

Hagopian, Elaine. *Civil Rights in Peril: The Targeting of Arabs and Muslims.* London:
Pluto, 2004.

Harth, Erica. *Last Witnesses: Reflections on the Wartime Internment of Japanese
Americans.* New York: Palgrave for St. Martin's Press, 2001.

Harvey, Gardiner. *Pawns in a Triangle of Hate: The Peruvian Japanese and the United
States.* Seattle: University of Washington Press, 1981.

Houston, Jeanne W., and James D. *Farewell to Manzanar: A True Story of Japanese
American Experience During and After the World War II Internment.* Boston:
Houghton Mifflin, 1973.

Hoyt, Edwin. *The Palmer Raids, 1919–1920: An Attempt to Suppress Dissent.* New
York: The Seabury Press, 2003.

Inada, Lawson Fusao. *Only What We Could Carry: The Japanese American Internment
Experience.* [S.l.]: Heyday, 2001.

Irons, Peter. *Justice at War.* New York: Oxford University Press, 1983.

Johnson, Haynes B. *The Age of Anxiety: McCarthyism to Terrorism.* Orlando, FL:
Harcourt, Inc., 2005.

Leone, Richard, and Greg Anrig. *The War on Our Freedoms: Civil Liberties in an Age
of Terrorism.* New York: BBS Public Affairs, 2003.

Meeropol, Rachel, and Reed Brody. *America's Disappeared: Detainees, Secret Imprisonment, and the "War on Terror."* An open media book. New York: Seven Stories Press, 2005.

Morgan, Ted. *Reds: McCarthyism in Twentieth-Century America.* New York: Random House, 2003.

Ngai, Mae. *Impossible Subjects: Illegal Aliens and the Making of Modern America. Politics and Society in Twentieth-Century America.* Princeton, NJ: Princeton University Press, 2004.

Parenti, Christian. *The Soft Cage: Surveillance in America: From Slavery to the War on Terror.* New York: Basic Books, 2003.

Preston, William. *Aliens and Dissenters: Federal Suppressions of Radicals, 1903–1933.* Cambridge, MA: Harvard University Press, 1963.

Rehnquist, William. *All the Laws but One: Civil Liberties in the Wartime.* New York: Alfred A. Knopf, 1998.

Robinson, Greg. *By Order of the President: FDR and the Internment of Japanese Americans.* Cambridge, MA: Harvard University Press, 2001.

Schrecker, Ellen. *Many Are the Crimes: McCarthyism in America.* Boston: Little, Brown, 1998.

Stanley, Jerry. *I Am An American: A True Story of Japanese Internment.* New York: Crown Publishers, 1994.

Takahashi, Jerald. *Nisei/Sansei: Shifting Japanese American Identities and Politics.* Philadelphia: Temple University Press, 1997.

Takezawa, Yasuko. *Breaking the Silence.* Ithaca, NY: Cornell University Press, 1995.

Yamamoto, Eric. *Race, Rights, and Reparation: Law and the Japanese American Internment.* Gaithersburg, MD: Aspen Law & Business, 2001.

9. John Chester and Alan M. Dershowitz, *Crisis in Freedom: The Alien and Sedition Acts* (Delanco, NJ: Notable Trials Library, 2002).

10. Hoyt, *Palmer Raids,* 14, 15.

11. Several scholars have written about the Palmer Raids. Following is a partial listing:

Coben, Stanley. *A. Mitchell Palmer: Politician.* New York: Columbia University Press, 1963.

Finan, Christopher. *From the Palmer Raids to the Patriot Act: A History of the Fight for Free Speech in America.* Boston: Beacon Press, 2007.

Hoyt, *Palmer Raids.*

Morgan, Ted. *Reds: McCarthyism in Twentieth-Century America.* New York: Random House, 2003.

Panunzio, Constantine. *The Deportation Cases of 1919–1920, Civil Liberties in American History.* New York: Da Capo Press, 1970 [ca. 1921].

12. Howard Zinn, *A People's History of the United States* (New York: Harper Collins, 2003).

13. Coben, *A. Mitchell Palmer.*

14. Daniels, Taylor, and Kitano, *Japanese Americans.*

15. Daniels, *Concentration Camps USA.*

16. Ibid.

17. Inada, *Only What We Could Carry.*

18. Fox, *American's Invisible Gulag*; Stephen Fox, *The Unknown Internment: An Oral History of the Relocation of Italian Americans During World War II* (Boston: Twayne, 1990).

19. Following is a partial list of scholars who have discussed the relationship between race and internment during World War II:
    Drinnon, *Keeper of Concentration Camps Dillon S. Myer and American Racism.*
    Takahashi, *Nisei/Sansei.*
    Takaki, Ronald. *Double Victory: A Multicultural History of America in World War II.* Boston: Little, Brown and Co., 2000.
    Yamamoto, *Race, Rights, and Reparation.*
20. Harvey, *Pawns in a Triangle of Hate.* Also see Casey Peek and Irum Shiekh, *Hidden Internment: The Art Shibayama Story,* Berkeley, CA: Peek Media, 2004.
21. A. Fried, *McCarthyism*; R. Fried, *Nightmare in Red.*
22. Ibid. A. Fried.
23. Iris Chang, *The Chinese in America: A Narrative History* (New York: Viking, 2003).
24. Amy Chen, *Chinatown Files* (New York: Filmakers Library Inc. 2002).
25. Richard Turner, *Islam in the African American Experience* Bloomington: Indiana University Press, 1997), 11.
26. Several scholars researched records and slave narratives to trace the lives and stories of Muslims among slaves who kept their faith despite encountering a foreign environment hostile to its practice. Among these include the following:
    Terry Alford, *Prince Among Slaves.* New York: Harcourt Brace Jovanovich, 1977.
    Allan Austin, *African Muslims in Antebellum America: Transatlantic Stories and Spiritual Struggles.* New York: Routledge, 1997.
    Sulviane Diouf, *Servants of Allah: African Muslims enslaved in the Americas.* New York: New York University Press. 1998.
27. Michael W. Suleiman, "Introduction: The Arab Immigrant Experience," in *Arabs in America: Building a New Future*, ed. Michael Suleiman (Philadelphia: Temple University Press, 1999), 3.
28. Yvonne Haddad, "Muslim Communities in North America: Introduction," in *Muslim Communities in North America*, ed. Yvonne Haddad and Jane Smith (Albany, NY: State University of New York Press, 1994), xviii.
29. Yvonne Haddad, "The Dynamics of Islamic Identity in North America," in *Muslims on the Americanization Path?*, ed. Yvonne Haddad and John Esposito (Atlanta, GA: Scholars Press, 1998), 19–46.
30. After the death of Wallace D. Mohammad in August 2008, the leadership has not been fully defined.
31. Haddad, "The Dynamics of Islamic Identity," 24.
32. Nilufer Ahmed, Gladis Kaufman, and Shamim Naim, "South Asian Families in the United States: Pakistani, Bangladeshi, and Indian Muslims," in *Family and Gender Among American Muslims*, ed. Barbara C. Aswad and Barbara Bilgé (Philadelphia: Temple University Press, 1996), 166.
33. The exact number of Muslims in the United States is contested; estimates range from 2 to 7 million. The Pew Research Center estimates the total population of Muslims to be at 2.35 million; see Pew Research Center, *Muslim Americans: Middle Class and Mostly Mainstream* (Washington, DC: Pew Research Center, 2007). Council on American-Islamic Relations (CAIR) estimated this number to be 7 million. See http://www.cair.com/aboutIslam/IslamBasics.aspx (accessed November 8, 2010).
34. Many scholars from various disciplines have discussed anti-Muslim sentiment. Following is a partial listing:

Haddad, Yvonne. "American Foreign Policy in the Middle East and Its Impact on the Identity of Arab Muslims in the United States." In *The Muslims of America*, edited by Yvonne Haddad. New York: Oxford University Press, 1991, 217–235.

Shaheen, Jack G. *Arab and Muslim Stereotyping in American Popular Culture*. Occasional Papers Series. Washington, DC: Center for Muslim-Christian Understanding, History and International Affairs, Edmund A. Walsh School of Foreign Service, Georgetown University, 1997).

Suleiman, Michael. "Islam, Muslims and Arabs in America: The Other of the Other of the Other...." *Journal of Muslim Minority Affairs* 19, no. 1 (1999): 33–47

———. "Introduction: The Arab Immigrant Experience."

35. Haddad, "American Foreign Policy in the Middle East."
36. Edward Said defines *orientalism* as a hegemonic discourse about the East instituted by orientalists as they invaded, possessed, and re-created the Orient to establish and maintain their superiority. In particular, orientalism uses modes of communication—including political accounts, journals, travel writing, history scholarships, and literature—to paint a seemingly objective picture of the East for Western eyes. The Western scholar's visit to the East earned him the credibility to decode the myth of the Orient and render it as objective reality, retrievable by the general public for informed discussions in parlors and at tea parties. Said argues that orientalism reveals less about the characteristics of the East than about the subjectivity, consciousness, and culture of the West. Nonetheless, orientalist discourse has been successful in creating stereotypes about the "Orientals" that linger today.
37. Edward W. Said, *Orientalism* (New York: Vintage Books, 1979).
38. Shaheen, *Arab and Muslim Stereotyping*, 12.
39. Jack G. Shaheen, *Reel Bad Arabs: How Hollywood Vilifies a People* (New York: Olive Branch Press, 2001).
40. The following documents discuss FBI sting operations and programs, which started to emerge in the late 1960s:

Gessert, Charles. "A Non-Arab Looks at an Anti-Arab-American Policy." In *The Civil Rights of Arab-Americans: "The Special Measures,"* edited by M.C. Bassiouni, 16–27. North Darthmouth, MA: Association of Arab-American University Graduates, 1974.

Jabara, Abdeen. "Operation Arab: The Nixon Administration's Measures in the United States after Munich." In *The Civil Rights of Arab-Americans: "The Special Measures,"* edited by M.C. Bassiouni, 1–15. North Darthmouth, MA: Association of Arab-American University Graduates, 1974.

Jones, Curtis. *ABSCAM, Its Operation and Political Consequences*. Public administration series—bibliography, no. P-1085. Monticello, IL: Vance Bibliographies, 1982.

Shah, Mowahid. *The FBI and the Civil Rights of Arab-Americans*. Washington, DC: American-Arab Anti-Discrimination Committee, 1980.

Shaheen, Jack G. *Abscam: Arabiaphobia in America*. Washington, DC: American-Arab Anti-Discrimination Committee, 1980.

41. American-Arab Anti-Discrimination Committee, "1998–2000 Report on Hate Crimes & Discrimination Against Arab Americans," American-Arab Anti-Discrimination Committee Research Institute, Washington DC. 2001, 29.

42. Kathleen M. Moore, "A Closer Look at Anti-Terrorism Law: American-Arab Anti-Discrimination Committee V. Reno and the Construction of Aliens Rights," in *Arabs in America: Building a New Future*, ed. Michael Suleiman (Philadelphia: Temple University Press, 1999), 84.
43. Suad Joseph, "Against the Grain of the Nation—the Arab," in *Arabs in America: Building a New Future*, ed. Michael Suleiman (Philadelphia: Temple University Press, 1999), 261.
44. John Esposito, *The Islamic Threat* (New York: Oxford University Press, 1992), 5.
45. From here on, I use the terms *Special Interest, 9/11 detainee*, and *immigration detainee* interchangeably. FBI and immigration officials coined this term for internal use; therefore, it is difficult for the public to determine which of the 9/11 detainees were "of interest."
46. Office of the Inspector General, *The September 11 Detainees: A Review of Aliens Held on Immigration Charges in Connection with the Investigation of the September 11 Attacks* Washington, DC. U.S. Department of Justice, April 2003), 1.
47. Dan Eggen, "Count of Released Detainees Is Hard to Pin Down," *Washington Post*, November 6, 2001.
48. The total number of detentions is very hard to pin down. Many newspapers, including the *New York Times* and *Washington Post*, tried to keep a tally initially but eventually gave up. I personally interviewed individuals arrested in December 2001 who were detained in the MDC under suspicion of terrorism. However, I don't dwell on the total number of 9/11 detentions because that is not the focus of this book.
49. The Office of the Inspector General report was released to the public in June 2003, but on the cover page, it is dated April 2003. Many public agencies received their copies in April 2003. In 2003 the Office of the Inspector General (OIG) released two reports about 9/11 detainees. The first one, dated April 2003 and released in June 2003, was entitled *The September 11 Detainees*. In December 2003, OIG released a supplemental report, which concentrated on the ninth floor of the MDC of Brooklyn, New York, and Passaic County (NJ) Jail. This report is entitled *Supplemental Report on September 11 Detainees' Allegations of Abuse at the Metropolitan Detention Center in Brooklyn, New York* (Department of Justice, December 2003). Throughout the document, I refer to it as "supplemental report."
50. OIG, *September 11 Detainees*, 5.
51. Ibid, 2.
52. Examples include Mohammed Azmath, who was eventually deported on a credit card charge, and Ansar Mahmood, who was eventually deported for a criminal charge of helping undocumented immigrants. The OIG's report does not provide specific names of the cases and, therefore, it is not clear if individuals like Azmath or were included in their definition of Special Interest Cases. Azmath was initially arrested for an expired visa, and criminal charges of credit card fraud were added in December 2001.
53. OIG, *September 11 Detainees*, 2.
54. Ibid., 21.
55. Ibid. Some French, British, and German citizens were held in the MDC. My conversations with the MDC detainees helped me understand that these nationals were originally born in Pakistan and Egypt and moved to the United States for better opportunities.

56. Human Rights Watch, *Presumption of Guilt: Human Rights Abuses of Post-September 11 Detainees* (Washington, DC: Human Rights Watch, 2002), 10.

57. Some scholars may argue that the large number of Pakistanis arrested after 9/11 corresponds to the fact that the intelligence community has identified Pakistan as a haven for Al-Qaeda supporters. However, using this argument, more individuals from Afghanistan should have been arrested, given that Al-Qaeda and the Taliban originated from Afghanistan. The majority of the Afghani population in the United States lives on the West Coast in places far away from the 9/11 attacks, like Fremont and Concord, California. I believe this distance explains why the number of Afghanis arrested after 9/11 remained low. Moreover, the fact that several Sikhs from India were mistakenly arrested as members of the Taliban clearly shows that the intelligence community was not provided training in how to go about finding suspicious people. Instead, they decided to detain individuals based on racial profiling and stereotypes.

58. *USA Today*, "Official: 15 of 19 Hijackers Were Saudis," February 6, 2002, http://www.usatoday.com/news/world/2002/02/06/saudi.htm (accessed July 11, 2009). One was from Egypt, two were from the United Arab Emirates, and one was from Lebanon.

59. The exact number is not provided in the OIG report, but the graph bar height for Saudi Arabia is equal to countries like India and Morocco. OIG, *September 11 Detainees*, 21.

60. Zogby polls ranked Michigan's Arab American population as the second largest in the United States, after California. However, the Southeast Michigan area has the highest concentration of Arab Americans in the United States—compared to California, where the population is spread out. "Arab Detroit," http://www.arab-detroit.com/arabamericans.php, March 24, 2008. Also, see Pew Research Center, *Muslim Americans*, 2007.

61. The OIG report does not provide detention statistics for Michigan or any other states. OIG, *September 11 Detainees*, 22.

62. Imad Hamad (director of American Arab Anti-Discrimination Committee), interview with author, Dearborn, MI, October 10, 2003. I held conversations with some community organizers as well.

63. Personal conversations held with several Arab American community leaders in Dearborn, Michigan, April 2004.

64. OIG, *Supplemental Report*, 4.

65. The U.S. Census does not provide demographics for Muslims because it does not collect data based on religion. However, it is estimated that between 2 and 7 million Muslims live in the United States (Pew Research Center 2007 and CAIR 2010) States like New York, New Jersey, Michigan, and Florida have large populations of Muslims and Arabs. The U.S. Department of State fact sheet states that of American Muslims, 32.2 percent live on the East Coast, 25.3 percent live in the South, 24.3 percent in the Central/Great Lakes Region, and 18.2 percent in the West.

66. The FBI discovered that the 19 hijackers lived in San Diego, California; Southern Florida; and New Jersey. Only one hijacker had lived in New York and San Diego. See FBI Press Release, "The FBI Releases 19 Photographs of Individuals Believed to Be the Hijackers of the Four Airlines that Crashed on September 11, 01," September 27, 2001, http://www.fbi.gov/pressrel/pressrel01/092701hjpic.htm (accessed July 12, 2009).

67. Figure 3 of the OIG report has redacted statistics for states other than New York and New Jersey. It is unknown how many individuals were arrested from California and Florida. See OIG, *September 11 Detainees*, 22.

68. Muzaffar Chishti, America's Challenge: Domestic Security, Civil Liberties, and National Unity After September 11 (Washington, DC: Migration Policy Institute, 2003), appendix E.

69. Ibid., appendix A.

70. OIG, *September 11 Detainees*, 1.

71. Steven Brill, *After: The Rebuilding and Defending of America in the September 12 Era* (New York: Simon & Schuster, 2003), 38.

72. OIG, *September 11 Detainees*, 1.

73. Scott Shane and Lowell Bergman, "FBI Struggling to Reinvent Itself to Fight Terror," *New York Times*, October 10, 2006.

74. Daniel Sneider, "Lack of Arabic Speakers Is a Crack in US Security," *Mercury News*, (San Jose, CA, October 5, 2004).

75. Tips came from the FBI hotline, which encouraged individuals to report suspicious people.

76. Human Rights Watch, *Presumption of Guilt*, 14.

77. Nina Bernstein, "In FBI, Innocent Detainee Found Unlikely Ally," *New York Times*, June 30, 2004.

78. Erica Noonan, "Fighting Terrorism Impact on New England/Ceremonial Garb; Sikh Is Prosecuted for Sword," *Boston Globe*, October 11, 2001.

79. OIG, *September 11 Detainees*, 12.

80. Ibid., 17.

81. Coleen Rowley, "Balancing Civil Liberties With the Need for Effective Investigation," in *Patriotism, Democracy and Common Sense: Restoring America's Promise at Home and Abroad*, ed. Alan Curtis (Lanham, MD: Rowman & Littlefield Publishers, 2004, 349–366.

82. Ibid. 358.

83. OIG, *September 11 Detainees*, 15–17.

84. Ibid., 1.

85. Brill, *After*, 38, 117, and 147.

86. Human Rights Watch, *Presumption of Guilt*, 65.

87. Many of the reports prepared about 9/11 detentions affirm this statement; for example, see OIG, *September 11 Detainees*. See note 104.

88. Andrea Elliott, "Militant's Path from Pakistan to Times Square," *New York Times*, June 22, 2010.

89. Sandra Nichols, interview with author, tape recording, New York, NY, January 2003.

90. Michael Welch, *Detained: Immigration Laws and the Expanding I.N.S. Jail Complex* (Philadelphia: Temple University, 2002), 43.

91. Cole. *Enemy Aliens.*

92. Irum Shiekh, "Racializing, Criminalizing, and Silencing 9/11 Deportees," in *Keeping Out the Other*, ed. David C. Brotherton and Philip Kretsedemas (New York: Columbia University Press, 2008), 81–107.

93. INS memo, Office of Field Operations, "Memorandum for Regional Directors, from Michael A. Pearson, Ins Executive Associate Commissioner," Washington. DC, 10-23-2001.

94. Information on the PATRIOT Act and additional programs, policies, and laws approved immediately after 9/11 can be found at the following sites:

Butterfield, Jeanne. *Executive Branch Actions*. Washington. DC, American Immigration Lawyers Association, 2002. http://www.aila.org/ (accessed August 15, 2002).

Network for Immigrants and Refugee Rights. *September 11: A Chronology of the "War Against Terrorism" & Immigrants Rights*. Network for Immigrants and Refugee Rights, Oakland, CA, Summer 2002.

Lawyers Committee for Human Rights. *A Chronology of the Government's Restrictions on Civil Liberties*, 2002. http://www.lchr.org/us_law/loss/time-line/sep_01.htm (accessed September 13, 2003).

95. U.S. Department of Homeland Security, *An Assessment of United States Immigration and Customs Enforcement's Fugitive Operations Teams* (Washington, DC: U.S. Department of Homeland Security, 2007), 4.

96. Office of Deputy Attorney General, *Guidance for Absconder Apprehension Initiative* (Washington DC: Office of Deputy Attorney General, January 25, 2002).

97. *[67 FR 155 at 52583, 8–12–02]*. The proposed rule appeared in the June 13, 2002, federal register *[67 FR 114 at 40581]*. Comments on the proposed rule were due July 15, 2002. The final rule is effective September 11, 2002 *[67 FR 173 at 57032]*.

98. American Civil Liberties Union (ACLU), "ACLU Says New Border Fingerprinting System Likely to Sow Confusion, Tracking of Arab and Muslims Based on National Origin Will Continue," January 5, 2004, http://www.aclu.org/safefree/general/16930prs20040105.html, (accessed March 28, 2008).

99. Michael Welch, *Scapegoats of September 11th: Hate Crimes & State Crimes in the War on Terror* (New Brunswick, NJ: Rutgers University Press, 2006), 85.

100. Abdus Ghazali, "Pakistanis' Exodus to Canada Accelerate," *Dawn, http://www.dawn.com/-*, March 16, 2003; (accessed April 5, 2004). Margaret Philp, "Pakistanis Flocking to Canada," *Globe and Mail*, March 15, 2003. http://www.theglobeandmail.com/ (accessed April 5, 2003).

101. Since 2002, Special Registration laws have gone through several changes, and today they are also called the National Security Entry-Exit Registration System. The latest information about Special Registration or the National Security Entry-Exit Registration System can be found at http://www.ice.gov/pi/specialregis-tration/index.htm. Because of the government's continuous focus on Muslim males, for data analysis, I use those 24 countries that became subject to Special Registration requirements in 2002. The following countries became subject to Special Registration in 2002: Afghanistan, Algeria, Bahrain, Bangladesh, Egypt, Eritrea, Indonesia, Iran, Iraq, Jordan, Kuwait, Lebanon, Libya, Morocco, North Korea, Oman, Pakistan, Qatar, Saudi Arabia, Somalia, Sudan, Syria, Tunisia, United Arab Emirates, Yemen. Of these, North Korea is the only country which is not predominantly Muslim and is not included in the graph. Source: US Bureau of Immigration and Customs Enforcement, Special Registration Archives: http://www.ice.gov/nseers/archive.htm (accessed February 3, 2004).

102. Eric Lichtblau, "US Report Faults the Roundup of Illegal Immigrants after 9/11," *New York Times*, June 3, 2003.

103. A partial list of reports is provided by date:

Amnesty International. *Memorandum to the US Attorney General—Amnesty International's Concerns Relating to the Post September 11 Investigations*. Amnesty International, November 2001.

Amnesty International. *Amnesty International's Concerns Regarding Post September 11 Detentions in the USA*. Amnesty International, 2002.

American Civil Liberties Union. *Civil Liberties After 9–11: The ACLU Defends Freedom*. New York: American Civil Liberties Union, 2002.

Human Rights Watch, *Presumption of Guilt*.

Council on American-Islamic Relations. *The Status of Muslim Civil Rights in the United States: Stereotypes and Civil Liberties*2002. http://www.cair.com/CivilRights/CivilRightsReports/2002Report.aspx (accessed April 3, 3003).

Lawyers Committee for Human Rights. *A Year of Loss*. New York: Lawyers Committee for Human Rights, 2002.

American-Arab Anti-Discrimination Committee, *Report on Hate Crimes & Discrimination Against Arab Americans: The Post-September 11 Backlash, September 11, 2001 to October 11, 2001*. Washington, DC: American-Arab Anti-Discrimination Committee Research Institute, 2003.

OIG. *September 11 Detainees*.

Migration Policy Institute. *America's Challenge: Domestic Security, Civil Liberties, and National Unity after September 11*. Washington, DC. Migration Policy Institute, 2003.

OIG. *Supplemental Report*.
104. Amnesty International, *Memorandum to the US Attorney General*, 1.
105. Ibid., 1, 6.
106. Human Rights Watch, *Presumption of Guilt*, 5.
107. OIG, *September 11 Detainees* and *Supplemental Report*.
108. Ibid., 59.
109. Ibid., 97.
110. Ibid., 164.
111. Brill, *After*, 627–639.
112. Ibid., 612.
113. Ibid., 149.
114. Cole, *Enemy Aliens*.
115. Welch, *Scapegoats of September 11*.
116. Nancy Chang and the Center for Constitutional Rights, *Silencing Political Dissent, How Post-September 11 Anti-Terrorism Measures Threaten Our Civil Liberties* (New York: Seven Stories Press, 2002).
117. Vijay Prashad, "The Green Menace: McCarthyism After 9/11," *Subcontinental* 1 no. 1 (Spring 2003): 65–75.
118. Tram Nguyen, *We Are All Suspects Now: Untold Stories from Immigrant America After 9/11* (Boston: Beacon Press, 2005).
119. Moazzam Begg and Victoria Brittain, *Enemy Combatant: My Imprisonment at Guantánamo, Bagram, and Kandahar* (New York: New Press, 2006).
120. James Yee, *For God and Country: Faith and Patriotism Under Fire* (New York: Public Affairs, 2005).
121. David Cole and Jules Lobel, "Are We Safer, A Report Card on the War on Terror," *Los Angeles Times*, November 18, 2007.
122. Ali Saleh Kahlah Al-Marri, arrested in December 2001. Additional information about his case can be accessed from various websites, including Human Rights First, Law and Security, http://www.humanrightsfirst.org/us_law/inthecourts/supreme_court_al_marri.htm.

123. New York University, *Terrorist Trial Report Card: September 11, 2001–September 11, 2009, U.S. Edition* (New York: Center on Law and Security, NYU School of Law, 2009); Serrin Turner and Stephen J. Schulhofer, "The Secrecy Problem in Terrorism Trials" (New York: Brennan Center for Justice at NYU School of Law, (2005); http://www.brennancenter.org/content/resource/the_secrecy_problem_in_terrorism_trials/ (accessed September 20, 2009), Richard B. Zabel and James J. Benjamin Jr., "Human Rights First, In Pursuit of Justice: Prosecuting Terrorism Cases in the Federal Courts" (2008). http://www.humanrightsfirst.info/pdf/080521-USLS-pursuit-justice.pdf (accessed November 5, 2009).

124. Welch, *Scapegoats of September 11.*

125. Some of the intelligence claimed that additional terrorist attacks might be coming, and they were sometimes referred to as the "Next Wave" or "Another Wave of Violence." See OIG, *September 11 Detainees*, 11, 74.

126. Michel Foucault, *Discipline and Punish: The Birth of the Prison* (New York: Random House, 1975).

127. Antonio Gramsci, *Selections from the Prison Notebooks of Antonio Gramsci*, trans. Quentin Hoare and Geoffrey Nowell Smith (New York: International Publishers, 1972).

128. Ibid.

129. Michael Parenti, *Lockdown America* (New York: Verso, 1999). Like Parenti, I argue that beyond economic interests, there are other larger political interests that necessitate the manufacturing of Muslim terrorists.

130. OIG, *September 11 Detainees*, 21.

131. The FBI had completed numerous background checks on the detainees before they released or deported them, and I knew, therefore, that these individuals did not have any connections with terrorism.

132. Irum Shiekh, "Insider/Outsider: Government Spy or a Terrorist? Dilemmas of Academic Research in the Post 9/11 Setting," *Amerasia Journal* 33 no. 2 (Fall 2007): 26–40. .

133. Calvin Pryluck, "Ultimately We Are All Outsiders: The Ethics of Documentary Filming," *Journal of the University Film Association* 28 no. 1 (Winter 1976): 21–29.

134. The recreation area also became a punitive device. Depending on the moods of the prison guards, detainees were placed in the cold for over five hours without any warm clothes.

135. OIG's description of the Administrative Maximum (ADMAX) Special Housing Unit matches the description provided by detainees.

136. Steven Watt is one of the many attorneys who worked on Mohamed E******'s case. Conversation held with the author in New York, April 2004.

137. Zacarias Moussaoui was arrested in August 2001 in Minnesota and charged with an immigration violation. He was enrolled in a flight school.

138. The overwhelming majority of individuals arrested had minor immigration violations; in cases in which individuals were not out of status (one example is included in this book, Ansar Mahmood), the government added charges such as harboring illegal immigrants after they could not find any immigration violation to justify their detentions.

139. A generalized response I got from various officials.

140. Brill, *After.*

141. OIG, *September 11 Detainees* and *Supplemental Report.*

142. In some cases, more than one attorney represented the case. I had the opportunity to talk to at least one attorney for each case.

143. I provide the file number for each legal case in the appropriate chapter.
144. For a list of major media articles written for each narrative, see the beginning of each chapter.
145. Some examples of oral histories of Japanese Americans are listed below:

Bahr, Diana M. *The Unquiet Nisei: An Oral History of the Life of Sue Kunitomi Embrey*. New York: Palgrave Macmillan, 2007.

Hansen, Arthur. *Japanese American World War II Evacuation Oral History Project*. Westport, CT: Meckler, 1990.

Houston and Houston, *Farewell to Manzanar*. Boston: Houghton Mifflin,

Stanley, Jerry. *I Am an American: A True Story of Japanese Internment*. New York: Crown Publishers, 1994.

Tateishi, John. *And Justice for All: An Oral History of the Japanese American Detention Camps*. New York: Random House, 1984.

Uchida, Yoshiko. *Desert Exile: The Uprooting of a Japanese American Family*. Seattle: University of Washington Press, 1984.

146. Pub.L.No. 104–132, 110 Stat. 1214 (1996) (the Act).

Chapter I The Transnational Implications of 9/11 Detentions

1. Throughout this chapter Mohammed Azmath is referred to as both Azmath and as Mohammed. The author follows the way his name appears in his legal files—Mohammed Azmath is his legal name but the author calls him Azmath on an informal basis.
2. This narrative primarily focuses on Azmath Mohammed. Ayub Khan was not available for an interview in 2003. I held some conversations with Ayub in my later visits, and we communicated through e-mail and letters. I incorporate some of those conversations in the narrative.
3. A partial listing of news articles about Azmath and Ayub is listed below:

Arena, Kelli, Susan Candiotti, and Eileen O'Connor. "Ashcroft Says More Attacks May Be Planned," *CNN.com*, September 18, 2001. http://archives.cnn.com/2001/US/09/17/inv.investigation.terrorism/index.html (accessed April 17, 2007).

Drew, Christopher. "After the Attacks: The Plot; Four People Flown to New York for Questioning in Connection With Attacks," *New York Times*, September 17, 2001.

Drew, Christopher, and Ralph Blumenthal. "A Nation Challenged: The Detained: Arrested Men's Shaved Bodies Drew Suspicion of the F.B.I.," *New York Times*, October 26, 2001.

Drew Christopher, and William Rashbaum. "2 Found With Box Cutters Remain Silent Suspects," *New York Times*, October 24, 2001.

Hedges, Chris. "After the Attacks: The Plot; New Jersey," *New York Times*, September 17, 2001.

Hirschkorn, Phil, and Jamie Colby. "Indian Men Look Back in Anger at U.S. Detainment," *CNN.com*, May 26, 2003 (accessed June 15, 2003).

Kovaleski, Serge F., and Fredrick Kunkle. "Focus Continues on Two New Jersey Men: Longtime Friends Facing Charges of Falsifying Passports in Native India," *Washington Post*, September 28, 2001.

Kovaleski, Serge F., and Rama Lakshmi. "Money Sent to India by 2 Detainees is Probed," *Washington Post*, October 7, 2001.

Milloy, Ross. "F.B.I. Holds Men Traveling with Knives," *New York Times*, September 14, 2001.

Van Natta, Don. "Arrests Have Yielded Little So Far, Investigators Say," *New York Times*, October 21, 2001.

Weiser, Benjamin. "Man Suspected of Terror Role Faces Deportation for Fraud," *New York Times*, June 7, 2002.

Worth, Robert. "Man Detained After 9/11 Says Rights Were Ignored," *New York Times*, May 11, 2002.

4. Drew and Blumenthal, "A Nation Challenged."
5. Mohammed Azmath, e-mail to author, September 9, 2007.
6. U.S. District Court, Southern District of New York, *United States v. Mohammed Azmath* (02-Cr. 45, Trial Transcripts, September 18, 2002).
7. U.S. District Court, Western District of Texas, "Application and Affidavit For Search Warrant," September 15, 2001.
8. Hirschkorn and Colby, "Indian Men Look Back."
9. Milloy, "F.B.I. Holds Men."
10. Arena, Candiotti, and O'Connor, "Ashcroft Says More Attacks."
11. Azmath told me he did not have a box cutter or a knife. Ayub Khan had a few box cutters, but that is not unusual given that he worked for a newspaper stand and box cutters are standard tools for the job. Possession of a box cutter does not make someone a terrorist.
12. Ayub Khan, e-mail to author, September 8, 2007.
13. Zacarias Moussaoui is a French Algerian national who was arrested in August 2001 in Minneapolis. He was attending a flight school, and after 9/11, he became a prime suspect in the 9/11 investigation. Moussaoui was convicted for the 9/11 attacks and sentenced to life in prison. See *BBC News*, "Moussaoui Is Spared Death Penalty: Al-Qaeda Plotter Zacarias Moussaoui is to face life in jail rather than execution, for his role in the 9/11 attacks, a US jury has decided," May 4, 2006 available at http://news.bbc.co.uk/2/hi/americas/4943196.stm assessed April 8, 2008. However, many scholars don't like to include him in analyses of 9/11 detention cases because he was arrested before the 9/11 attacks. Also see David Johnston and Philip Shenon, "A Nation Challenged: The Suspects: FBI Curbed Scrutiny of Man Now a Suspect in the Attacks," *New York Times*, October 6, 2001.
14. Emily Colborn, "Staging the Home Front: Spectacle, Spectatorship, and Post-Pearl Harbor Raids" (Paper presented at the Dokkyo International Forum on Performance Studies, Japan, December 2002).
15. Irum Shiekh, "Racializing, Criminalizing, and Silencing 9/11 Deportees," in *Keeping Out the Other*, ed. David C. Brotherton and Philip Kretsedemas (New York: Columbia University Press, 2008) 81–107.
16. Office of the Inspector General, *Supplemental Report on September 11 Detainees' Allegations of Abuse at the Metropolitan Detention Center in Brooklyn, New York* (Department of Justice, December 2003), 46.
17. Ibid, 4.
18. Alison Beigh Cowan, "5 Young Israelis, Caught in Net of Suspicion," *New York Times*, October 8, 2001. These young men were arrested on September 11 in midday after someone reported them as suspicious (I assume based on their Middle

Eastern looks). One of the five young men carried box cutters, one had $4,000 in cash, some had pictures of the World Trade Center wreckage, and all of them had immigration violations. However, their cases were never publicized like Azmath's case, and all five of them were released approximately two months after the detention. The article also mentions that the Israeli consulate intervened and tried to clarify the situation for the American authorities. Such privileges and interventions were not available for the Muslim detainees. Of course, most of the Muslim consulates (i.e., Pakistan and Egypt) did not have the same resources and networks.

19. Anthony Ricco, Letter to the Judge Hon. Shira A. Scheindlin, May 24, 2002; retrieved from *United States v. Mohammed Azmath* (02-Cr. 45).
20. Anthony Ricco and Steven Legon worked on Azmath's case together.
21. Serge F. Kovaleski and Rama Lakshmi, "Money Sent to India by 2 Detainees Is Probed," *Washington Post*, October 7, 2001.
22. Omer Farooq, "Pakistani Woman Escapes Deportation," *BBC News*, September 23, 2002.
23. Video interview with an anyonymous friend of Azmath, Hyderabad, India, October 2008.
24. U.S. District Court, District of New Jersey, "Application and Affidavit for Search Warrant," September 14, 2001.
25. Drew and Blumenthal, "A Nation Challenged."
26. U.S. District Court, Southern District of New York, *United States v. Mohammed Azmath* (02-Cr. 45, Trial Transcripts, September 18, 2002), 11, 12.
27. Ibid., 13, 14.
28. Syed Gul Mohammed Shah, a/k/a Ayub Ali Khan, "Sworn Statement for an Affidavit in Support of Motion to Suppress Statements, and Physical Evidence," May 1, 2002 (02-CR-44).
29. The *New York Times* has prepared special archives for Omar Abdel Rahman, the blind Egyptian imam, who has been considered a spiritual force behind the 1993 attacks. Some hold him responsible for the 2001 attacks also. See *New York Times*, "Omar Abdel Rahman: News about Abdel Rahman, including commentary and archival articles published in the New York Times", http://topics.nytimes.com/top/reference/timestopics/people/a/omar_abdel_rahman/index.html?8qa&scp=1-spot&sq=omar+Abdel+Rahman&st=nyt (accessed April 2, 2008).
30. I did not find a reference to Azmath being considered the 20th hijacker in any major newspaper. However, a web page referring to Azmath and Ayub as the 20th and 21st hijackers does exist. See Ewing2001, "The 20th Hijacker," December 22, 2003, http://911review.org/inn.globalfreepress/20th_Hijacker_AA43.html (accessed July 7, 2003). An unidentified FBI officer in charge of the operation was the source for this term.
31. As referenced earlier, an FBI agent made a sworn statement and called him a pilot. See U.S. District Court, District of New Jersey, "Application and Affidavit for Search Warrant," September 14, 2001.
32. Drew and Blumenthal, "A Nation Challenged."
33. Conversations held with various individuals who practice Sunni Islam.
34. Bureau of Prisons, File Records, Request for Administrative Remedy, dated July 17, 2002; provided to author in March 2003 by Azmath Mohammed.
35. Bureau of Prisons, File Records, Inmate Azmath Mohammed, Reg. No 51428–054, dated August 9, 2002, signed by Luis Penn Ann for Michael Zenk, Warden; provided to author in March 2003 by Azmath Mohammed.

36. Alison Mitchell, "U.S. Widens Charges in Trade Center Bombing," *New York Times*, May 27, 1993.

37. In September 2002, a nurse in Georgia reported that she overheard three young men saying, "They mourned on 9/11 and they are going to mourn again on 9/13." Various law enforcement agencies chased these young men and closed portions of Interstate 75 in Florida. Nationwide headlines depicted the three young men—Ayman Gheith, Omer Choudhary, and Kambiz Butt, all U.S. citizens and medical students—as potential terrorists. Detained for hours, Ayman, Omer, and Kambiz were finally cleared of all charges. In a press conference the next day, all three of the students denied making any reference to September 11. Ultimately, they were unable to continue their residency at the Dominica medical school in Florida and were reassigned. See David Kidwell, "Trio Stopped After Georgia Woman's Tip," *Miami Herald*, September 14, 2002.

38. Several community organizations—like Desis Rising Up and Moving, Islamic Circle of North America, Justice for Detainees, and Shubh Mathur—fought for Azmath's release, held protests, and issued press releases.

39. Many individuals use different names and passports to acquire a visa to travel outside the country. Many of these individuals don't consider this a crime because their purpose is to make some money for their families, not commit crimes.

40. Between February and May 2002, communal riots between Muslims and Hindus killed approximately 2,000 individuals in the state of Gujarat in India. The overwhelming majority were Muslims. Many young women and girls were raped before being killed. Several sources document these tragic riots; see Human Rights Watch, "We Have No Orders to Save You, State Participation and Complicity in Communal Violence in Gujarat," April 2002, http://www.hrw.org/reports/2002/india/ (accessed April 3, 2008).

41. Human Rights Watch, "After Gujarat Riots, Witnesses Face Intimidation: State Government Fails to Provide Protection; Time for New Delhi to Step In," September 24, 2004, http://www.hrw.org/english/docs/2004/09/23/india9383.htm (accessed April 8, 2008).

42. Reference to the Miami case, mentioned earlier, when three young doctors became suspects; see Kidwell, "Trio Stopped."

43. Many individuals—especially in the Middle East, South Asia, and other Islamic regions—believe that Muslims did not carry out the 9/11 attacks. See Pew Global Attitudes Project, "The Great Divide: How Westerns and Muslims View Each Other, Europe Muslims More Moderate," June 13, 2007, http://pewglobal.org/reports/display.php?PageID=832 (accessed April 2, 2008). This report confirms that a large sector of the Muslim world believes for various reasons that Muslims did not carry out the attacks. Although readers may not accept the validity of these statements, it is important to place them in the proper context: sometimes they simply reflect the belief that Muslims don't hate America. One funny explanation came from a young Pakistani man, who said, "Muslims are always late getting anywhere. How can they get to four airports and fly four planes on time? It can't be Muslims." Various conspiracy theories about the 9/11 attacks continue to float around within the United States and Europe.

44. Melinda Henneberger, "Terror in Oklahoma: Bias Attacks: Muslims Continue to Feel Apprehensive," *New York Times*, April 24, 1995.

45. Mohammad Atta, the Egyptian leader of the 9/11 hijackers.

46. Glen Johnson, "Probe Reconstructs Horror, Calculated Attacks on Planes," *Boston Globe*, November 23, 2001.
47. Drew and Blumenthal, "A Nation Challenged."
48. Dina Temple-Raston, "Enemy Within? Not Quite," *Washington Post*, September 9, 2007. Seven U.S. citizens of Yemeni heritage from Buffalo, New York, were arrested in September 2002 with the help of an informant.
49. Jeff Kearns, "Lodi Muslims: Under the 'Eye of Suspicion,'" *Frontline*, October 10, 2006, http://www.pbs.org/wgbh/pages/frontline/enemywithin/lodi/lodislide.html (accessed April 8, 2008).
50. Irum Shiekh, "Insider/Outsider: Government Spy or a Terrorist? Dilemmas of Academic Research in the Post 9/11 Setting," *Amerasia Journal* 33 no. 2 (Fall 2007):26–40.
51. Hirschkorn and Colby, "Indian Men Look Back."
52. Azmath is referring to Zacarias Moussaoui, who was arrested in August 2001. Some individuals have been arrested in connection with the 9/11 attacks outside U.S. borders. An example is Khalid Shaikh Mohammed, who was captured in March 2003 from Pakistan. Currently, he is detained in Guantanamo Bay. See *CNN.com*, "Khalid Sheikh Mohammed Confesses 9/11 Role," March 15, 2007. A few other individuals arrested in connection with 9/11 attacks are also being kept in secret prisons and at Guantanamo Bay. Also see Human Rights Watch, "List of 'Ghost Prisoners' Possibly in CIA Custody" (List of Detainees Published by Human Rights Watch, updated on December 1, 2005), http://hrw.org/english/docs/2005/11/30/usdom12109_txt.htm (accessed March 27, 2008).
53. Azmath is referring to the 1988 Civil Liberties Act, when the U.S. government decided to provide $20,000 to each surviving Japanese American who had been interned by the U.S. government during World War II.

Chapter 2 Lifelong Deportation: The Punishment for Helping a Friend

1. Susan Davies took detailed notes and shared them with me.
2. *United States of America v. Ansar Mahmood* (01-CR-441) and *Ansar Mahmood v. United States of America* (03-CV-15).
3. A partial list of media articles written about Ansar's case appears here:
    Foderaro, Lisa. "A 9/11 Lesson: Don't Photograph the Water," *New York Times*, June 6, 2004.
    Garcia, Michelle. "Detainee to Be Deported on Immigration Charges; Supporters Allege Racial Profiling in Case," *Washington Post*, June 30, 2004.
    Rosin, Hanna. "Ansar Mahmood's American Dream: A Pakistani Immigrant Waits for Deliverance in Jail Rather Than to Be Deported Back Home," *Washington Post*, September 28, 2003.
    ———. "Snapshot of an Immigrant's Dream Fading: A Legacy of Sept. 11 Sweeps Pakistani to the Point of No Return: Deportation," *Washington Post*, March 24, 2002.
    Semple, Kirk. "Man Arrested Over Photos After 9/11 Is Deported," *New York Times*, August 14, 2004.

Shapiro, Walter. "Hype and Glory: Unfortunate Photo Shatters One Man's American Dream," *USA Today*, July 1, 2004.

Younge, Gary. "America Just Loves Immigration—It's Immigrants Who Aren't Popular. As Muslims Are Now Finding Out," *UK Guardian*, July 14, 2003.

4. Kent Sprotbery, personal interview held with Susan Davies and author, written notes, Upstate New York, September 2007.

5. Tina Sciocchetti and Mr. Jaquith, personal meeting held with author, written notes, Albany, New York, September 21, 2007.

6. Many other Syeds whom I know on a personal level don't believe in such inequality. Islam does not suggest that a lineage to the Prophet Mohammad provides higher status. Many Muslim scholars suggest that one of the primary reasons that the Prophet Mohammad did not have a son was to avoid such claims for respect and power in the future. However, as Ansar mentioned, this kind of discrimination exists in some villages in Pakistan.

7. Majeed, interview with author and Susan Davies, Hudson, New York, September 2007.

8. Fatima, interview with author, tape recording, Gujarat, February 2003; Yusuf, interview with author, tape recording, Gujarat, February 2003.

9. Steven Brill, *After: The Rebuilding and Defending of America in the September 12 Era* (New York: Simon & Schuster, 2003), 147.

10. I could not find the television program reporting the arrest of Fatima, Yusuf, and Ansar. A separate article published on October 11, 2001, called her a Palestinian. See "Photographer at City Water Plant Arouses Suspicion," *Hudson (NY) Register Star*, October 11, 2001. At the end of the article, Deputy Mayor Bryan Cranna made the following statement:

   "We live in very different times now, and everyone is quite aware of the warnings and the concerns that we all have, so when we were met with a situation like this we reacted to it in a way that we thought was appropriate." Cranna was referring to possible terrorist activity in the aftermath of the World Trade Center attack.

11. Trial transcripts, *United States v. Ansar Mahmood* (01-CR-441, October 16, 2001), 22.

12. Kent Sprotbery, interview with Susan Davies and author, written notes, September 2007.

13. Rosin, "Snapshot of an Immigrant's Dream" and "Ansar Mahmood's American Dream."

14. Rich Azzoparti, "Detainee Gains Senators' Sympathy and Staff," *Hudson (NY) Register Star*, October 2, 2003; John Mason, "Pizza Man 'Terrorist' Could Walk," *Hudson Valley (NY) Newspaper*, January 4, 2003.

15. Tina Sciocchetti, "Government Opposition to Petition for a Writ of Habeas Corpus," *Ansar Mahmood v. United States of America* (03-CV-15), March 7, 2003.

16. "Free Ansar Mahmood," http://www.chathampeace.org/.

17. Ellen Wulfhurst, "New York Town Unites to Help Immigrant Fight Deportation," *Reuters*, October 28, 2003; Brian Mann, *All Things Considered: Profile*, National Public Radio, August 5, 2003.

18. Abdus S. Ghazali, "Pakistanis' Exodus to Canada Accelerates," *Dawn*, March 16, 2003;www.dawn.com (accessed April 5, 2004). Margaret Philip, "Pakistanis Flocking to Canada," *Globe and Mail*, March 15, 2003. http://www.theglobeandmail.com/ (accessed April 5, 2003).

19. The Migration Policy Institute issued a report that provided statistical analysis of approximately 406 individuals detained in the aftermath of 9/11. It stated that of the detainees for whom information regarding employment was available, 51 percent worked as nonprofessionals. See Migration Policy Institute, "America's Challenge: Domestic Security, Civil Liberties, and National Unity after September 11" (Migration Policy Institute, 2003), 1.

20. U.S. Senate Letter to "The Honorable Tom Ridge, US Department of Homeland Security," May 21, 2004. The following senators signed the letter: Russell D. Feingold, Patrick J. Leahy, Edward Kennedy, Richard Durbin, and Jon S. Corzine. A similar letter with signatures of Congress members including Rep. Michael Honda was sent to Tom Ridge. The letter said, "We write to urge the Department's due consideration of Mr. Ansar Mahmood...petitions for release under an order of supervision and deferred action on his deportation."

21. Bill Cleary, *Letter to Mr. Ansar Mahmood, Reference...*, U.S. Department of Homeland Security, U.S. Immigration and Customs Enforcement, Buffalo, New York, March 2005.

22. Pub.L.No. 104–132, 110 Stat. 1214 (1996) (the Act).

Chapter 3 Uprooting Immigrants, Uprooting Families

1. A Migration Policy Institute report on 406 detainees notes that more than 90 percent of the people included in their analysis were males and approximately 70 percent of the detainees were between 20 and 49 years old. The report also recognizes that "in those instances where detainees had wives who were out of status, the wives were for the most part disregarded for enforcement purposes." See Muzaffar Chishti. *America's Challenge: Domestic Security, Civil Liberties, and National Unity After September 11*. Washington, D.C.: Migration Policy Institute, 2003.," appendix A.1.

2. Order of the Immigration Judge, *United States Department of Justice v. Anser Mehmood*, File number withheld, December 5, 2001. *United States of America v. Anser Mehmood* (02-Cr 637(BSJ)).

3. The following is a partial listing of media articles written about Anser, Uzma, and their family. Their case has been featured in a documentary called "Brothers and Others."

   Doty, Cate. "Gore Criticizes Expanded Terrorism Law," *New York Times*, November 10, 2003.

   Fainaru, Steve. "Detainees Offer Glimpse of Life in N.Y. Facility; 3 in September Probe Say They Were Abused in Top Security," *Washington Post*, April 17, 2002.

   Jacinto, Leela. "Family Desperate as Breadwinner Languishes in Jail," *ABC News*, January 11, 2002. http://abcnews.go.com/US/story?id=90031&page=1 (accessed April 4, 2008).

   Rohde, David. "Threats and Responses: Crackdown; US-Deported Pakistanis: Outcasts in 2 Lands," *New York Times*, January 20, 2003.

   Sachs, Susan. "A Nation Challenged: Detainees: Dispute That Prevented New Jersey Deportations Is Resolved," *New York Times*, April 27, 2002.

Standley, Jane. "America's 11 September Detainees," *BBC News*, February 7, 2002. http://news.bbc.co.uk/1/hi/world/americas/1804086.stm (accessed April 4, 2008).

4. Farhat Haq, "Rise of the MQM in Pakistan: Politics of Ethnic Mobilization," *Asian Survey* 35, no. 11 (November 1995): 990–1004.

5. Two of Uzma's brothers lived in the United States. The first one, Mauzam Ali, came to the United States in the early 1980s.

6. U.S. Department of Justice, "Notice of Action, Case Type, I130, Immigrant Petition for Relative, Finance (E) or Orphan, Petitioner, Ali, Mauzam, Beneficiary, Abaysi, Uzma." Receipt number withheld, received May 18, 2001. Immigration and Naturalization Service. Notice date, August 1, 2001.

7. Last name unknown.

8. Ahmar Abaysi, interview with author, audio recorded, Lahore, Pakistan, February 2003.

9. U.S. Department of Justice, "Notice of Action, Case Type, I130."

10. U.S. Department of Justice, "Affidavit in an Administrative Proceeding, Regarding Anser Mehmood" (201 Varick Street, New York, New York, October 3, 2001).

11. Emily Colborn, "Staging the Home Front: Spectacle, Spectatorship, and Post-Pearl Harbor Raids" (Paper presented at the Dokkyo International Forum on Performance Studies, Japan, December 2002). Many scholars, including Emily Colborn, have discussed the theatrical performance that the FBI created through raids of Japanese Americans during World War II for anxious neighbors, outraged politicians, and sensation-hungry journalists.

12. Abaysi, interview.

13. As the introduction points out, a few non-Muslims were kept on the ninth floor of the MDC.

14. Zacarias Moussaoui is a French Algerian national who was arrested in August 2001 in Minneapolis. He was attending a flight school, and after September 11, he became a prime suspect in the 9/11 attacks. Moussaoui was convicted for the 9/11 attacks and sentenced to life in prison. See *BBC News*, "Moussaoui Is Spared Death Penalty: Al-Qaeda Plotter Zacarias Moussaoui is to face life in jail rather than execution, for his role in the 9/11 attacks, a US jury has decided," May 4, 2006. However, he was arrested before the 9/11 attacks, and therefore, many scholars tend not to include him in the 9/11 detention cases. Also see David Johnston and Philip Shenon, "A Nation Challenged: The Suspects: FBI Curbed Scrutiny of Man Now a Suspect in the Attacks," *New York Times*, October 6, 2001.

15. Indifference from community members was not unique to Uzma, and others in Uzma and Anser's situation got similar responses because FBI tactics such as placing informants in Muslim communities had caused mistrust between friends and neighbors.

16. Several newspapers published Anser's story, see note 3.

17. Some Muslims believe that Jews were responsible for the 9/11 attacks. Many individuals whom I talked to directly or indirectly implicated Israel and Jewish people for the 9/11 attacks. Also see Steven Stalinsky, "Arab Press Says Jews Perpetrated 9/11 Attacks," *New York Sun*, http://www2.nysun.com/article/38781 (accessed April 2, 2008).

18. *Desis* is an Urdu/Hindi word for people from the same nation. It generally refers to people from India, Pakistan, and Bangladesh.

19. *Revolutionary Worker* (April 7, 2002): 13. The article includes a photograph of Uzma speaking at a press conference in Union Square, New York City, January 19, 2002.

20. Many immigrants believe that being out of status is not a major offense because they see millions of undocumented individuals working in various capacities throughout the country. This makes them believe that it is all right for them to join the workforce. Some immigrants are also familiar with the fact that the United States annexed portions of Mexico and challenge the legality of the takeover. In a sense, the prevalence of undocumented immigrants in the United States has made violating immigration regulations such as overstaying visas more acceptable.

21. Debbie Lang, "The Story of Uzma Naheed," The article refers to Harris Anser speaking at a February 20, 2002, National Day of Solidarity with Arab, Muslim, and South Asian immigrants. The children also spoke on a television program, *Now with Bill Moyers*, aired on PBS, March 15, 2002.

22. As the introduction illustrates, the FBI did not arrest anyone connected with the 9/11 attacks within the United States after 9/11. Zacarias Moussaoui was arrested before 9/11. A few individuals suspected of involvement in the 9/11 attacks have been arrested outside U.S. borders. See *CNN.com*, "Khalid Sheikh Mohammed Confesses 9/11 Role," March 15, 2007. A few other individuals arrested in connection with 9/11 attacks are kept in secret prisons and at Guantanamo Bay. Also see Human Rights Watch, "List of 'Ghost Prisoners' Possibly in CIA Custody" (List of Detainees Published by Human Rights Watch, updated December 1, 2005), http://hrw.org/english/docs/2005/11/30/usdom12109_txt.htm (accessed March 27, 2008).

23. The trial transcripts reveal that the judge did not take an in-depth look at any options for Anser to stay in the United States. The lawyer tried to discuss the pending immigration application and the pending labor certification, but the judge did not seem interested. See trial transcripts, *US Department of Justice v. Anser Mehmood*, October 25, 2002.

24. Neil Donovan, *FBI Special Agent Report Prepared in Bond Proceedings re Anser Mehmood* (U.S. Department of Justice, Executive Offices for Immigration Review, Immigration Court, In Bond Proceedings Re Anser Mehmood, October 11, 2001, New York).

25. Leela Jacinto, "Wife of Detainees Packs Her Bags: Wife of Detainee Ready to Leave America After Harrowing Time," *ABC News*, February 21, 2002, http://abcnews.go.com/US/Story?id=91882&page=1 (accessed September 10, 2005).

26. *United States Department of Justice v. Anser Mehmood Asylum, Withholding of Removal and Protection Under the Convention Against Torture* (December 5, 2001).

27. FBI coined the term *PENTTBOM* to refer to all 9/11-related investigations.

28. Office of the Inspector General, *The September 11 Detainees: A Review of Aliens Held on Immigration Charges in Connection With the Investigation of the September 11 Attacks* (U.S. Department of Justice, April 2003), 76.

29. Uzma is referring to the overall response of criminal lawyers. Before Martin, she had an immigration lawyer who was helping her in the immigration proceedings.

30. The Pakistani media was reporting about the detention of Pakistanis in the United States. *Dawn*, "24 Pakistanis Detained in US for September 11 Attacks," November 5, 2001.

31. Public Broadcasting Station, "Society and Community: A Family Divided," *Now with Bill Moyers*, March 15, 2002, http://www.pbs.org/now/transcript/transcript109_full.html (accessed August 21, 2007).
32. "Protest Secret Detentions at MDC this Saturday," a flyer from Martha Cameron, Justice for Detainees. Also see Sarah Ferguson, "A Peaceful Movement Emerges," *Village Voice*, October 7, 2002.
33. Public Broadcasting Station, "Society and Community."
34. Ibid.
35. He is trying to convert rupees into dollars.
36. It is notable that this experience led them to align themselves to other groups and communities who have suffered in the past.
37. Scholars estimate that over 1,000 individuals were detained in the two years following 9/11. Graph 1, included in the introduction, indicates that over 2,000 individuals were deported to predominately Muslim countries. Also see David Cole and Jules Lobel, "Are We Safer, a Report Card on the War on Terror," *Los Angeles Times*, November 18, 2007.
38. *BBC News*, "Pakistanis Deported From US," March 14, 2003.

Chapter 4 Loss of Civil Liberties for Muslims after 9/11: The National Security System's Guinea Pig

1. Palestinian citizenship is a tricky term to explain, especially in the absence of a valid Palestinian state. Residents of the West Bank carry passports issued by the Palestinian Authority, which provide them international travel privileges. People living in Palestinian Territories and in diaspora also identify themselves Palestinians; however, Palestine does not exist on a current world map.
2. According to the legal file, Nabil and his family had expired visas, and they tried to help their family friends enter into the United States from the Canadian border. The court found them guilty of alien smuggling, an aggravated felony by immigration law standards.
3. His lawyer told me that on the police report, it said that he was stopped for an expired inspection sticker and that he was driving with a suspended license.
4. Maria Panaritis, "Illegal Alien to be Deported," *Philadelphia Inquirer*, April 23, 2003.
5. Thanks to Grant McCool for providing me with Nabil's telephone number in Palestine.
6. *Nightline*, "Nightline Detainees," *ABC News*, December 27, 2002. Nabil Ayesh's name is misspelled as Nabil Ajaz.
7. Alison Maclean and Tobias Perse, *Persons of Interest* (Brooklyn, NY: First Run/Icarus Films, 2004).
8. Many individuals, especially in the Middle East, South Asia, and other areas of the Islamic world, believe that Muslims did not carry out the 9/11 attacks. See Pew Global Attitudes Project, "The Great Divide: How Westerns and Muslims View Each Other, Europe Muslims More Moderate," June 13, 2007, http://pewglobal.org/reports/display.php?PageID=832 (accessed April 2, 2008).

9. Office of the Inspector General, *Supplemental Report on September 11 Detainees' Allegations of Abuse at the Metropolitan Detention Center in Brooklyn, New York* (U.S. Department of Justice, December 2003), 4.

10. Ibid., 33–35.

11. Alison B. Cowan, "5 Young Israelis, Caught in Net of Suspicion," *New York Times*, October 8, 2001.

12. Some Muslims believe that Jews were responsible for the 9/11 attacks. Many individuals whom I talked to directly or indirectly implicated Israel and Jews for the 9/11 attacks. Also see Steven Stalinsky, "Arab Press Says Jews Perpetrated 9/11 Attacks," *New York Sun*, http://www2.nysun.com/article/38781 (accessed April 2, 2008).

13. Mukkaram Ali was arrested right after 9/11 as a material witness for Zacarias Moussaoui's case. Ali shared an apartment with Zacarias before 9/11. He denied having any knowledge about Zacarias's plan or any information about the 9/11 attacks. Based on an e-mail conversation held with his attorney, Sandra Nicholas, on April 4, 2004, I learned that he was eventually deported for an immigration violation and joined his family in Saudi Arabia.

14. The OIG report states that an FBI clearance was required for all Special Interest Cases. See OIG, *September 11 Detainees*, 25, 188.

15. Ali Yaghi was another Special Interest Case arrested from Albany, New York, for an immigration violation. He was married to a U.S. citizen and had three U.S.-born children. Ali was eventually deported to Jordan. Shokeria Yaghi (Yaghi's wife), interviews with author, New York, December and April 2003.

16. Nabil is referring to Mohammad Azmath; see Azmath's narrative, chapter 1.

17. Maclean and Perse, *Persons of Interest.*

18. *Nightline*, "Nightline Detainees."

19. Grant McCool, "US Finds Way to Deport Palestinians with No State," *Reuters*, July 28, 2003.

20. Ibid.

21. *Turkmen v. Ashcroft*, 02-civ-2307 (Eastern District of New York (E.D.N.Y.) filed April 17, 2002).

22. I heard of this anonymous person during one of my trips to Pakistan and the Middle East and briefly talked to him on the phone. He did not explain to me the reasons for his departure; however, the U.S. immigration office had told him something that forced him to leave. His departure confirms that the U.S. government wanted to get rid of all MDC detainees within its national boundaries.

Chapter 5 Propagating and Maintaining the Global War on Terror

1. *US Department of Justice v. E****** Mohamed* (rest of the file number withheld, as it provides his Alien ID number). I don't think that I got a complete set of Mohamed's legal files. The Freedom of Information Office sent me about 200 pages of legal files, which did not include any trial transcripts. I submitted another request and got the exact same set of legal files.

2. ACLU, "Worlds Apart: How Deporting Immigrants After 9/11 Tore Families Apart and Shattered Communities" (New York: ACLU, December 2002), 17, 18.

3. I received several e-mails and letters through Adem Carroll while Mohamed E****** was in jail in Egypt. The following is a list of this correspondence:

   Author unknown. "Some Notes" (provides legal background on Mohamed's immigration case and disappearance), ca. October 2002.

   Carroll, Adem. "Letter to His Excellency Ahmed Maher El Sayed" (Egyptian Ambassador to the United States), October 11, 2002. This letter provides background on Mohamed's case and was signed by several organizations, including Islamic Circle of North America, Coalition for the Human Rights of Immigrants, Coney Island Avenue Project, Asian American Legal Defense and Education Fund, the Interfaith Center, Muslim Community Support Services, and Justice for Detainees.

   E******, Hesham. E-mail to several organizations, including Amnesty International, "Held in Jail in Egypt," December 28, 2002.

   Mohamed, Swsan (Mohamed's mother). E-mail to Shubh Mathur, "Looking for Mohamed E******," October 16, 2002.

4. Immigration News Brief, "New Jersey Detainee 'Disappeared'" (press release, October 13, 2002), http://ww4report.com/static/56.html (accessed March 31, 2008); Gustavo Capdevila, "Rights-U.N.: ACLU Files Complaint Over Detained US Muslims" (Inter Press Service, January 27, 2004).

5. I discuss some of these attitudes toward the United States in Irum Shiekh, "9/11 Detainees and Deportees: Are They Transforming Images of the United States?," in *Democracy and Homeland Security, Strategies, Controversies and Impact*, ed. Nawal H. Ammar (Kent, OH: Kent State University Press, 2004).

6. Some Middle Eastern people refer to Spanish-speaking people as *Spanish*. I maintain the use of this term in the narrative.

7. Some of the other legal statements about Mohamed's case and ACLU reports also refer to his marriage to a U.S. citizen. Although someone could argue that maybe it was a marriage of convenience, the government had not disputed the legality of this marriage.

8. Office of the Inspector General, *The September 11 Detainees: A Review of Aliens Held on Immigration Charges in Connection With the Investigation of the September 11 Attacks* (U.S. Department of Justice, April 2003), 111.

9. I found the telephone number of the lawyer who helped Mohamed in his second immigration case. I called him several times, but he never returned my phone calls.

10. I tried to contact the Pakistani lawyer who worked with ACLU, but she was no longer working with the organization. I found her e-mail address and tried to contact her, but I did not get any response.

11. The five other narratives included in the book reveal that deportation experiences differed from one person to the other. For example, Yasser Ebrahim got clothes that were too big for him. Ansar Mahmood, in contrast, had the opportunity to wear his own clothes. Deportation officers accompanied a very limited number of deportees. Sending two deportation officers to Egypt is expensive, and someone in the upper management must have allocated the budget for this trip.

12. Do James Carroll, "Significant Incident Report" (Newark, NJ: U.S. Department of Justice, 2002). Mohamed gave me a copy of this official document.

13. 8 CFR Part 208-Procedures for Asylum and Withholding of Removal (part revised effective 4/1/97; 62 FR 10312) Sec. 208.6. Disclosure to Third Parties (Revised effective 1/5/01; 65 FR 76121) (a).
14. Swsan Mohamed, "Looking for Mohamed E******."
15. As I mentioned in the beginning of this chapter, I heard about Mohamed's case through Adem and saw several requests signed by human and legal rights organizations for his release. This international pressure also contributed to his quick transfer from the emergency jail.
16. *BBC News*, "CIA Agents Guilty of Italy Kidnap," November 4, 2009, http://news.bbc.co.uk/2/hi/europe/8343123.stm (accessed June 6, 2010).
17. Amnesty International. *United States of America: Below the Radar: Secret Flights to Torture and Disappearance.* London, U.K.: Amnesty International, International Secretariat, 2006.
18. Human Rights Watch, "List of 'Ghost Prisoners' Possibly in CIA Custody" (List of Detainees published by Human Rights Watch, updated December 1, 2005), .

Chapter 6 Reclaiming Our Civil Rights and Liberties

1. The brothers spell their last names slightly differently.
2. Last name unknown.
3. I saw two versions of Ramy's name: Ramy Ahmed and Ramy A. Abd El-Rahman Shehata.
4. Yasser Ebrahim, written statement received via e-mail to author, June 4, 2003.
5. Yasser Ebrahim has two legal cases. The first one is an immigration file, which includes his case for the expired visa, U.S. Department of Immigration, Executive Office for Immigration Review, *Yasser Ebrahim*, Trial Transcripts of November 6, 2001. The CCR gave me only the public portion of the file. The immigration court refused to provide me any documentation for the immigration file. The second legal file is the lawsuit that Yasser filed in the beginning of 2002, *Turkmen v. Ashcroft*, in the Eastern District Court of New York, *Turkmen v. Ashcroft* (02-Cv-2307, 2002). Extensive contents of this lawsuit are available from the following website: *Turkmen v. Ashcroft*, http://www.ccr-ny.org/v2/legal/september_11th/sept11Article.asp?ObjID=35KQUuFROg&Content=96.
6. Kim Barker, "Federal Tactics Criticized in Roundup of 1,100; FBI Defends Detention Policy, but Some Courts Aren't Convinced," *Chicago Tribune*, September 11, 2002; Tom Hays, "Muslims Beaten and Threatened at Brooklyn Jail: 'What We Said About All the Suffering Was True," *Toronto Star*, June 23, 2003.
7. Ahmad Khalifa and Walid, interview with author, tape recording, Alexandria, Egypt, April 2003.
8. Ramy Ahmed, interview with author, tape recording, Alexandria, Egypt, April 2003.
9. *Turkmen v. Ashcroft* (02-Cv-2307, 2002).
10. Ibid. *Turkmen v. Ashcroft* is a class-action civil rights lawsuit filed on behalf of a class of Muslim, South Asian, and Arab noncitizens who were arrested after September 11 in connection with the investigations around the 9/11 attacks. In November 2009, Yasser and four other plaintiffs accepted a settlement with the U.S. government for $1.26 million. Currently, the CCR is seeking permission

from the district court to amend the complaint and add six new plaintiffs—former MDC detainees. For additional development on the legal case, see http://ccr-justice.org/ourcases/current-cases/turkmen-v.-ashcroft (accessed June 2, 2010).

11. Chapter two provides documentation from the OIG report on the September 11 detainees.

12. Ramy Ahmed, interview.

13. The court transcripts of Yasser's file are dated November 6, 2001.

14. Office of the Inspector General, *The September 11 Detainees: A Review of Aliens Held on Immigration Charges in Connection with the Investigation of the September 11 Attacks* (U.S. Department of Justice, April 2003), 37, 38.

15. U.S. Department of Immigration, Executive Office for Immigration Review, *Yasser Ebrahim*, Trial Transcripts of November 6, 2001.

16. No one knows the reasons for these discrepancies. I think that bureaucracy, inefficiency, and indifference played a major role in these delays. FBI field officers did not care whether they kept these detainees for another week or for another month. It was not a priority for them or for the administration.

17. I interviewed Mohammad Maddy in Cairo, Egypt, in April 2003 and he confirmed the loss of his radio. He was also angry that they never gave him back the radio or the money that he spent to buy the radio.

18. Ramy Ahmed, interview. He also corroborated Yasser's story.

19. Yasser and many other individuals whom I interviewed started to see the United States in a different way. Some of them started to compare themselves to other people of color, especially Japanese Americans and Latinos (see the narratives of Anser Mehmood and Ansar Mahmood). Also see Irum Shiekh, "9/11 Detainees and Deportees: Are They Transforming Images of the United States?" in *Democracy and Homeland Security, Strategies, Controversies and Impact* (Kent, OH: Kent State University, 2004).

20. I discuss this loss of personal security in the conclusion.

21. Center for Constitutional Rights, "Appeals Court Rules in Case Challenging Racial Profiling of Muslim, Arab, South Asian Men in Post-9/11 Sweeps: Leaves Open Possibility for Holding High Level Officials Accountable," December 18, 2009, http://ccrjustice.org/newsroom/press-releases/appeals-court-rules-case-challenging-racial-profiling-muslim,-arab,-south-as (accessed June 2, 2010).

22. *Turkmen v. Ashcroft* (02-Cv-2307, 2002). Center for Constitutional Rights, Docket: *Turkmen v. Ashcroft*, http://www.ccr-ny.org/v2/legal/september_11th/sept11Article.asp?ObjID=35KQUuFROg&Content=96 (accessed May 21, 2007).

23. *Turkmen v. Ashcroft* (02-Cv-2307, 2002). Center for Constitutional Rights, http://ccrjustice.org/ourcases/current-cases/turkmen-v.-ashcroft (accessed June 2, 2010).

Conclusion

1. Steven Brill, *After: The Rebuilding and Defending of America in the September 12 Era* (New York: Simon & Schuster, 2003); Office of the Inspector General, *The September 11 Detainees: A Review of Aliens Held on Immigration Charges in Connection with the Investigation of the September 11 Attacks* (U.S. Department of Justice, April 2003).

2. Brill, *After*, 37.
3. Ibid., 38.
4. Ibid., 149.
5. Center for Constitutional Rights, "Description for *Turkmen v. Ashcroft*," http://ccrjustice.org/ourcases/current-cases/turkmen-v.-ashcroft (accessed June 2, 2010). In November 2009, five of the seven named *Turkmen* plaintiffs have settled their claims for $1.26 million from the United States. Currently, CCR is seeking permission from the district court to amend the complaint to add six new MDC plaintiffs, which would allow them to hold the former attorney general John Ashcroft, the former FBI director Robert Mueller, and the former INS director James Ziglar responsible for the illegal roundups and abuse.
6. Ibid.
7. Ibid., 15.
8. OIG, *September 11 Detainees*, 47.
9. A composite response based on over 40 personal interviews. For specific examples, see narrative of Anser Mehmood.
10. OIG, *September 11 Detainees*, 44.
11. The OIG report does not explain the reasons for not sending the memo. However, this memo reveals that staff within the office were thinking and talking about these issues.
12. Ibid., 65n50.
13. OIG, *September 11 Detainees*, 46.
14. Ibid., 78.
15. Ibid., 46.
16. Nina Bernstein, "In FBI, Innocent Detainee Found Unlikely Ally," *New York Times*, June 30, 2004.
17. Al-Badr Al-Hazmi, a Saudi national detained in Texas by the INS on September 17, 2001, was released on September 24, 2001. His private attorney, Gerald Goldstein, was able to get him out and even testified before the Senate Judiciary Committee that the INS did not let him talk to his client for five days despite his and his client's numerous requests for counsel. Most of the detainees were unable to get such counsel and secure quick releases after 9/11. U.S. Senate Committee on the Judiciary, *Testimony of Gerald Goldstein, Attorney, National Association of Criminal Defense Lawyers, Department of Justice Oversight: Preserving Our Freedom While Defending against Terrorism*, Hearing Before the S.Comm. on the Judiciary, 107th Congress, December 4, 2001.)
18. Section 241(a) of the Immigration and Nationality Act (INA) provides that "except as otherwise provided in this section, when an alien is ordered removed, the Attorney General shall remove the alien from the United States within a period of 90 days (in this section referred to as the 'removal period'). 8 U.S.C. &123(a)(1)(A). The statue provides exceptions when removal within the 90-day period is not possible (such as when the alien's country of citizenship will not accept the alien). It also permits detention to continue beyond the 90-day period for aliens charged with certain types of immigration violations who have not been removed or when the attorney general determines that the aliens present a risk to the community or a risk of flight. OIG, *September 11 Detainees*, 91.

19. In *Turkmen v. Ashcroft*, the CCR challenged the government on the length of detention. In December 2009, the Second Circuit Court of Appeals decided that the government has the right under immigration law to detain noncitizens on the basis of religion, race, or national origin and to hold them indefinitely without explanation. Civil rights lawyers and organizations criticized the court's decision and found it disturbing. Rachel Meeropol, the lead attorney for the case, stated, "This ruling leaves millions of non-citizens vulnerable. After 9/11 Attorney General John Ashcroft decided to use any means he could to hold Muslims and Arabs, based only on their race and religion, so he could investigate whether they had any ties to terrorism. This is racial and religious profiling. It is not only bad law enforcement policy, it is also unconstitutional." See Center for Constitutional Rights, "Appeals Court Rules in Case Challenging Racial Profiling of Muslim, Arab, South Asian Men in Post-9/11 Sweeps: Leaves Open Possibility for Holding High Level Officials Accountable," Press Release, December 18, 2009, New York, NY, http://www.ccrjustice.org/newsroom/press-releases/appeals-court-rules-case-challenging-racial-profiling-muslim%2C-arab%2C-south-as (accessed June 14, 2010).

20. Brill, *After*, 147–148.

21. *Turkmen v. Ashcroft*, http://ccrjustice.org/ourcases/current-cases/turkmen-v.-ashcroft (accessed June 2, 2010).

22. U.S. Department of Justice, *Testimony of Attorney General John Ashcroft: Senate Committee on the Judiciary* [Prepared remarks] (December 6, 2001), http://www.usdoj.gov/ag/testimony/2001/1206transcriptsenatejudiciarycommittee.htm. (accessed May 2, 2003).

23. Committee on the Judiciary U.S. Senate, *Testimony of Michael Chertoff, Assistant Attorney General, Criminal Division, Preserving Our Freedom While Defending Against Terrorism*, November 28, 2001.

24. U.S Department of Justice, Testimony of Attorney General John Ashcroft.: Senate Committee on the Judiciary , December 6, 2001.

25. Viet Dinh, "Freedom and Security after September 11," *Harvard Journal of Law & Public Policy* 399 (2002): 399.

26. "President Convenes Homeland Security Advisory Council: Remarks by the President at Meeting of Homeland Security Advisory Council, the Indian Treaty Room," *Office of the Press Secretary*, June 12, 2002, http://www.whitehouse.gov/news/releases/2002/06/20020612–3.html (accessed July 23, 2004).

27. Coleen Rowley, "Letter to FBI Director, Mr. Robert Muller," *New York Times*, March 6, 2003.

28. Brill, *After*, 119.

29. Ibid., 38.

30. Ibid., 213.

31. Ibid., 392, 587.

32. Ibid., 587.

33. Matthew Purdy and Lowell Bergman, "Where the Trail Led: Between Evidence and Suspicion: Unclear Danger: Inside the Lackawanna Terror Case," *New York Times*, October 12, 2003.

34. Ibid.

35. James Bamford, "Television Review: Looking Beneath the Surface of a Terrorism Case," *New York Times*, October 10, 2006.

36. The Center on Law and Security, *Terrorist Trial Report Card: September 11, 2001–September 11, 2009* (New York: New York University, School of Law, January 2010), 46.

37. Project Salam, Support and Legal Advocacy for Muslims, http://www.project-salam.org/index.html (accessed June 10, 2010).

38. Racialization is a sociopolitical process through which frameworks for defining racial difference are manipulated by institutional actors and used to subjugate specific groups. This usually results in the creation of a field of discourse that imputes negative stereotypes to racialized minorities.

39. Jeff Stein, "Can You Tell a Sunni From a Shiite?" *New York Times*, October 17, 2006.

40. Allan Lengel, "Secret Service Suspends Agent for Islam Slur Words Scrawled on Calendar at Muslim Suspect's Home," *Washington Post*, July 26, 2002. From a separate source, I learned that the Jordanian guy was the brother of a congressman in the Jordan parliament, who used his resources to put the Secret Service agent under investigation; otherwise, his actions could have gone unnoticed.

41. As of December 27, 2002, there were only 25 FBI agents who could speak Arabic. See Susan Schmidt, "Help Still Wanted: Arabic Linguists, Agencies Rushed to Fill Void, but Found Screening New Hires Takes Times," *New York Times*, December 27, 2002.

42. Anjum Shiekh, interview with author, written notes, Oakland, California, April 2004.

43. Council on American-Islamic Relations, "The Status of Muslim Civil Rights in the United States: Stereotypes and Civil Liberties," Washington D.C. 2002, 26.

44. Syed Ali, interview with author, tape recording, Safron, New York, January 2003.

45. Steve Fainaru, "Detainees Offer Glimpse of Life in N.Y. Facility, 3 in Sept. 11 Probe Say They Were Abused in Top Security," *Washington Post*, April 17, 2002.

46. Office of the Inspector General, *Supplemental Report on September 11 Detainees' Allegations of Abuse at the Metropolitan Detention Center in Brooklyn, New York* (Department of Justice, December 2003), 4.

47. Ibid.

48. This statement does not imply that Muslim detainees endured the same hardships as slaves, but the patterns of racialization combined with cruel treatment and the helplessness of detainees reminded me of the conditions of slavery.

49. The Center on Law and Security, *Terrorist Trial Report Card*, iii, 20.

50. *Nightline*, "Nightline Detainees," ABC News, December 27, 2002.

51. National Immigration Forum, *Immigrants and the Economy*, http://www.immigrationforum.org/pubs/articles/economy2002.htm (accessed April 13, 2004).

52. Gretchen Peters, "Pakistan Takes Hunt for Al-Qaeda to Cities: The FBI is Working with Local Officials to Root Out Terrorists in Urban Areas Such as Karachi," *Christian Science Monitor*, October 29, 2002. The Human Rights Watch report listed in the following note provides a list of several Pakistanis nationals arrested by the joint efforts of Pakistani and American intelligence. I heard about the presence of FBI officials several times from other sources and local and national Urdu newspapers.

53. Human Rights Watch, "List of 'Ghost Prisoners' Possibly in CIA Custody" (List of Detainees published by Human Rights Watch, updated December 1, 2005), http://hrw.org/english/docs/2005/11/30/usdom12109_txt.htm (accessed March 27, 2008).

54. Ibid.

55. Ibid.

56. Dana Priest, "CIA Holds Terror Suspects in Secret Prisons: Debate is Growing Within Agency About Legality and Morality of Overseas System after 9/11," *Washington Post*, November 5, 2005; Stephen Grey, *Ghost Plane: The True Story of the CIA Torture Program* (New York: St. Martin's Press, 2006).

57. Scott Shane, "Obama Orders Secret Prisons and Detention Camps Closed," *New York Times*, January 22, 2009.

58. David Johnston, "U.S. Says Rendition to Continue, but With More Oversight," *New York Times*, August 25, 2009.

59. Beth Duff-Brown, "Deported Man Gets Apology: Canadian Tortured in Syria Compensated $8.9 Million," January 27, 2007, http://seattlepi.nwsource.com/national/301439_canada27.html (accessed March 27, 2008). Several media articles document the case, including Arar's website, which provides a detailed description and timeline for the case: http://www.maherarar.ca/.

60. *CBS News*, "Cleric Alleges Torture after CIA Kidnap: Egyptian Man Abducted in Italy, Released From Prison in Egypt Shows 'Scars of Torture,'" February 22, 2007, http://www.cbsnews.com/stories/2007/02/22/world/main2502447.shtml (accessed March 27, 2008).

61. Dana Priest, "Wrongful Imprisonment: Anatomy of a CIA Mistake: German Citizen Released after Months in 'Rendition,'" *Washington Post*, December 4, 2005.

62. Ibid.

63. Moazzam Begg and Victoria Brittain, *Enemy Combatant: My Imprisonment at Guantánamo, Bagram, and Kandahar* (New York: New Press, 2006). Many other scholars have criticized the U.S. government for its operation of Guantanamo. I don't discuss Guantanamo detainees in this book since most of them were arrested outside U.S. borders and their cases come under international laws.

64. Amnesty International, *Denying the Undeniable Enforced Disappearances in Pakistan* (London: Amnesty International, 2008), http://www.amnesty.org/en/library/asset/ASA33/018/2008/en/0de43038–57dd-11dd-be62–3f7ba2157024/asa330182008eng.pdf (accessed June 11, 2010).

65. *Dawn*, "Rally Held for Recovery of Missing Persons," June 1, 2010, http://www.dawn.com/wps/wcm/connect/dawn-content-library/dawn/the-news-paper/local/islamabad/rally-held-for-recovery-of-missing- (accessed June 12, 2010).

66. *Turkmen v. DOJ*, 02-Cv-2307 (2002).

67. Center for Constitutional Rights, *Turkmen v. Ashcroft*, http://www.ccr-ny.org/v2/legal/september_11th/sept11Article.asp?ObjID=35KQUuFROg&Content=96 (accessed June 2, 2010).

68. Nina Bernstein, "2 Men Charge Abuse in Arrests after 9/11 Terror Attack," *New York Times*, May 3, 2004.

69. Nina Bernstein, "U.S. Is Settling Detainee's Suit in 9/11 Sweep," *New York Times*, February 28, 2006.

70. See Center for Constitutional Rights, "CCR Statement on Supreme Court Ruling Against Holding High-Level Officials Accountable for Post-9/11 Domestic Sweeps," http://ccrjustice.org/newsroom/press-releases/ccr-statement-supreme-court-ruling-against-holding-high-level-officials-acco (accessed September 9, 2009); also see Adam Liptak, "Justices Void Ex-Detainee's Suit Against 2 Officials," *New York Times*, May 19, 2009.
71. Liptak, "Justices Void Ex-Detainee's Suit."
72. *Korematsu v. United States*, 323 U.S. 214 (1944), challenged the United States on its Executive Order 9066. The U.S. Supreme Court sided with the government and upheld the internment for the need to protect the nation.
73. In 1988 U.S. president Ronald Reagan signed the Civil Liberties Act of 1988, which provided reparations and an apology for the unjust actions of World War II.

Index

PALGRAVE Studies in Oral History

Series Editors: Linda Shopes and Bruce M. Stave

The Order Has Been Carried Out: History, Memory, and Meaning of a Nazi Massacre in Rome, by Alessandro Portelli (2003)

Sticking to the Union: An Oral History of the Life and Times of Julia Ruuttila, by Sandy Polishuk (2003)

To Wear the Dust of War: From Bialystok to Shanghai to the Promised Land, an Oral History, by Samuel Iwry, edited by L. J. H. Kelley (2004)

Education as My Agenda: Gertrude Williams, Race, and the Baltimore Public Schools, by Jo Ann Robinson (2005)

Remembering: Oral History Performance, edited by Della Pollock (2005)

Postmemories of Terror: A New Generation Copes with the Legacy of the "Dirty War," by Susana Kaiser (2005)

Growing Up in the People's Republic: Conversations between Two Daughters of China's Revolution, by Ye Weili and Ma Xiaodong (2005)

Life and Death in the Delta: African American Narratives of Violence, Resilience, and Social Change, by Kim Lacy Rogers (2006)

Creating Choice: A Community Responds to the Need for Abortion and Birth Control, 1961–1973, by David P. Cline (2006)